NEGOTIATING THE SUSTAINABLE DEVELOPMENT GOALS

The Sustainable Development Goals (SDGs) are a universal set of seventeen goals and 169 targets, with accompanying indicators, which were agreed by UN member states to frame their policy agendas for the fifteen-year period from 2015 to 2030. Written by three authors who have been engaged in the development of the SDGs from the beginning, this book offers an insider view of the process and a unique entry into what will be seen as one of the most significant negotiations and global policy agendas of the twenty-first century.

The book reviews how the SDGs were developed, what happened in key meetings and how this transformational agenda, which took more than three years to negotiate, came together in September 2015. It dissects and analyzes the meetings, organizations and individuals that played key roles in their development. It provides fascinating insights into the subtleties and challenges of high-level negotiation processes of governments and stakeholders, and into how the SDGs were debated, formulated and agreed. It is essential reading for all interested in the UN, sustainable development and the future of the planet and humankind.

Felix Dodds is a Senior Fellow at the Global Research Institute and a Senior Affiliate at the Water Institute at the University of North Carolina, USA, and also an Associate Fellow at the Tellus Institute, Boston, USA. Felix has edited or written fourteen books on sustainable development and UN-related issues and was Chair of the 2011 UN DPI NGO Conference 'Sustainable Societies Responsive Citizens'. From 1992 to 2012 he was Executive Director of the Stakeholder Forum for a Sustainable Future.

Ambassador David Donoghue is Ireland's Permanent Representative to the United Nations in New York, USA. He co-facilitated, with the Permanent Representative of Kenya, the negotiations at the UN which produced the 2030 Agenda for Sustainable Development. He also co-facilitated, with the Permanent Representative of Jordan, the negotiations which agreed the outcome of the High Level Meeting on large movements of refugees and migrants held at the UN on 19 September 2016.

Jimena Leiva Roesch is a Senior Policy Analyst at the International Peace Institute. Previously she was a diplomat for the Permanent Mission of Guatemala to the United Nations in New York, USA. She was a lead negotiator for the 2030 Agenda for Sustainable Development and for climate change. She offers hands-on training on multilateral negotiations to diplomats and students worldwide. Jimena was an active member of the Security Council team when Guatemala was an elected member in 2012–2013.

"Learning from the process that engaged so many stakeholders at national and international level is important for future multilateral negotiations. This contribution from three actors intimately involved in the process offers rare insights into a long, challenging and ultimately fruitful process. I hope many readers will enjoy the insights presented in this book and be inspired to realise that the impossible is possible through compromise, partnership and leadership."

– **from the foreword by Mary Robinson,** *President of the Mary Robinson Foundation: Climate Justice, Former President of Ireland (1990–1997) and Former UN High Commissioner for Human Rights (1997–2002)*

"This is an important book that charts the journey we went on and the challenges faced in agreeing the 2030 Agenda for Sustainable Development. I hope it will help people understand what was achieved and help those now, and in the future, engaged in the implementation of this agenda."

– **from the foreword by Ambassador Macharia Kamau,** *Permanent Representative of Kenya to the United Nations in New York, USA, co-chair of the negotiations for the Sustainable Development Goals (2012–2014) and co-facilitator of Transforming Our World: the 2030 Agenda for Sustainable Development (2014–2015)*

"Having participated in various negotiations on sustainable development since 1992, this overview of the process leading to the ambitious and important Sustainable Development Goals allows us to see the big picture and helps make the journey ahead possible."

– **Julia Marton-Lefevre,** *former Director General of IUCN, the International Union for Conservation of Nature*

"As the most prolific writer on issues of sustainable development and the multilateral system, Felix Dodds has done it again; on this occasion, working with Ambassador David Donoghue and Jimena Lieva Roesch. These three authors have brought their individual and collective knowledge and expertise to review the 2030 development agenda, consolidated in a recently articulated set of Sustainable Development Goals (SDGs). Offered by people who were immersed in the process, theirs is a necessary and timely analysis of how the multilateral system works, the consultations and negotiations out of which the SDGs evolved and their intended objectives.

Given their backgrounds and proximity to what took place, the authors have brought to their subject the quality of information and analysis likely to be useful to those who will be engaged in fulfilling this agenda within the multilateral system and its myriad stakeholders. When compared with the MDGs, the very large number of sustainable development goals and targets suggest very high ambition and an enormous undertaking at both the national and international levels. For students of development and international relations this will be an essential book. It will become a useful tool for peer review of the attainment of the SDGs. Coming so soon after consensus on the SDGs and the new development agenda were reached, the authors engage in an important discussion on which future books on this area will draw and be assessed.

All three authors are to be congratulated for this important piece of work."

*– **Liz Thompson,** former UN Assistant Secretary General for Rio+20*
and Barbados Minister of Energy and Environment

"Experienced journalists covering UN negotiating meetings on sustainable development issues tend to make a bee-line for Felix Dodds to discover what is going on. Now he, and his equally well-informed co-authors – Ambassador David Donoghue and Jimena Leiva Roesch – are doing everyone a service by extending the privilege through this book, which traces the often tortuous process that led to the agreement last September of the Sustainable Development Goals.

Though AS OF YET little-known outside the international environment and development community, the Goals are – as the authors write – 'a blueprint for the development of humanity and the planet in the 21st century'. Their adoption marks the moment when a decades-old argument was finally won.

This book charts how that happened and suggests how the victory should be followed up with action."

*– **Geoffrey Lean,** award-winning environmental journalist*

"*Negotiating the Sustainable Development Goals* is an important and timely contribution to global development policymaking that will further our understanding of how the SDGs became the new overarching framework for a comprehensive development agenda – and help inspire and guide their implementation."

*– **Mark Suzman,** President of Global Policy and Advocacy and*
Chief Strategy Officer, Bill and Melinda Gates Foundation

NEGOTIATING THE SUSTAINABLE DEVELOPMENT GOALS

A transformational agenda for an insecure world

Felix Dodds, Ambassador David Donoghue and Jimena Leiva Roesch

LONDON AND NEW YORK

from Routledge

First published 2017
by Routledge
2 Park Square, Milton Park, Abingdon, Oxon OX14 4RN

and by Routledge
711 Third Avenue, New York, NY 10017

Routledge is an imprint of the Taylor & Francis Group, an informa business

© 2017 Felix Dodds, Ambassador David Donoghue and Jimena Leiva Roesch

The right of Felix Dodds, Ambassador David Donoghue and Jimena Leiva Roesch to be identified as authors of this work has been asserted by them in accordance with sections 77 and 78 of the Copyright, Designs and Patents Act 1988.

All rights reserved. No part of this book may be reprinted or reproduced or utilised in any form or by any electronic, mechanical, or other means, now known or hereafter invented, including photocopying and recording, or in any information storage or retrieval system, without permission in writing from the publishers.

Trademark notice: Product or corporate names may be trademarks or registered trademarks, and are used only for identification and explanation without intent to infringe.

British Library Cataloguing in Publication Data
A catalogue record for this book is available from the British Library

Library of Congress Cataloging in Publication Data
Names: Dodds, Felix, author. | Donoghue, David, author. | Leiva Roesch, Jimena, author.
Title: Negotiating the sustainable development goals / Felix Dodds, Ambassador David Donoghue and Jimena Leiva Roesch.
Description: London ; New York : Routledge, 2017. | Includes bibliographical references and index.
Identifiers: LCCN 2016023183 | ISBN 9781138695078 (hbk) | ISBN 9781138695085 (pbk) | ISBN 9781315527093 (ebk)
Subjects: LCSH: Sustainable development—International cooperation. | Rio+20 (Conference) (2012 : Rio de Janeiro, Brazil)
Classification: LCC HC79.E5 .D6219 2017 | DDC 338.9/27—dc23
LC record available at https://lccn.loc.gov/2016023183

ISBN: 978-1-138-69507-8 (hbk)
ISBN: 978-1-138-69508-5 (pbk)
ISBN: 978-1-315-52709-3 (ebk)

Typeset in Bembo
by Apex CoVantage, LLC

CONTENTS

FIGURES

TABLES

BOXES

FOREWORD

'Negotiating the Sustainable Development Goals: A transformational agenda for an insecure world' documents, celebrates and analyses the historic 2030 Agenda adopted in September 2015. I am grateful to the authors for taking the time to record the many steps on the journey from the Earth Summit in 1992 and the Millennium Development Goals (MDGs) in 2000, through Rio+ 20 to the 17 Sustainable Development Goals (SDGs). Agenda 2030 is a unique accomplishment owing to the scale of the vision, the ambition of the Goals, how it was negotiated and due its universal nature. Learning from the process that engaged so many stakeholders at national and international level is important for future multilateral negotiations. This contribution from three actors intimately involved in the process offers rare insights into a long, challenging and ultimately fruitful process.

Ambassador David Donoghue and his co–facilitator Ambassador Macharia Kamau built on the fine work of Ambassadors Kamau and Körösi as co-chairs of the Open Working Group, and this involved an unprecedented engagement of states, civil society, business, academics and citizens. Managing this inclusive process was challenging, as this book shows, but also rewarding and informative. As a result Agenda 2030 belongs to many people. This broad ownership bodes well for its implementation which requires the commitment of stakeholders around the world.

Two aspects of the Goals I would like to highlight are their universality and their indivisibility. The universal nature of the new sustainable development agenda was hard won and transformative. No longer are we talking about development with a donor-recipient mind-set. No country has achieved sustainable development. Every country is challenged, in different ways, to achieve the 17 goals. Only through action at home and cooperation internationally can transformation be achieved. Universality means leadership is required of every country. Solidarity and cooperation mean that, by working together as a United Nations of sovereign states, all countries can be enabled to achieve their goals. Many of the goals, like Goal 13 on climate change and Goal 14 on oceans, can only be achieved through global cooperation.

The integrated and indivisible nature of the Goals results from learning from the MDGs. Experience has shown that a siloed approach to development yields limited results. From my own perspective, working as President of the Mary Robinson Foundation- Climate Justice and as the UN Secretary General's Special Envoy on Climate Change in 2015, an important signal of the linkages between global challenges was the inclusion of the climate Goal in the SDGs. Science warns us that sustainable development is contingent on our ability as an international community to limit global warming to 1.5°C and well below 2°C above pre industrial levels. Recognition of climate action as a component of sustainable development will also drive the coherent development of policies at national level to jointly deliver both the SDGs and climate commitments.

The commitment to leave no one behind in the implementation of the SDGs is again informed through learning from the past and the inability of the MDGs to reduce inequality even as progress was made on other development indicators. Goal 10 to reduce inequalities, Goal 7 on gender equality and the commitment by all member states to a follow up and review process, will help to ensure that this time everyone benefits from sustainable development. Linked to this is the commitment to reach the furthest behind first. For me this brings to mind the many millions of women who live without access to electricity or clean cooking, and the absolute need to ensure that, by 2030, their lives have been transformed by access to sustainable energy. We will have to target these women carefully to ensure that, although they may be the hardest to reach, we will get to them first.

Agenda 2030 is a blueprint for the development of humanity and the planet in the 21st century. The key to delivering the vision and transforming peoples' lives lies in how seriously governments, the UN, international organisations, civil society and business take their roles, together and in partnership, in implementing the SDGs. It is an agenda for the people, by the people and with the people. It is founded on the premise that every person matters, and it sets out to ensure dignity and human rights for all. Implementation of the Agenda started in January 2016 and must continue apace. 15 years is a short time to achieve such a transformative vision. But to fail is unacceptable, morally and in terms of the long term stability of human society. In an increasingly tumultuous period of history, we know that empowering people, realising their rights and giving them an equal opportunity to thrive is a cornerstone of peaceful societies.

Implementing the SDGs will be a mammoth task; but the rewards will be reaped by generations now and into the future. The SDGs are a means to allow dreams to become a reality; so that no girl is refused entry to school, no father watches his children go hungry, no mother is unable to find decent work and no child breathes dirty air that makes them ill. I hope many readers will enjoy the insights presented in this book and be inspired to realise that the impossible is possible through compromise, partnership and leadership.

Mary Robinson
President of the Mary Robinson Foundation: Climate Justice
Former President of Ireland (1990–1997)
Former UN High Commissioner for Human Rights (1997–2002)

FOREWORD

I dedicated over four years of my professional life to a global project premised on the rather noble and quaint idea that if the world were to come together it might be possible to address the worst scourges and threats of modern civilization and also possibly turn back the clock of time and undo some of the most damaging consequences of nineteenth- and twentieth-century industrialization and modernization.

The promise of this project was predicated on the surprisingly refreshing text entitled "The Future We Want" that had emanated from the Rio UN Conference on Sustainable Development. The text was heady stuff, which, intellectually and programmatically, excited all of us who wished for a better world and who believed that we had the means and the organizational capabilities within the United Nations and among all nations of the world to respond to the great historical challenges of our time, challenges that appeared to be engulfing humanity at the dawn of the twenty-first century.

The moment of truth came together in 2012. The Rio Conference had been a resounding success; its outcome was ambitious and expansive with hugely transformative and universal dimensions that promised a sea change in how global development cooperation would be understood moving forward. The Millennium Development Goals (MDGs) of the latter part of the twentieth century have been successful, but they were limited in ambition, reach and impact. The deadline for the MDGs of 2015 was upon the world, and time was running out. The MDGs, however, had pointed the way to what could be done if the world came together around a common program for development and how time-bound initiatives in a structured framework could produce amazing outcomes that could have real impact on people, saving millions of lives and pulling millions of others out of poverty. The idea of successor goals for the MDGs, mooted as the Sustainable Development Goals, had gained ground prior to the Rio Summit in 2012 and had taken root during the summit and gotten acceptance in the final outcome text. There was now a headline "sustainable development goals", the general principles of which were also agreed upon, but no one had any clear idea what shape or character they would take nor how many there would be. That task to scope and define the SDGs was undone, and this was left to the SDG OWG.

The UN General Assembly Open Working Group of the Sustainable Development Goals was set up in June 2012 and after six months of hard negotiations on how it should be structured and function, it was ready to commence its two and a half years of work in December 2012.

Equally important, and as contextually parallel to these events, was the unfolding global climatic, environmental and social reality. The perfect storm of weather disruptions and climatic disasters, biodiversity collapse and species decimation, social unrest and persistent grinding poverty, and the rise of inequality accompanied by historic economic crises had left the entire world on edge. The consequence of ten decades of unregulated industrialization and explosive urbanization was everywhere, resulting in the pumping of megatons of greenhouse gases into the atmosphere and the release of a wide range of poisonous and ruinous chemicals into the biosphere. The result was that the world was choking on its own pollutants and the climate was spiraling dangerously out of control. The Earth's biodiversity was in turn being decimated and food stocks consumed in a manner likely to up-end global food chains and biogenetic life cycles. It was a scary and seminal time in human history. It had become pressingly clear that something needed to be done and to be done so urgently.

The question, however, was what? What was to be done, and how was it to get done? "The Future We Want" had pointed to what the world desired. But how was the world to get there? What was the world to prioritize? How was a world of 193 independent, sovereignty-minded governments to agree on what was to be done? And after decades of globalization how was business, both transnational and local, to be brought together into a single solution-finding process, recognizing that the greater part of the financing, innovation and technology for driving "the future we want" was to come from the private sector? And how would the world publics, now a vastly more integrated force joined at the hip by social media, the Internet and transnational values on ethics and human rights, to be included and integrated in helping define the solutions for the future we want? And how would we make sure that in the future no one was left behind—that all people enjoyed the full potential of a better world?

These were the organizational and negotiation conundrums that had to be confronted and overcome. The work of the co-chairs and co-facilitators was to help find the path that all groups could walk to a coherent outcome, one of high ambition and purpose.

Luckily the science was clear. Decades of academic, scientific and United Nations–related work had established the parameters of the debate, and the science and the policy boundaries were broadly mapped out. There was general agreement that human actions in both consumption and production were at the core of the existential Armageddon that the world faced. But until 2012 no single global effort had yet been attempted to find a broad, credible, global solution to the global challenges and questions of our time. The task of finding and negotiating the global solutions to these global challenges is the story that unfolds in this book. This is a story that will be written many times over and that will be studied rigorously around the world for many years to come.

After three and a half years and countless official and informal meetings, retreats, and breakfast, lunch and dinner consultations, and after travel to dozens of countries around the world on all continents and while still doing my day job as Kenya's Ambassador to the United Nations, it was with great satisfaction and a big sigh of relief when we finally adopted the Sustainable Development Goals in June 2014 and, a year later, "The 2030 Agenda for Sustainable Development". Undertaking these twin tasks turned out to be the greatest intellectual, technical and emotional professional challenge of my life. It was a time of great anxiety and debate, but also a time of great exhilaration and satisfaction. Working with my co-chair, Ambassador Csaba Körösi of Hungary and my co-facilitator Ambassador David Donoghue of Ireland on the OWG and the Post-2015 Agenda, respectively, we led processes that gave the world the SDGs and the 2030 Agenda for Sustainable Development. It was a historical achievement. And it was an honor and privilege to have been tasked to lead these processes.

This is an important book that charts the journey we went on and the challenges faced in agreeing to the 2030 Agenda for Sustainable Development. I hope it will help people understand what was achieved and help those now, and in the future, engaged in the implementation of this agenda.

Ambassador Macharia Kamau
Permanent Representative of Kenya to the United Nations in New York, USA
Co-chair of the negotiations for the Sustainable Development Goals (2012–2014)
Co-facilitator of Transforming Our World: the 2030 Agenda for
Sustainable Development (2014–2015)

ACRONYMS AND ABBREVIATIONS

AAAA	Addis Ababa Action Agenda
AMR	Annual Ministerial Review
AOSIDS	Alliance of Small Island Developing States
ART	antiretroviral therapy
CBD	UN Convention on Biological Diversity
CBDR	Common But Differentiated Responsibilities
CEB	Chief Executives Board
CELAC	Community of Latin American and Caribbean States
CLEW	Climate, Land, Energy and Water
CoF	co-facilitators
CSD	Commission on Sustainable Development
DESA	Department for Economic and Social Affairs
ECOSOC	Economic and Social Council
ESG	environment, social and governance
EU	European Union
FDI	Foreign Direct Investment
FfD	Financing for Development
GA	General Assembly
G77	Group of 77
GDP	Gross Domestic Product
GEG	Global Environmental Goals
GNP	gross national product
GMOs	genetically modified foods
HLPF	High-Level Political Forum
HOSG	heads of state or government
ICESDF	Intergovernmental Committee of Experts on Sustainable Development Finance

ICT	information and communications technology
IDP	internally displaced person
IMF	International Monetary Fund
IMO	International Maritime Organization
IGN	Intergovernmental Negotiations
IPCC	Intergovernmental Panels on Climate Change
IPR	intellectual property rights
IPU	Inter-Parliamentary Union
ISO	International Standards Organization
IFSD	Institutional Framework for Sustainable Development
JPoI	Johannesburg Plan of Implementation
LDCs	Least Developed Countries
LGBT	lesbian, gay, bisexual, and transgender
LLDCs	Landlocked Developing Countries
MDGs	Millennium Development Goals
MOI	means of implementation
MGoS	Major Groups and other Stakeholders
NCSD	National Councils for Sustainable Development
NGOs	Nongovernmental Organizations
NRG4SD	Network for Regional Government for Sustainable Development
NSDGS	National Sustainable Development Goals Strategy
ODA	Official Development Assistance
OECD	Organization for Economic Co-operation and Development
OWG	Open Working Group
PGA	President of the General Assembly
QCPR	Quadrennial Comprehensive Policy Review
RE	renewable energy
SCP	Sustainable consumption and production
SDGs	Sustainable Development Goals
SDSN	Sustainable Development Solutions Network
SEI	Stockholm Environment Institute
SFSF	Stakeholder Forum for a Sustainable Future
SG	Secretary General
SIDS	Small Island Developing States
SIWI	Stockholm International Water Institute
TFM	Technology Facilitation Mechanism
UNCTAD	United Nations Conference on Trade and Development
UNCSD	United Nations Conference on Sustainable Development
UNCCD	United Nations Convention to Combat Desertification
UNDESA	United Nations Department of Economic and Social Affairs
UNDG	United Nations Development Group
UNGA	UN General Assembly
UNDP	United Nations Development Program
UNDPI	United Nations Department of Public Information

UNEP   United Nations Environmental Program
UNESCO   United Nations Educational, Scientific and Cultural Organization
UNFCCC   United Nations Framework Convention on Climate Change
UNSFSA   Straddling Fish Stocks and Highly Migratory Fish Stocks
UNV   United Nations Volunteers
WEOG   Western Europe and Other Group
WHO   World Health Organization
WPSA   World Society for Animal Protection
WRI   World Resource Institute
WSSD   World Summit on Sustainable Development
WTO   World Trade Organization

AUTHOR BIOGRAPHIES

Felix Dodds

Felix Dodds is a Fellow at the Global Research Institute, a Senior Affiliate at the University of North Carolina and an Associate Fellow at the Tellus Institute. Previously he was the Executive Director of Stakeholder Forum for a Sustainable Future (1992–2012). In 2014 he was also the co-director of the Nexus Conference on Water, Food, Energy and Climate.

In 2011 he chaired the UN NGO DPI conference 'Sustainable Societies Responsive Citizens' and from 1997 to 2001 he was the Co-chair of the NGO Coalition at the UN Commission on Sustainable Development. In 1996 he introduced the concept of Stakeholder Dialogues through the UN General Assembly for Rio+5, and helped run what is recognized as some of the most successful ones at Bonn Water (2001) and Bonn Energy (2004). For Rio+20 he was on the Advisory Boards for the Bonn 2011 Nexus Conference (November 2011) and the Planet Under Pressure conference, which was the global science conference (March 2012). He has been an advisor to the UK and Danish Governments and the European Commission.

He has written or edited thirteen books, the sister books to this one being *Building a Bridge to a Sustainable Future – From Rio+20 to a New Development Agenda* (October 2013) with Jorge Laguna-Celis and Liz Thomson and *Only One Earth – The Long*

Road via Rio to Sustainable Development (May 2012) with Michael Strauss and Maurice Strong. Other books include a trilogy on the issue of environment and security. In 2010 Green Eco Services listed him as one of the twenty-five environmentalists ahead of their time.

He has been a contributor to the BBC website and enjoys blogging on sustainable development and sometimes on films from film festivals. He has two amazing children, Merri and Robin.

Ambassador David Donoghue

Ambassador David Donoghue is Ireland's Permanent Representative to the United Nations in New York.

Ambassador Donoghue acted as co-facilitator, with the Permanent Representative of Kenya, of the UN intergovernmental negotiations which in August 2015 reached agreement on the 2030 Agenda for Sustainable Development. This agreement was formally adopted at a special summit of world leaders held at the UN in New York in September 2015. In February 2016, Ambassador Donoghue was appointed as co-facilitator, with the Permanent Representative of Jordan, for the high level meeting on large movements of refugees and migrants which took place in September 2016 at the UN in New York.

The Ambassador, who is a career diplomat, entered Ireland's Department of Foreign Affairs in 1975. He served in the Anglo-Irish Division, dealing with Northern Ireland and Anglo-Irish relations, where he would serve again on two further occasions. Adding in periods spent at the Irish Embassy in London (1988–91) and as head of the Anglo-Irish Secretariat in Belfast (1995–99), he spent a combined total of seventeen years working on the Northern Ireland problem and Anglo-Irish relations. He was closely involved in the negotiation of both the Anglo-Irish Agreement and the Good Friday Agreement.

From 1999 to 2001, he served as Irish Ambassador to the Russian Federation. In 2001, he became Director-General of the Irish government's development cooperation programme (known as Irish Aid). From 2004 to 2006, he served as Irish Ambassador to Austria and the Vienna-based UN agencies. From 2006 to 2009, he was the Irish Ambassador to Germany. From 2009 to August 2013, he was the Political Director of the Department of Foreign Affairs and Trade in Dublin (with overall responsibility for Irish foreign policy). He took up his present position in New York in September 2013.

Jimena Leiva Roesch

Jimena Leiva Roesch is a Senior Policy Analyst at the International Peace Institute. From 2009 to March 2015, Jimena was at the Permanent Mission of Guatemala to the UN in New York, where she last served as Counselor. She was Guatemala's lead negotiator for the Sustainable Development Goals and the 2030 Agenda. Guatemala had the honor to share a seat with Colombia in the Open Working Group. From 2009 to 2015, Jimena was also Guatemala's focal point for the United Nations Framework Convention on Climate Change (UNFCCC). Jimena was an active member of Guatemala's Security Council team from 2012 to 2013, when Guatemala was a non-permanent member, under the leadership of Ambassador Gert Rosenthal. Jimena offers hands-on training on leadership and diplomacy at the United Nations University in Tokyo and other institutions.

INTRODUCTION

*Felix Dodds, Ambassador David Donoghue
and Jimena Leiva Roesch*

> The 2030 Agenda for Sustainable Development embodies the yearnings of
> people everywhere for lives of dignity on a healthy planet. It shows what
> Member States can achieve when they work together in solidarity.
>
> *(Ban Ki-moon, 2015)*

This book is part of a trilogy of books on sustainable development at the global
level. The sister books are *Only One Earth: The Long Road via Rio to Sustainable
Development* written by Felix Dodds, Michael Strauss and Maurice Strong, which
tells the story from the 1960s through to before Rio+20 (2012). The second book
is *From Rio+20 to a New Development Agenda: Building a Bridge to a Sustainable Future*
by Felix Dodds, Jorge Laguna-Celis and Liz Thompson and explains the Rio+20
process and its significance in re-establishing the sustainable development narrative
at the global level. This third book, which you are now reading, picks up the themes
of the previous two and takes the reader through the development, agreement and
first steps to start implementation of the Sustainable Development Goals (SDGs) and
the Addis Ababa Action Agenda on Financing Development and the Paris Agreement. It concludes by looking at some of the emerging issues that could affect the
delivery of these agendas.

It is written by three authors who took part in the process – one Ambassador
who co-facilitated the intergovernmental negotiations leading to the adoption of
the SDGs in September 2015, an official from one of the governments who developed the idea of the SDGs and a stakeholder leader. We hope this gives the book a
unique and perceptive insight and informs the next generation of government officials and stakeholders who will be part of the implementation of this transformative
agenda and those who will at some point start to think of what should replace the
SDGs in 2030.

The book is broken down into the following five chapters and one annex:

Chapter 1 – A new beginning: conceiving the Sustainable Development Goals

It starts with the journey from the Rio Earth Summit (1992) and takes the reader through the development of the Millennium Development Goals (MDGs) and how the SDGs were first promoted. It recognized the critical role played by Colombia and then supported by Guatemala, Peru and the United Arab Emirates (UAE). It chronicles the development of the idea and the key stages leading to the Rio+20 Conference.

Although the path to agreeing to the SDGs was not easy, it managed to mobilize the input from a large number of governments, intergovernmental organizations and stakeholder groups around the world.

Chapter 2 – Understanding complexity: development or sustainable development parallel paths emerging as one

The key outcomes from Rio+20 started to be implemented with the setting up of the Sustainable Development Goals Open Working Group (SDG OWG) with Ambassador Csaba Körösi (Hungary) and Ambassador Macharia Kamau (Kenya) as co-chairs. An Intergovernmental Committee of Experts on Sustainable Development Finance (ICESDF) was set up and finally a process to launch a Technology Facilitation Mechanism (TFM). The UN Secretary General started a parallel process to prepare the ground for the replacement of the Millennium Development Goals. This included the setting up of a High-Level Panel on the Post-2015 Development Agenda co-chaired by the Presidents of Indonesia and Liberia and the UK prime minister. To engage stakeholders, Jeffrey Sachs was asked by the Secretary General to set up what became the Sustainable Development Solutions Network (SDSN). Finally, there were over 100 national consultations and eleven thematic consultations. This chapter explores how these parallel paths converged in a single one. It also looks at the outcome of the 2013 special meeting of the General Assembly that took place to review progress of the MDGs and to chart the way forward in relation to the 2030 Agenda.

The chapter also explores how the SDGs where crafted and how complex issues were resolved to achieve consensus on the 17 goals and 169 targets.

Chapter 3 – The big year: the preparatory process

Shortly after the completion of the Open Working Group, two Ambassadors were appointed as co-facilitators for the wider Intergovernmental Negotiations (IGN), which were required to agree on the post-2015 development agenda. These were Ambassador Macharia Kamau of Kenya and Ambassador David Donoghue of Ireland.

As the IGN process started, we wondered: Would the agreement reached on the SDGs hold together, or would the forces that wanted fewer goals and targets manage to reopen the agreement? What narrative would frame the new goals and targets? How would the UN system, government and stakeholders coalesce around an agreement that heads of state and government agreed to in September 2015? What role would the Addis Ababa Financing for Development Conference and the Climate Change Conference play?

Chapter 4 – A transformational agenda: outcomes from 2015 and what they mean

The key to delivering the Sustainable Development Goals in a truly transformational way would be how serious governments, intergovernmental bodies and stakeholders take their role, singularly or in partnership, in their implementation. This chapter looks at what the next stages could look like for their implementation at the global, regional, national and subnational level. It also addresses the unanswered questions from 2015 regarding how the UN system would reorganize around these goals. It reviews what roles different stakeholders, including the private sector, can play.

The SDGs have been framed as a 'We the People' document, rather than taking only a state-centric approach. Its achievement will lie in their ability to inspire people around the world.

Chapter 5 – Understanding the future: from 2015 to 2030, the challenges ahead

Over the coming fifteen years, the SDGs will be implemented in a more complex and insecure environment. This chapter suggests what the emerging issues are that will have an impact on the SDGs and how this transformational agenda will address these challenges while still working to achieve the goals and targets agreed to in 2015.

Annex – Transforming our world: the 2030 Agenda for Sustainable Development

To enable the reader to have a full understanding of the outcome document (UN, 2015) we have enclosed it as an annex to the book. We would hope you read it after you have read the five chapters.

Thanks

We have a number of people to thank for this book's development. In particular, we thank Leah Komada, Jeannet Lingan, Tanner Patrick Glenn, Ross, Bailey, David Banisar, David Le Blanc, Zak Bleicher, Maruxa Cardama, Naiara Costa Chaves, Josko Emrich, John Gilroy, Thomas Frey, Jeffery Huffines, Emine Isciel, Mohamed Khalil, Farrukh Khan, Paul Ladd, Syahda Guruh L. Samudera, Ambassador Martin Sajdik, Hugo-Maria Schally, Jan-Gustav Strandenaes, Liz Thompson, David Trouba, Borg Tsien Tham, Stacey Wilenkin and Paula Caballero.

We dedicate this book to all the delegates, UN staff and stakeholders who spent more time working on this collective endeavor than with their families and close ones. The 2030 Agenda is the work of many more people than we could name here and even identify. To all who helped build this new vision: thank you.

While writing this book, the father of sustainable development, Maurice Strong, died. He started us on the journey in 1972 as Secretary General of the first UN Conference on the Human Environment, re-energized us through the Rio Earth Summit in 1992 and laid down the foundations for the 2015 Paris Climate Agreement. In what would be his final speech to the UN General Assembly (read, not given, because of ill health) in September 2014, addressing the SDG OWG outcome document he said:

> Our essential unity as peoples of the Earth must transcend the differences and difficulties which still divide us. You are called upon to rise to your historic responsibility as custodians of the planet in taking the decisions in the next year that will unite rich and poor, North, South, East and West, in a new global partnership to ensure our common future.
>
> *(Strong, 2014)*

References

Ki-moon, B. (2015) Opening remarks at press conference, 16 September 2015, UN, New York. Available online at: www.popefrancisvisit.com/schedule/address-to-united-nations-general-assembly/

Strong, M. (2014) Speech to the UN General Assembly high-level stocktaking event on the post-2015 development agenda: Contributions to the Secretary General's synthesis report, strong. Available online at: http://blog.felixdodds.net/2014/09/maurice-strongs-statement-to-unpga.html

United Nations (2015) Transforming our world: The 2030 agenda for sustainable development. Available online at: https://sustainabledevelopment.un.org/post2015/transformingourworld

1

A NEW BEGINNING

Conceiving the Sustainable Development Goals

Introduction

The story of sustainable development is a remarkable one. The year 2015 not only saw the adoption of the Sustainable Development Goals (SDGs) but also of the Addis Ababa Action Agenda on Financing for Development (AAAA) and the Paris Agreement on Climate Change. Coincidentally, these three processes originated in Rio de Janeiro at the Earth Summit in June 1992. Together, these three political agreements define a vision for a more sustainable, equitable world and a roadmap for achieving it.

Although the path to agreeing on the SDGs was not easy, it managed to mobilize an important number of governments, intergovernmental organizations and stake-holder groups from around the world. To understand why this process generated such mobilization, it is important to go back to the 1990s and the origin of the Millennium Development Goals (MDGs).

The Millennium Development Goals

The 1990s was a decade of important UN conferences and summits. It started with the World Summit for Children (New York, 1990) and continued with the United Nations Conference on Environment and Development or the Rio Earth Summit (Rio de Janeiro, 1992), International Conference on Population and Development (Cairo, 1994), World Summit on Social Development (Copenhagen, 1995), Fourth World Conference on Women (Beijing, 1995), Second United Nations Conference on Human Settlements (Istanbul, 1996) and the World Food Summit (Rome, 1996). Each conference or summit agreed on a comprehensive action plan. In addition, the Rio Earth Summit introduced legally binding conventions such as the UN Convention on Biological Diversity (CBD) and the United Nations Framework Convention on Climate Change (UNFCCC). During the same decade, two further legally binding agreements were approved: the United Nations Convention to Combat Desertification (UNCCD, 1994) and the United Nations Conservation and Management of Straddling Fish Stocks and Highly Migratory Fish Stocks (UNSFSA, 1995).

In the context of these conferences, the turn of the new millennium was seen as a great opportunity to secure renewed commitments from governments to implement these action plans. As such, the General Assembly decided to articulate the outcomes of these past conferences and bring them together in the Millennium Summit. In preparation for this summit, the United Nations Secretary General produced the 'Millennium Report: We the Peoples: The Role of the United Nations in the 21st Century' (April 2000). The report put forward a list of goals and objectives for poverty eradication. This report, together with the International Development Goals that the Organization for Economic Cooperation and Development (OECD) agreed to in 1996 (Hulme, 2007), fed into the outcome of the Millennium Summit. In September 2000, 189 United Nations member states adopted the Millennium Declaration as a set of values and broad objectives for poverty eradication to guide international relations in the twenty-first century.

It was not until August 2001 that UNDP and other United Nations departments, the OECD and the World Bank came together to create the eight MDGs and their twenty-one quantifiable targets (and subsequently sixty indicators). The goals were presented in September 2001 in the report 'Road map towards the implementation of the Millennium Declaration' by UN Secretary General Kofi Annan. The goals were not negotiated by governments, nor was input given from stakeholders.

It is important to recognize that the MDGs were the first time that international cooperation would focus around a set of goals to put poverty eradication at the center of a global development agenda. It would acknowledge the multidimensional character of poverty, i.e., that this was beyond just the issue of below US$1.25/day.

At the time, there was a great deal of criticism of the way the MDGs came into existence. In particular, they were seen as addressing the symptoms of poverty rather than its underlying causes. This, along with the lack of ownership in their development, is the reason it took a number of years before stakeholders and many governments focused on them. What later helped with their implementation was that, after a decade of reduction of Official Development Assistance (ODA), ODA started to rise again. It returned to 1992 levels of US$64 billion in 2000 and grew to approximately US$150 billion by 2014 (US$135.4 billion of this from developed countries). Furthermore, it also started to be refocused around the MDGs.

The progress toward delivering the MDGs was reviewed by United Nations General Assemblies three times: once in 2005, again in 2010 and at a special event in 2013 to accelerate progress toward their full implementation by 2015.

The 2005 Heads of State UN review of the MDGs established a formalized monitoring and review system by setting up an Annual Ministerial Review (AMR) within the United Nations Economic and Social Council. This would create a formal space for progress on the MDGs to be monitored annually to help keep governments focused on delivering the goals and to learn from one another's experience.

BOX 1.1 2015 UNDP REVIEW OF THE MILLENNIUM DEVELOPMENT GOALS AND THEIR TARGETS

Goal 1: Eradicate extreme poverty and hunger

- Target 1A: Halve, between 1990 and 2015, the proportion of people living on less than US$1.25 a day.

By 2015: Extreme poverty has declined significantly over the last two decades. In 1990, nearly half of the population in the developing world lived on less than US$1.25 a day; that proportion dropped to 14 percent in 2015 (United Nations, 2015).

By 2015: Globally, the number of people living in extreme poverty has declined by more than half, falling from 1.9 billion in 1990 to 836 million in 2015. Most progress has occurred since 2000 (United Nations, 2015).

- Target 1B: Achieve decent employment for women, men and young people.

By 2015: The number of people in the working middle class – living on more than US$4 a day – has almost tripled between 1991 and 2015. This group now makes up half the workforce in the developing regions, up from just 18 percent in 1991 (United Nations, 2015).

- Target 1C: Halve, between 1990 and 2015, the proportion of people who suffer from hunger.

By 2015: The proportion of undernourished people in the developing regions has fallen by almost half since 1990, from 23.3 percent in 1990–1992, to 12.9 percent in 2014–2016 (United Nations, 2016).

Goal 2: Achieve universal primary education

- Target 2A: By 2015, all children can complete a full course of primary schooling, girls and boys.

By 2015: The primary school net enrollment rate in the developing regions has reached 91 percent in 2015, up from 83 percent in 2000 (United Nations, 2015).

By 2015: The number of out-of-school children of primary school age worldwide has fallen by almost half, to an estimated 57 million in 2015, down from 100 million in 2000 (United Nations, 2015).

By 2015: The literacy rate among youth aged 15 to 24 has increased, globally, from 83 percent to 91 percent between 1990 and 2015. The gap between women and men has narrowed (United Nations, 2015).

Goal 3: Promote gender equality and empower women

- Target 3A: Eliminate gender disparity in primary and secondary education, preferably by 2005, and at all levels by 2015.

By 2015: Many more girls are now in school compared to fifteen years ago. The developing regions, as a whole, have achieved the target to eliminate gender disparity in primary, secondary and tertiary education (United Nations, 2015).

By 2015: Women have gained ground in parliamentary representation in nearly 90 percent of the 174 countries, with data over the past twenty years. The average proportion of women in parliament has nearly doubled during the same period. Still, only one in five members is a woman (United Nations, 2015).

Goal 4: Reduce child mortality rates

- Target 4A: Reduce by two-thirds, between 1990 and 2015, the under-five mortality rate.

By 2015: The global under-five mortality rate has declined by more than half, dropping from 90 to 43 deaths per 1,000 live births between 1990 and 2015 (United Nations, 2015).

Goal 5: Improve maternal health

- Target 5A: Reduce by three-quarters, between 1990 and 2015, the maternal mortality ratio.

By 2015: Since 1990, the maternal mortality ratio has declined by 45 percent worldwide, and most of the reduction has occurred since 2000 (United Nations, 2015).

- Target 5B: Achieve by 2015 universal access to reproductive health.

By 2015: Contraceptive prevalence among women aged 15 to 49, married or in a union, increased from 55 percent in 1990 worldwide to 64 percent in 2015 (United Nations, 2015).

Goal 6: Combat HIV/AIDS, malaria and other diseases

- Target 6A: Have halted by 2015 and begin to reverse the spread of HIV/AIDS.

By 2015: New HIV infections fell by approximately 40 percent between 2000 and 2013, from an estimated 3.5 million cases to 2.1 million (United Nations, 2015).

- Target 6B: Achieve by 2010 universal access to treatment for HIV/AIDS for all those who need it.

By June 2014: An estimated 13.6 million people living with HIV were receiving antiretroviral therapy (ART) globally, an immense increase from just 800,000 in 2003. ART averted 7.6 million deaths from AIDS between 1995 and 2013 (United Nations, 2015).

- Target 6C: Have halted by 2015 and begun to reverse the incidence of malaria and other major diseases.

By 2015: Over 6.2 million malaria deaths have been averted between 2000 and 2015, primarily of children under 5 years of age in sub-Saharan Africa. The global malaria incidence rate has fallen by an estimated 37 percent and the mortality rate by 58 percent (United Nations, 2015).

Between 2000 and 2013, tuberculosis prevention, diagnosis and treatment interventions saved an estimated 37 million lives. The tuberculosis mortality rate fell by 45 percent and the prevalence rate by 41 percent between 1990 and 2013 (United Nations, 2015).

Goal 7: Ensure environmental sustainability

- Target 7A: Integrate the principles of sustainable development into country policies and programs; reverse loss of environmental resources.

By 2015: Ozone-depleting substances have been virtually eliminated since 1990, and the ozone layer is expected to recover by the middle of this century (United Nations, 2015).

- Target 7B: Reduce biodiversity loss, achieving by 2010 a significant reduction in the rate of loss.

By 2015: Terrestrial and marine protected areas in many regions have increased substantially (United Nations, 2015).

- Target 7C: Halve by 2015 the proportion of the population without sustainable access to safe drinking water and basic sanitation.

By 2015: Over half of the global population (58 percent) now enjoys this higher level of service. Globally, 147 countries have met the drinking water target (United Nations, 2015).

By 2015: Worldwide, 2.1 billion people have gained access to improved sanitation. The proportion of people practicing open defecation has fallen almost by half since 1990. Ninety-five countries have met the sanitation target (United Nations, 2015).

- Target 7D: By 2020 achieve a significant improvement in the lives of at least 100 million slum dwellers.

By 2015: The proportion of the urban population living in slums in the developing regions fell from approximately 39.4 percent in 2000 to 29.7 percent in 2014 (United Nations, 2015).

Goal 8: Develop a global partnership for development

- Target 8A: Develop further an open, rule-based, predictable, nondiscriminatory trading and financial system.

By 2015: Official development assistance from developed countries increased by 66 percent in real terms between 2000 and 2014, reaching US$135.2 billion (United Nations, 2015).

By 2015: In 2014, 79 percent of imports from developing to developed countries were admitted duty free, up from 65 percent in 2000 (United Nations, 2015).

- Target 8B: Address the special needs of the Least Developed Countries (LDCs).

By 2015: The proportion of ODA to LDCs and SIDS only slightly increased from 1990, but did nearly double from 2000 (United Nations, 2015).

- Target 8C: Address the special needs of landlocked developing countries Small Island Developing States (SIDS).
- Target 8D: Deal comprehensively with the debt problems of developing countries through national and international measures in order to make debt sustainable in the long term.

By 2015: The proportion of external debt service to export revenue in developing countries fell from 12 percent in 2000 to 3 percent in 2013 (United Nations, 2015).

- Target 8E: In cooperation with pharmaceutical companies, provide access to affordable, essential drugs in developing countries.

By 2015: Global and regional data are lacking, but a limited number of surveys undertaken at different times from 2007 to 2014 in low-income and lower-middle-income countries indicate that, on average, generic medicines were available in 58 percent of public health facilities (United Nations, 2015).

- Target 8F: In cooperation with the private sector, make available the benefits of new technologies, especially information and communications.

By 2015: Ninety-five percent of the world's population is covered by a mobile-cellular signal.

By 2015: The number of mobile-cellular subscriptions has grown almost tenfold in the last fifteen years, from 738 million in 2000 to over 7 billion in 2015 (United Nations, 2015).

By 2015: Internet penetration has grown from just over 6 percent of the world's population in 2000 to 43 percent in 2015. As a result, 3.2 billion people are linked to a global network of content and applications (United Nations, 2015).

There were to be real problems in measuring the MDG targets, as in many places governments were not yet collecting the relevant data.

The global financial crisis and the role of the UN

The 2008 economic crisis, which has been acknowledged as the greatest financial crisis since the 1920s, was caused, according to the US Senate's Levin-Coburn Report, by "high risk, complex financial products; undisclosed conflicts of interest; the failure of regulators, the credit rating agencies, and the market itself to rein in the excesses of Wall Street" (Levin & Coburn, 2011).

The impact on so many people's lives and livelihoods was huge. By the fourth quarter of 2008, the primary developed countries experienced a decline in Gross Domestic Product (GDP) of over 7 percent. The Least Developed Countries (LDCs) saw their growth rate, which had been an average 7.3 percent achieved from 2001 to 2010, fall in 2011 to only 4 percent (UN-OHRLLS, 2013). The only economies that were more resilient were the emerging economies such as Brazil, India and China. In fact, during the aftermath (2011) of the crisis, Brazil overtook the United Kingdom as the sixth largest economy in the world (Llana, 2011).

The crisis also had an impact on the environment and development agenda. Just as banks succeeded in privatizing the profits and socializing the losses as they led the global economy to the brink of collapse, the danger was growing that the same would happen with the environment.

In this context, many governments wanted the United Nations to play a role in discussing the national and international impacts of the global crisis. The G20, which was set up in 1999, became a major center for key governments to discuss policies addressing the crisis. Many countries felt excluded by the G20 – this was expressed at the United Nations Interactive Panel on the Global Economic Crisis held by the President of the United Nations General Assembly, Miguel d'Escoto Brockmann from Nicaragua. Sentiments of exclusion were expressed in the summary of the meeting when they:

> Made an urgent call for the United Nations to play a central role in the search for solutions and the implementation of decisions. The United Nations system can credibly ensure that the creation of new mechanisms and policy decisions will reflect input by all 192 Member States which will help credibility and restore legitimacy to the international financial system.
>
> *(United Nations, 2008)*

There had been a recommendation from the 2006 High Level Panel on United Nations System-Wide Coherence that the United Nations should set up a Global Leaders Forum within the Economic and Social Council. It was suggested that such a body would provide leadership and guidance to the international community on issues related to development and to global public goods and to develop a long-term strategic policy framework to secure consistency in the policy goals of the major international organizations (United Nations, 2006). This was not followed up on, but did in part become an outcome from Rio+20 in the establishment of the High-Level Political Forum (HLPF).

The United Nations continued to address the crisis through the 2009 Conference on the World Financial and Economic Crisis and Its Impact on Development. It identified actions for a "coordinated response to the crisis" (United Nations, 2009):

- Safeguarding economic, development and social gains and providing adequate support for developing countries to address the human and social impacts of the crisis.
- Fostering an inclusive, green and sustainable recovery and providing continued support for sustainable development efforts by developing countries.
- Strengthening the role of the United Nations development system in responding to the economic crisis and its impact on development.
- Reforming and strengthening the international financial and economic system and architecture, as appropriate, to adapt it to current challenges (UN, 2009).

In preparation for the conference, the President of the General Assembly convened a Commission of Experts headed by Nobel laureate Joseph Stiglitz. It produced a report on reforms of the international monetary and financial system.

The conference and the Commission had a lasting impact contributing to the improvement of governance and accountability in the International Monetary Fund (IMF) and the World Trade Organization (WTO). One other outcome was that the G20 would consult with the larger UN membership before each G20 meeting.

The global financial crisis that began in 2008 was, of course, a major blow to progress on the MDGs. A 2010 report of the IMF, entitled, 'The impact of the financial crisis of 2008' estimated that one of the impacts of the crisis was that it pushed a further 53 million people into poverty (defined as less than US$1.25 a day). The shock waves generated by the crisis did not just affect the international financial institutions and the G8, but also the United Nations. What role should the United Nations play as a venue for discussing the crisis? Many countries argued that the United Nations has universal membership and is therefore a more legitimate decision-making body, so it should have a role.

Also in 2010, what was to become known as the Arab Spring erupted in response to an increase in inequality, rising unemployment (particularly youth unemployed) and aspirations for social freedom in Arab states. This was an attempt to bring more democracy to states that had seen little of it. This movement spread in countries like the United States through the "Occupy" movement. As Annie Lowrey observed in the *Washington Post* on 6 October 2012:

> The top 1 percent of households took a bigger share of overall income in 2007 than they did at any time since 1928.
>
> *(Lowrey, 2012)*

Put in a slightly different way, Joseph Stiglitz commented:

> Growing inequality is the flip side of something else: shrinking opportunity. Whenever we diminish equality of opportunity, it means that we are not using some of our most valuable assets – our people – in the most productive way possible.
>
> *(Stiglitz, 2011)*

Inequality was to become a topic of Rio+20 and the post-2015 agenda.

The death and rebirth of sustainable development

The World Summit on Sustainable Development (WSSD) in 2002 should have added substantively to the MDGs; however, it happened in the wake of the 9/11 terrorist attack. The focus of member states had moved from addressing poverty and sustainable development toward peace and security. As the Rio Declaration stated in 1992:

> Principle 25: Peace, development and environmental protection are interdependent and indivisible.
>
> *(United Nations, 1992)*

Because of the impact of 9/11 the Johannesburg Plan of Implementation (JPoI) only secured the addition of one target on sanitation to the MDGs:

> Halve, by the year 2015, the proportion of people who do not have access to basic sanitation.
>
> *(United Nations, 2002)*

People leaving Johannesburg did so realizing that the next few years were going to be very difficult years for sustainable development. This turned out to be an understatement – at least at the global level. By September 2006, addressing the United Nations General Assembly, President Mbeki of South Africa declared that:

> We have not implemented the Monterrey Consensus on Financing for Development, thus making it difficult for the majority of the developing countries, especially those in Africa, to achieve the Millennium Development Goals, and have reduced the Johannesburg Plan of Implementation to an insignificant and perhaps forgotten piece of paper.
>
> *(Mbeki, 2006)*

Also in 2006, Swiss President Moritz Leuenberger suggested at the Global Ministerial Environment Forum in Dubai that the UNEP should develop a list of Global Environmental Goals (GEGs) (UNEP, 2006).

The Swiss proposal called for goals, targets and indicators and proposed that:

> They should be general in character and establish a universal objective for safeguarding the environment in a specific field . . . targets should reflect primary international measures or obligations for achieving the overarching goals.
>
> *(Perrez & Ziegerer, 2008)*

The dire state of the environment as expressed by President Mbeki became worse in 2007. The United Nations Commission on Sustainable Development (CSD) would, for the first time, fail to agree on any policy outcome on the critical issues of energy and climate. This would be followed in 2011 by the CSD again failing to agree to an outcome document – this time on sustainable consumption and production (SCP). The global consensus on where we needed to go – and how – was coming apart.

As custodian for Agenda 21, the sustainable development blueprint for the twenty-first century agreed to in 1992, the Government of Brazil picked up the challenge to resurrect sustainable development as an overarching concept. In a speech to the United Nations General Assembly in September 2007, the President of Brazil, Lula da Silva, called for a new sustainable development summit in 2012 – twenty years after the original Rio Conference. The Brazilian Ambassador, Maria Luiza Ribeiro Viotti, led the discussions in New York and secured first the support of 134 developing countries, the members of the Group of 77 (G77) and then of the General Assembly.

In 2009, sustainable development again suffered a considerable blow with the failure of the climate negotiations in Copenhagen. Most delegates left the Copenhagen Climate Summit on 18 December in a despondent mood. Those returning to New York six days later started to rebuild. On 24 December, the General Assembly agreed to a new United Nations Conference on Sustainable Development (UNCSD), otherwise known as Rio+20, which would be held in 2012.

This conference had three objectives:

• Securing renewed political commitment for sustainable development.
• Assessing the progress and implementation gaps in meeting previous commitments.
• Addressing new and emerging challenges.

The official discussions had two main themes:

• How to build a green economy to achieve sustainable development and lift people out of poverty, including support for developing countries that would allow them to find a green path for development.
• How to improve international coordination for sustainable development by building an institutional framework.

The Rio+20 preparatory process

The two co-chairs of the Rio+20 preparatory process, who, with the larger bureau, would guide the process, were Ambassador John W. Ashe of Antigua and Barbuda and Ambassador Kim Sook of the Republic of Korea.

Several governments were reluctant to agree to an extensive preparatory process. In fact, they agreed to three formal meetings lasting only seven days (Rio 1992 lasted forty days). It takes time to build levels of trust among member states that enable agendas to move forward.

Core input often comes from member states to the UN, who engaged in consultation with their national stakeholders before developing their position. This would then have to be negotiated within any political groupings of which they are members, such as the G77[1] or the European Union,[2] before being presented in the formal or informal meetings.

The original Rio Summit in 1992 had been a huge breakthrough in terms of stakeholder engagement in a UN conference. This was the first conference to identify individual responsibilities for nine stakeholder groups (which Agenda 21 called Major Groups[3,4,5]). The CSD further developed the innovative participatory processes in the UN to involve stakeholders. This included multistakeholder dialogues with member states on the issues that the Commission was discussing. It is therefore not surprising that Rio+20 also focused on engaging and expanding stakeholders' participation throughout the preparatory process. From the very start, the development of the Rio+20 zero draft drew not only on member states' inputs but also on those of stakeholders'. For the negotiations themselves, none of the formal or informal processes for Rio+20 excluded stakeholders from participating.

In addition to the involvement of stakeholders, the UN system as a whole brought its expertise and institutional memory to the process. For the original Rio, the initial chapters of Agenda 21 were drafted by the UN system; this time around, they would reflect the input of governments, the UN and stakeholders.

It became clear that, as the process toward Rio+20 gained momentum, the original program of preparatory meetings would not be enough. Three further intersessional meetings were added, totally an additional seven days and another seventeen days of 'informal-informal' meetings. This brought the total up from seven to thirty-four days.

The UN Development Group's initial ideas on SDGs

A paper produced by Paul Ladd of the UNDP in May 2011 echoed much of what Colombia and later Guatemala, UAE and Peru would propose conceptually in July 2011. However, it started to identify within the UN what could be an ambitious plan that:

> Would seek to re-frame a new set of goals around the shared challenges currently faced by the planet and its people, thereby making significant changes from the original MDG framework.

(Ladd, 2011)

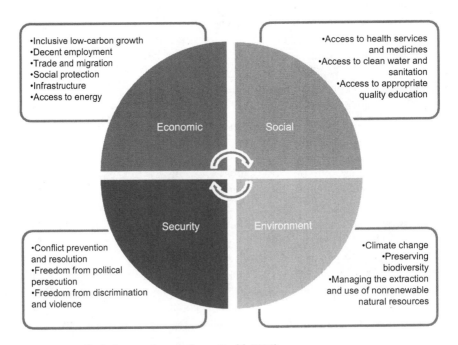

FIGURE 1.1 Goals for people and planet (Ladd, 2011)

The birth of the SDGs

It always seems impossible until it's done.

Nelson Mandela

This is a "new sustainable development era" (Sachs, 2016). Scientists, academics, politicians and business leaders now recognize that the world is shifting in a new policy direction. Yet, in 2010, the thought that the MDGs would be followed by a "universal" and "sustainable" development agenda was as remote as, for example, the idea prior to 2007 that the United States might have an African American as president.

In 2009, the UN agreed to host the Rio+20 Conference in June 2012. This global event would celebrate forty-two years of progress since Stockholm, particularly in the environment field. The conferences in 1972 and in 1992 had established the basic tenets of international cooperation in many fields, including climate change (the UN climate convention was born in 1992), biodiversity and desertification. The 1972 and 1992 conferences had inspired countries to establish ministries for the environment and to develop national policies to meet these international agreements.

As part of the preparatory process, in the fall of 2010 the UN sent a survey to all governments asking them what expectations they had for Rio+20. Colombia, like all other countries, received the survey, and the task of completing it fell to the new Director of Economic Social and Environmental Affairs at the Ministry of Foreign Affairs, Ms. Paula Caballero.

From the beginning, Paula considered that the MDGs, although perhaps not perfect, had changed how many agents were engaged on key development priorities, and had helped to galvanize concrete action, however, she was also keenly aware of their limitations. So she proposed a new metric, but one that would encompass the complexity of development challenges – recognizing that it is impossible to deliver on social challenges without bringing in the economic and environmental drivers and opportunities. She also proposed that these SDGs should be applicable to all countries, a significant departure from the Millennium Development Goals (MDGs). The Colombian vice-minister, Patti Londoño, did not blink when she heard of the novel idea of adopting a universal set of Sustainable Development Goals. Yet to discuss at Rio+20 what would come after the MDGs seemed out of place. Rio+20 was supposed to be dedicated only to environmental issues.

There was a strong pushback even against the idea of expanding MDG7 into a greater number of goals. The SDG proposal accordingly had to be framed in agreed-upon terms. The answer was simple: go back to Agenda 21. At that time, proposing that the SDGs would incorporate the 'unfinished business of the MDGs' and would replace the MDGs was unthinkable. Thus, the initial Colombian proposal kept the SDGs separate from the MDGs. However, the reaction of several delegations was one of concern that there could be two parallel tracks emerging from the Rio+20 Conference, one devoted to the MDGs and another to the SDGs.

As the proposal was circulated informally, it was met with disbelief and sometimes with outright anger. The SDGs were viewed as competing with the MDGs, and concerns were expressed, for example, that the three MDGs on health would be streamlined into a single SDG. The SDGs were seen as a direct threat to countries that had invested in the MDGs – which meant most UN member states. Some of Paula's colleagues discouraged her from moving forward as it was not perceived as a serious proposal.

Objections to the proposal came from all quarters. Developing countries feared that funding would be cut off if the agenda was going to be universally applicable. Bilateral aid agencies from many donor countries were not interested in changing the structure of their aid, which was largely based on the MDGs. Others thought that the SDG proposal would distract attention from the MDGs and from the issues that were central to Rio+20.

Paula recalled that "the SDGs were not discussed among the 193 countries; rather, they were discussed with over 700 delegates each of whom had a different opinion". Often delegates from the same country had opposing views on the SDGs. Paula used all international fora to present the SDG idea. It was also unthinkable that all countries, developed and developing, would apply the same goals and targets.

In July 2011, Indonesia hosted a meeting in Solo in preparation for Rio+20. Colombia presented its SDG proposal. In the corridors of that meeting, Paula received support from several colleagues, including Rita Mishaan from Guatemala, which soon afterward became the first country to endorse the Colombian proposal.

Many times, Paula sought the endorsement of the region for the idea of SDGs. However, the unclear relationship with the MDGs prevented countries from endorsing the proposal. Perhaps, regional rivalries also hampered the endorsement.

To increase momentum, on 4 November 2011 Colombia hosted an informal consultation in Bogota to which it invited delegates from all regions. Over forty countries participated, including representatives from the Netherlands, Norway, United States, Mexico, Kenya, India and Australia. Also attending was Felix Dodds from Stakeholder Forum. Many of these people would become essential allies in the coming months and years. The proposal gained traction. The meeting was a key turning point. Many delegates were now more open to the idea of SDGs.

A month later, with a twist of fate, the delegations met in the 17th Climate Conference (COP17) that was held in Durban, South Africa. Although the climate talks were a separate process, the outcome in Durban shared a similar characteristic with the SDGs: the new climate agreement had to be universally applicable. Although the connection between the Durban package and the SDGs was not evident at the time, the move on the part of the UN and its member states toward universality was significant.

After COP17 in Durban, delegations gathered in New York for a final consultation before the "zero draft" of the outcome document for Rio+20 was to be released. A revised version of the SDGs was presented at a side event organized by Colombia. The event attracted over 114 delegations, many of whom were hearing of the SDGs for the first time. At this time, Peru officially endorsed the proposal.

When the zero draft appeared in January 2012, something remarkable became clear: the SDGs had been included in it. This victory, however, did not mean that the SDGs would necessarily survive the next six months leading up to Rio+20. As negotiations advanced it became clear that reaching agreement on a full set of SDGs at Rio+20 would be highly ambitious, if not impossible. For Colombia, Guatemala and Peru, the end game for the conference was adjusted as follows:

1   Agreement on the concept of SDGs.
2   Defining a preliminary set of issue areas.
3   Most importantly, agreement on a process to negotiate the SDGs beyond Rio+20.

A strategic shift became necessary – it was important to gain the support of developing countries, particularly the Group of 77 and China. Vice minister Londoño traveled to New York in February with the sole purpose of persuading the G77 to support the SDGs. In March 2011, Paula and Patti on behalf of Colombia traveled east to present the SDGs to the Indian Government. By April 2012, Community of Latin American and Caribbean States (CELAC) member states agreed to support the proposal and accepted that Brazil, as the host of Rio+20, would take the lead in moving it forward. The negotiation process toward Rio gained speed; shortly afterward Colombia wrote a new version, and Peru and UAE endorsed the proposal. The G77 coordinator, Farrukh Khan from Pakistan, played a key role in bridging the divide amongst delegations.

Rio+20 Conference (13–22 June 2012): "the future we want"

While the concept of the SDGs was more or less palatable by the time delegations reached Rio, agreement on the SDGs was to hang in the balance until the final hours. There was one aspect that had to be resolved: the process to create the SDGs. The United States and the EU wanted a technical working group composed of scientists and experts in the field that would be appointed by the Secretary General. The G77 was split: some delegations wanted an 'open-ended working group' that would involve all member states and would adhere to the traditional negotiation setting of the UN, whereas others wanted a small group of government representatives that would be able to craft a concise SDG proposal. In the end, the G77+China met in the middle and agreed to an "Open (not open-ended) Working Group" – this meant that it would be open and transparent in its working methods but would only consist of a small number of delegations.

The compromise reached at Rio+20 was to set up this "Open Working Group". It would consist of only thirty government representatives. This small group would have the responsibility to craft a report containing the SDG proposal to be presented by the 68th session of the General Assembly (before September 2014). Delegates also agreed that the SDGs would be universally applicable and aspirational and would integrate economic, social and environmental dimensions. These principles were very different from the MDGs.

United Nations Environment Program Governing Council (2012)

Opening the UNEP Governing Council, the UN Secretary General outlined an agenda very close to what heads of state would endorse in September 2015. He had hoped that this might be possible for 2012, but the closer Rio+20 came, the clearer it became that Rio+20 could only be a staging post for 2015. Colombia, Guatemala and later on Peru and the UAE continued to promote the idea of SDGs as a game changer. Colombia hosted informal meetings with governments and stakeholders and a side event, which was billed as the SDGs building on the legacy of Stockholm (1972), Rio (1992) and Johannesburg (2002).

In 2012, the UNEP celebrated its fortieth anniversary as a UN program, bringing together all of the previous executive directors to discuss the lessons of the last forty years and the challenges ahead. Mostafa Tolba (1975–92) called for a concrete methodology to achieve the Sustainable Development Goals (ENB, 2012). The summary of the dialogue with the former executive directors declared that:

> UNEP must be at the forefront of sustainable development goals and ensure that the 'culture' of sustainable development is not lost.
>
> A need to think of the Millennium Sustainable Development Goals – and not just the Millennium Development Goals (MDGs) – which follow the idea of the sustainable development goals (SDGs).
>
> *(UNEP, 2012)*

The summary of the discussions by ministers and heads of delegation at the twelfth special session of the governing council/Global Ministerial Environment Forum of the UNEP also underlined the importance of a proposal for SDGs:

> UNEP's Governing Council played a vital role in helping to establish and promote the idea of the SDGs being part of not only Rio+20, but also of the post-2015 agenda.

Notes

1 The Group of 77 (G77) was established on 15 June 1964 by seventy-seven developing countries who were signatories of the 'Joint Declaration of the Seventy-Seven Developing Countries' issued at the end of the first session of the United Nations Conference on Trade and Development (UNCTAD) in Geneva. Beginning with the first "Ministerial Meeting of the Group of 77 in Algiers (Algeria) on 10–25 October 1967, which Adopted the Charter of Algiers", a permanent institutional structure gradually developed which led to the creation of chapters of the Group of 77 with liaison offices in Geneva (UNCTAD), Nairobi (UNEP), Paris (UNESCO), Rome (FAO/IFAD), Vienna (UNIDO) and the Group of 24 (G24) in Washington, DC (IMF and World Bank). Although the members of the G77 have increased to 134 countries, the original name was retained due to its historic significance.

2 The European Union (EU) is a politico-economic union of twenty-eight member states that are located primarily in Europe. The EU operates through a system of supranational institutions and intergovernmental-negotiated decisions by the member states. The institutions are the European Parliament, the European Council, the Council of the European Union, the European Commission, the Court of Justice of the European Union, the European Central Bank and the Court of Auditors. The European Parliament is elected every five years by EU citizens.

3 Agenda 21 identified nine stakeholder groups: Business and Industry, Children and Youth, Farmers, Indigenous Peoples, Local Authorities, NGOs, Scientific and Technological Community, Women and Workers and Trade Unions. For more on the Major Groups see: www. uncsd2012.org/majorgroups.html#sthash.vKefsyD7.dpuf.

4 The annual report of the Secretary General on accelerating progress toward the Millennium Development Goals included options for sustained and inclusive growth and issues for advancing the United Nations development agenda beyond 2015 (11 July 2011, A/66/126).

5 UN System Task Team on the Post-2015 UN Development Agenda Membership: Department of Economic and Social Affairs (DESA), Co-Chair and United Nations Development Program (UNDP), Co-Chair Convention on Biological Diversity (CBD), Department of Public Information (DPI), Economic Commission for Africa (ECA), Economic Commission for Europe (ECE), Economic Commission for Latin America and the Caribbean (ECLAC), Economic and Social Commission for Asia and the Pacific (ESCAP), Economic and Social Commission for Western Asia (ESCWA), Executive Office of the Secretary-General (EOSG), Food and Agricultural Organization of the United Nations (FAO), Global Environment Facility (GEF), International Atomic Energy Agency (IAEA), International Civil Aviation Organization (ICAO), International Fund for Agricultural Development (IFAD), International Labour Organization (ILO), International Maritime Organization (IMO), International Monetary Fund (IMF), International Organization for Migration (IOM), International Telecommunication Union (ITU), Joint United Nations Program on HIV/AIDS (UNAIDS), Non-Governmental Liaison Service (NGLS), Office of the Deputy Secretary-General (ODSG), Office of the High Commissioner for Human Rights (OHCHR), Office of the High Representative for the Least Developed Countries, Landlocked Developing Countries and Small Island Developing States (OHRLLS), Office of the Special Advisor on Africa (OSAA), Peace Building Support Office (PBSO), United Nations Children's Fund (UNICEF), United Nations Conference on Trade and Development (UNCTAD), United Nations Convention to Combat Desertification (UNCCD), United Nations Educational, Scientific and Cultural Organization (UNESCO), United Nations Entity for Gender Equality and Empowerment of Women, (UN Women), United Nations Environment Programme (UNEP), United Nations Framework Convention on Climate Change (UNFCCC), United Nations Fund for International Partnerships (UNFIP), United Nations Global Compact Office, United Nations High Commissioner for Refugees (UNHCR), United Nations Human Settlements Program (UN-HABITAT), United Nations Industrial Development Organization (UNIDO), United Nations International Strategy for Disaster Reduction (UNISDR), United Nations Institute for Training and Research (UNITAR), United Nations Millennium Campaign, United Nations Office for Outer Space Affairs (UNOOSA), United Nations Office for Project Services (UNOPS), United Nations Office on Drugs and Crime (UNODC), United Nations Population Fund (UNFPA), United Nations Relief and Works Agency for Palestinian Refugees in the Near East (UNRWA), United Nations Research Institute for Social Development (UNRISD), United Nations System Chief Executives Board for Coordination Secretariat (CEB), United Nations University (UNU), United Nations Volunteers (UNV), United Nations World Tourism Organization (UNWTO), Universal Postal Union (UPU), World Bank, World Food Program (WFP), World Health Organization (WHO), World Intellectual Property Organization (WIPO), World Meteorological Organization (WMO) and World Trade Organization (WTO).

References

Colombia (2011a) First SDG proposal, New York (paper not online).
Colombia (2011b) Second SDG proposal, New York (paper not online).

Earth Negotiations Bulletin (2012) Summary of the twelfth special session of the UNEP Governing Council/Global Ministerial Environment Forum. Available online at: www. iisd.ca/vol16/enb1698e.html

Hulme, D. (2007) *The Making of the Millennium Development Goals: Human Development Meets Results-Based Management in an Imperfect World*, pp. 10–11. Working Paper 16, BWPI, Manchester.

IMF (2010) Global monitoring report 2010: The MDGs after the crisis (GMR). Available online at: http://siteresources.worldbank.org/INTGLOMONREP2010/Resources/6911301–1271698910928/GMR2010WEB.pdf

Ladd, P. (2011) Comments on a post-2015 development framework: Goals for people and planet? Personal paper. Available online at: https://post2015.files.wordpress.com/2014/10/comments-on-a-post-2015-framework-may-2011.pdf

Levin, C. and Coburn, T. (2011) Wall Street and the financial crisis: Anatomy of a financial collapse, Washington US Senate. Available online at: www.hsgac.senate.gov//imo/media/doc/Financial_Crisis/FinancialCrisisReport.pdf?attempt=2

Llana, M. S. (2011) Brazil bumps Britain to become world's sixth largest economy, *Christian Science Monitor* (Dec. 27, 2011). Available online at: www.csmonitor.com/World/Americas/Latin-America-Monitor/2011/1227/Brazilbumps-Britain-to-become-world-s-sixth-largest-economy

Lowrey, A. (2012) Who Are the 1 Percent, *Washington Post*, October 6, 2011, Washington. Available online at: www.washingtonpost.com/blogs/ezra-klein/post/who-are-the-1-percenters/2011/10/06/gIQAn4JDQL_blog.html

Mbeki, T. (2006) Addressing the United Nations General Assembly. Available online at: www.un.org/webcast/ga/61/pdfs/south_africa-e.pdf

Perrez, F. and Ziegerer, D. (2008) A Non-Institutional Proposal to Strengthen International Environmental Governance. *Environmental Policy and Law* 38/5, 253–261.

Solo Message (2011) Solo Message, Solo, Indonesia. Available online at: www.uncsd2012.org/content/documents/Chairs%20Summary%20from%20Solo%20meeting.pdf

Stiglitz, J. (2011) The Economics of Occupy Wall Street, *Washington Post*, October 5, 2011, Washington. Available online at: www.slate.com/articles/business/moneybox/2011/10/occupy_wall_street_says_the_top_one_1_percent_of_americans_have_.html

United Nations (1992) Rio Declaration, principle 25. Available online at: www.United Nations.org/documents/ga/conf151/aconf15126-1annex1.htm

United Nations (2002) Johannesburg plan of implementation. Available online at: http://www.un.org/esa/sustdev/documents/WSSD_POI_PD/English/WSSD_PlanImpl.pdf

United Nations (2006) Report of the Secretary General's high-level panel on system-wide coherence: 'Delivering as one'. Available online at: http://www.un.org/events/panel/resources/pdfs/HLP-SWC-FinalReport.pdf

United Nations (2008) The interactive panel of the United Nations General Assembly on the global financial crisis. Available online at: www.un.org/ga/president/63/interactive/gfc/report_gfc101108.pdf

United Nations (2009) Report of the Commission of Experts of the President of the United Nations General Assembly on Reforms of the International Monetary. UN, New York . Available online at: www.un.org/ga/econcrisissummit/docs/FinalReport_CoE.pdf.

United Nations (2015) Millennium Development Goals Report 2015. Available online at: www.un.org/millenniumgoals/2015_MDG_Report/pdf/MDG%202015%20rev%20(July%201).pdf

United Nations Environment Programme (2006) Proceedings of the Governing Council/global ministerial environment forum at its ninth special session, 7–9 February 2006.

UNEP Document UNEP/GCSS.IX/11, § 15. Available online at: www.unep.org/GC/GCSS%2DIX

United Nations Environment Programme (2012) Summary of the dialogue with former executive directors. Available online at: www.unep.org/gc/gcss-xii/docs/Proceedings/K1280542%20-%20e-GCSS-XII-14.pdf

United Nations Office of the High Representative for the Least Developed Countries, Land-locked Developing Countries and Small Island Developing States (2013) State of the least developed countries 2013: Follow up of the implementation of the Istanbul programme of action for the least developed countries. Available online at: http://unohrlls.org/custom-content/uploads/2013/10/State-of-the-LDCs-2013.pdf

2

UNDERSTANDING COMPLEXITY

Development or sustainable development parallel paths emerging as one

Introduction

Rio+20 was, at the time, criticized by the media and by some NGO leaders for not achieving more. It was clear that it compared poorly to the 1992 Rio Earth Summit. What the critics had perhaps not understood when considering the comparison was that the 1992 conference was built on the back of the Brundtland Commission Report "Our Common Future" of 1987 and that it would have been appropriate to judge it against that report. It was that report to which Rio+20 should have been compared. What Rio+20 achieved was creating the possibility of bringing the environment and development communities back together and developing a joint agenda for the challenges of the next fifteen years.

Preparations for 2015

In retrospect it is clear that without Rio+20, the post-2015 agenda would not look the way it does today. In particular, Rio+20 set up:

- A new vehicle for monitoring implementation of the eventual Sustainable Development Goals (SDGs) – the High-Level Political Forum (HLPF). The terms of reference were still to be agreed upon.
- An intergovernmental process for agreeing the SDGs – the Open Working Group (SDG-OWG) – to be followed by wider intergovernmental negotiations.
- An Intergovernmental Committee of Experts on Sustainable Development Finance (ICESDF) – as an input to the upcoming Third International Conference on Financing for Development.
- A process to agree to a Technology Facilitation Mechanism (TFM) – something that had not been possible in the previous twenty years.

As people left Rio in June 2012, most of the work to establish the SDGs was still to be undertaken. There was now a process, and that process was intergovernmental. It would work with a number of initiatives which the UN Secretary General had undertaken:

- A High-Level Panel of Eminent Persons on the Post-2015 Development Agenda.
- A sustainable development solutions network.
- National consultations.
- Thematic consultations.

If 2011 and 2012 had been hectic years for the intergovernmental process, 2014 and 2015 were looking like big years for coffee producers – delegates would need something to give them energy. Many late nights and weekend meetings were on the horizon.

High-Level Panel of Eminent Persons on the Post-2015 Development Agenda

In July 2012, the UN Secretary General launched a High-Level Panel of Eminent Persons. This aimed to give guidance and recommendations on the Post-2015 Development Agendas. He successfully bridged the MDG and SDG agenda within the terms of reference of the panel, asking it to consider not just the Millennium Declaration but also the outcomes of Rio+20.

He proposed three chairs: President Susilo Bambang Yudhoyono of Indonesia, President Ellen Johnson Sirleaf of Liberia, and Prime Minister David Cameron of the United Kingdom. There were twenty-four other members, drawn predominantly from governments, with a few additions from the private sector, academia, NGOs, local authorities and other stakeholders (see Box 2.1) The individual choices caused some strong criticism from stakeholders.

BOX 2.1 LIST OF PEOPLE CHOSEN TO BE MEMBERS OF THE HIGH-LEVEL PANEL OF EMINENT PERSONS

H.E. Mr. Susilo Bambang Yudhoyono, President of Indonesia, Co-Chair.
H.E. Ms. Ellen Johnson Sirleaf, President of Liberia, Co-Chair.
H.E. Mr. David Cameron, Prime Minister of the United Kingdom, Co-Chair.

Fulbert Gero Amoussouga (Benin) heads the Economic Analysis Unit of the President of the Republic of Benin, current Chair of the African Union.
Vanessa Petrelli Corrêa (Brazil) is President of Brazil's Institute for Applied Economic Research.

Yingfan Wang (China) is a current member of the Secretary General's MDG Advocacy Group.

Maria Angela Holguin (Colombia) is the current Foreign Minister of Colombia.

Gisela Alonso (Cuba) is the current President of the Cuban Agency of Environment.

Jean-Michel Severino (France) was the General Director of the French Development Agency.

Horst Kohler (Germany) is a former President of the Federal Republic of Germany (2004–10).

Naoto Kan (Japan) is a former Prime Minister of Japan.

H.M. Queen Rania of Jordan (Jordan) is an Eminent Advocate for UNICEF and Honorary Chairperson for the United Nations Girls' Education Initiative (UNGEI).

Betty Maina (Kenya) is the Chief Executive of Kenya's Association of Manufacturers.

Abhijit Banerjee (India) is currently the Ford Foundation International Professor of Economics at the Massachusetts Institute of Technology.

Andris Piebalgs (Latvia) is the current Commissioner for Development for the European Commission.

Patricia Espinosa (Mexico) is the current Secretary of Foreign Affairs for Mexico.

Paul Polman (Netherlands) is the Chief Executive Officer of Unilever.

Ngozi Okonjo-Iweala (Nigeria) is the Minister of Finance for the Federal Republic of Nigeria.

Elvira Nabiullina (Russian Federation) is currently the Economic Advisor to Russian President Vladimir Putin.

Graça Machel (South Africa) is a current Member of The Elders.

Sung-Hwan Kim (Republic of Korea) is the current Minister of Foreign Affairs and Trade for the Republic of Korea.

Gunilla Carlsson (Sweden) is the current Minister for International Development Cooperation of Sweden.

Emilia Pires (Timor-Leste) is the Minister of Finance of Timor-Leste.

Kadir Topbaş (Turkey) is the current Mayor of Istanbul and President of United Cities and Local Governments.

John Podesta (United States of America) is Chair of the Center for American Progress.

Tawakel Karman (Yemen) is a young Yemini journalist, human rights activist and politician who was awarded the 2011 Nobel Prize.

Amina J. Mohammed (ex officio) is the Special Advisor of the Secretary General on post-2015 development.

Homi Kharas, who had been at the World Bank, but was now a senior fellow and deputy director in the Global Economy and Development program of the Brookings Institution in Washington, DC, was appointed lead author and executive secretary of the High-Level Panel Secretariat. By November 2012, the panel came up with four key areas to guide its work and consultations:

1 Lessons learned and context.
2 The shape of a post–2015 development framework.
3 Themes and content of a new framework.
4 Partnership and accountability for development.

The panel started by looking at the lessons to be learned from the MDG process and how the world had changed since 2000. It also decided to address two key questions: "what should be the architecture of the next framework? And what is the role of the SDGs in a broader post–2015 framework?".

There were hopes that the panel would take note of the national and thematic consultations overseen by the UN Development Group, which were held from December 2012 to July 2013. In the event, they set up their own consultation process (MDF, 2016, p. 18). Prior to each meeting, a stakeholder preparatory session was held which engaged panel members and the panel secretariat and focused the input of stakeholders on the panel's deliberation.

The panel published its report in May 2013. It went further than expected by putting forward its own set of twelve illustrative goals and targets. These promoted more than the MDG agenda which had been broadly expected of the panel. It reflected the beginning of a real acceptance by many that a transformational agenda might be possible. The leadership of developing countries in securing this cannot be underestimated.

BOX 2.2 THE REPORT OF THE HIGH-LEVEL PANEL OF EMINENT PERSONS ON THE POST-2015 DEVELOPMENT AGENDA

Goal 1: End poverty

a) Bring the number of people living on less than US$1.25 a day to zero and reduce by x percent the share of people living below their country's 2015 national poverty line.
b) Increase by x percent the share of women and men, communities and businesses with secure rights to land, property, and other assets.
c) Cover x percent of people who are poor and vulnerable with social protection systems.
d) Build resilience and reduce deaths from natural disasters by x percent.

Goal 2: Empower girls and women and achieve gender equality

a) Prevent and eliminate all forms of violence against girls and women.
b) End child marriage.

c) Ensure equal rights of women to own and inherit property, sign a contract, register a business and open a bank account.

d) Eliminate discrimination against women in political, economic and public life.

Goal 3: Provide quality education and lifelong learning

a) Increase by x percent the proportion of children able to access and complete preprimary education.

b) Ensure every child, regardless of circumstance, completes primary education able to read, write and count well enough to meet minimum learning standards.

c) Ensure every child, regardless of circumstance, has access to lower secondary education, and increase the proportion of adolescents who achieve recognized and measurable learning outcomes to x percent.

d) Increase the number of young and adult women and men with the skills, including technical and vocational, needed for work by x percent.

Goal 4: Ensure healthy lives

a) End preventable infant and under-5 deaths.

b) Increase by x percent the proportion of children, adolescents, at-risk adults and older people who are fully vaccinated.

c) Decrease the maternal mortality ratio to no more than x per 100,000.

d) Ensure universal sexual and reproductive health and rights.

e) Reduce the burden of disease from HIV/AIDS, tuberculosis, malaria, neglected tropical diseases and priority noncommunicable diseases.

Goal 5: Ensure food security and good nutrition

a) End hunger and protect the right of everyone to have access to sufficient, safe, affordable and nutritious food.

b) Reduce by x percent stunting, wasting by y percent and anemia by z percent for all children under 5.

c) Increase agricultural productivity by x percent, with a focus on sustainably increasing smallholder yields and access to irrigation.

d) Adopt sustainable agricultural, ocean and freshwater fishery practices and rebuild designated fish stocks to sustainable levels.

e) Reduce postharvest loss and food waste by x percent.

Goal 6: Achieve universal access to water and sanitation

a) Provide universal access to safe drinking water at home and in schools, health centers and refugee camps.
b) End open defecation and ensure universal access to sanitation at school and work, and increase access to sanitation at home by x percent.
c) Bring freshwater withdrawals in line with supply and increase water efficiency in agriculture by x percent, industry by y percent and urban areas by z percent.
d) Recycle or treat all municipal and industrial wastewater prior to discharge.

Goal 7: Secure sustainable energy

a) Double the share of renewable energy in the global energy mix.
b) Ensure universal access to modern energy services.
c) Double the global rate of improvement in energy efficiency in buildings, industry, agriculture and transport.
d) Phase out inefficient fossil fuel subsidies that encourage wasteful consumption.

Goal 8: Create jobs, sustainable livelihoods and equitable growth

a) Increase the number of good and decent jobs and livelihoods by x.
b) Decrease the number of young people not in education, employment or training by x percent.
c) Strengthen productive capacity by providing universal access to financial services and infrastructure such as transportation and information and communications technology (ICT).
d) Increase new start-ups by x and value added from new products by y through creating an enabling business environment and boosting entrepreneurship.

Goal 9: Manage natural resource assets sustainably

a) Publish and use economic, social and environmental accounts in all governments and major companies.
b) Increase consideration of sustainability in x percent of government procurements.
c) Safeguard ecosystems, species and genetic diversity.

d) Reduce deforestation by x percent and increase reforestation by y percent.

e) Improve soil quality, reduce soil erosion by x tons and combat desertification.

Goal 10: Ensure good governance and effective institutions

a) Provide free and universal legal identity, such as birth registrations.

b) Ensure that people enjoy freedom of speech, association, peaceful protest and access to independent media and information.

c) Increase public participation in political processes and civic engagement at all levels.

d) Guarantee the public's right to information and access to government data.

e) Reduce bribery and corruption and ensure officials can be held accountable.

Goal 11: Ensure stable and peaceful societies

a) Reduce violent deaths per 100,000 by x and eliminate all forms of violence against children.

b) Ensure justice institutions are accessible, independent, well resourced and respect due-process rights.

c) Stem the external stressors that lead to conflict, including those related to organized crime.

d) Enhance the capacity, professionalism and accountability of the security forces, police and judiciary.

Goal 12: Create a global enabling environment and catalyze long-term finance

a) Support an open, fair and development-friendly trading system, substantially reducing trade-distorting measures, including agricultural subsidies, while improving market access of developing-country products.

b) Implement reforms to ensure stability of the global financial system and encourage stable, long-term private foreign investment.

c) Hold the increase in global average temperature below 2° C above preindustrial levels, in line with international agreements.

d) Developed countries that have not done so need to make concrete efforts toward the target of 0.7 percent of gross national product (GNP) as official development assistance to developing countries and 0.15 to 0.20 percent of GNP of developed countries to Least Developed Countries; other countries should move toward voluntary targets for complementary financial assistance.

e) Reduce illicit flows and tax evasion and increase stolen-asset recovery by US$x.

f) Promote collaboration on and access to science, technology, innovation, and development data.

The Open Working Group: an unusual negotiation process

In September 2012, the then President of the sixty-eighth session of the UNGA, Mr. Vuk Jeremic, appointed Ambassador Maria Luiza Ribeiro Viotti (Brazil) as facilitator for the establishment of the Open Working Group of the Sustainable Development Goals (OWG).

Despite numerous meetings with regional groups organized by the Brazilian Ambassador, the different regions could not decide which countries should be nominated. The number of countries wanting to participate vastly exceeded the number of seats allocated. With thirty countries to be elected from the five different UN regions, the following formula was agreed to for the number of seats per region:

> Seven seats for Africa; seven seats for Asia and the Pacific; six seats for Latin America and the Caribbean; five Western European and others (WEOG) and; five seats for Eastern Europe.

After six months of discussions, which went nowhere, a new and creative format emerged: one seat could be shared by more than one country. The original group of thirty countries that had been envisaged increased eventually to seventy. On 22 January 2013, through decision 67/555, the OWG composition was established (see Table 2.1).

TABLE 2.1 Membership of the Sustainable Development Goals Open Working Group

African Group
1. Algeria/Egypt/Morocco/Tunisia
2. Ghana
3. Benin
4. Kenya
5. United Republic of Tanzania
6. Congo
7. Zambia/Zimbabwe

Asia Pacific
8. Nauru/Palau/Papua New Guinea
9. Bhutan/Thailand/Viet Nam
10. India/Pakistan/Sri Lanka
11. China/Indonesia/Kazakhstan
12. Cyprus/Singapore/United Arab Emirates
13. Bangladesh/Republic of Korea/Saudi Arabia
14. Iran (Islamic Republic of)/Japan/Nepal

Latin America and the Caribbean
15. Colombia/Guatemala
16. Bahamas/Barbados

Western European States and Others
21. Australia/Netherlands/United Kingdom
22. Canada/Israel/United States of America
23. Denmark/Ireland/Norway
24. France/Germany/Switzerland
25. Italy, Spain, Turkey

Eastern European States
26. Hungary
27. Belarus/Serbia
28. Bulgaria/Croatia
29. Montenegro/Slovenia
30. Poland/Romania

Little did anyone know at the time that the configuration of the OWG, with the multiple duos and troikas, would alter the traditional format of UN multilateral negotiations. The EU and the G77 made general statements, but their role was not as prominent as it usually is. The north–south divide was less evident given that countries were less constrained to follow the script of the group to which they belonged.

Although one troika – Japan/Nepal/Iran – never spoke collectively, with one exception, to thank the stellar work of the co-chairs, many of them – Denmark/Ireland/Norway and Colombia and Guatemala – kept up a virtually unbroken practice of speaking with one voice throughout the OWG.

With upwards of seventy countries participating, the discussions did on occasion become very long and repetitive; nevertheless this format made for a truly cross-regional and indeed universal process.

Working methods of the OWG

On 20 February 2013, the PGA appointed the Permanent Representatives of Hungary and Kenya, Ambassadors Csaba Kőrösi and Macharia Kamau, to organize the first meeting of the OWG.

The PGA had to choose two countries – one from the developed world and one from the developing world – to be at the helm of the OWG process. Hungary was the only developed country that was not in a pair or in a troika. African concerns about the SDGs potentially interfering with achievement of the MDGs may have been a factor in the appointment of the Ambassador of Kenya to the second co-chair post.

The first test of the duo was to establish the rules of procedure of the OWG. During the discussions with delegations, two questions emerged:

1   How 'open and inclusive' would the process be?
2   Would the report be adopted by consensus or could options be reflected where there was no agreement?

Member states who were not included in the OWG asked that all OWG meetings be open to all.

The rules of procedure leaned toward an open and inclusive process. On consensus, the co-chairs struck a balance between member states that wanted the report to be agreed to strictly by consensus and others who favored a slightly looser approach.

Having got delegations to agree to working methods for the OWG, at the group's first meeting, Ambassadors Kamau and Kőrösi were elected as co-chairs of the OWG. During the next eighteen months, they and their teams were to play a critical role in leading the process.

FIGURE 2.1   Ambassadors Csaba Körösi and Macharia Kamau, co-chairs, Open Working Group on Sustainable Development Goals, consulting

Photo by IISD/ENB (www.iisd.ca/sdgs/owg7/images/10Jan/2_IMG_5670_FR.jpg)

A global alignment

Many of the delegates involved in Rio+20 were now members of the OWG. For the next eighteen months, many negotiators traveled from capitals once a month to participate in the OWG. Member states showed deep commitment to the process by sending people regularly over the next year and a half.

The UN Department for Economic and Social Affairs (DESA) team was led by Mr. Nikhil Seth, with David O'Connor and others providing very able support. DESA and UNDP had been tasked to lead an interagency technical support team to offer relevant expert advice.

The work of the OWG was organized in two distinct phases. From March 2013 to February 2014. In this first phase, the work program focused on thematic areas that could then be transformed into goals and targets. By February 2014, delegations were anxious that almost a year had passed and negotiations in the strict sense had not started. Countries began to request more focused discussions based on a text. A vast amount of technical information relating to the potential goals and targets was now available. The challenge was to collate all these inputs into a limited number of goals and targets. The second phase of the OWG lasted from March to July 2014, during which the discussions were taken forward on the basis of a text presented by the co-chairs.

Universally applicable agenda

Throughout the OWG, the co-chairs maintained a sharp focus on universality. Although the MDGs were global in nature, they were not universally applicable. Despite a general agreement now on universality, developing countries pointed out that not all countries had the same level of capacity and development. At the center of this discussion was Rio principle 7 about Common But Differentiated Responsibilities (CBDR).

Many developing countries initially requested that CBDR be part of every goal. There were also proposals that involved different sets of targets for developed and developing countries. On the other hand, developed countries argued that CBDR was applicable only to the environmental field and was in any event not appropriate for actions that would be undertaken at the national level. A WEOG member suggested that CBDR would not be helpful in advancing specific health or education targets (UN, 2014b). In the co-chairs' text, the principle of CBDR was placed in the preamble rather than attached to specific goals.

Despite various pressures to fragment the SDG framework between north and south, and within the south between LDCs, LLDCS, SIDS, Africa and MICs, the OWG was able to maintain a universal vision.

In the OWG negotiations, the goal on sustainable consumption and production became an important test of commitment to a universal agenda. Whereas some SDGs involved a tilting of responsibility toward the south (such as education, water and sanitation), the pendulum on SCP clearly tilted toward the North and presented the latter with a significant challenge. This goal was addressing overconsumption in affluent societies and the impact this was having on the rest of the world.

The legacy of the MDGs and design of the SDGs

Delegations were facing an unusual challenge. The outcome of the OWG would not take the form of a traditional UN report; rather, agreement would have to be reached on a limited set of goals and targets with progress being measured in multifaceted ways. The MDGs would provide inspiration: they had been concise, easily understandable and involved measurable targets.

At the beginning, it was not clear whether the SDGs and the MDGs would be merged into one single vision. A group of countries still advocated for separate tracks. Manish Bapna of the World Resource Institute (WRI), who participated as a panelist, observed that the SDGs needed to build on the success of the MDGs but also needed to address some of the latter's shortcomings (UN, 2013).

As the OWG continued and trust was gained in the process, delegations began to incorporate the 'unfinished business of the MDGs' into the emerging SDGs. Unmet goals and targets of the MDGs were incorporated in the opening set of goals proposed in the co-chairs' text (i.e., poverty, hunger, education, health, gender equality and partnerships). Issues such as maternal and child mortality were also incorporated.

Moreover, the SDGs had to move beyond the scope of the MDGs. Ambassador Kamau pointed out often that delegations would have to deal with issues such as biodiversity, climate change and governance as "21st century issues" (UN, 2014c). The debate on having a stand-alone goal on inequality gained prominence as delegations from the north and south recognized the increased gap between the poor and the rich in their societies.

Moreover, the SDG framework needed to function holistically instead of in silos. Ambassador Körösi several times observed that if a country implemented one goal, it would be indirectly implementing at least five others because of the interconnectedness of the entire framework. The SDG functions as a network. There are interlinkages between targets, across different goals. For example, even though there is a dedicated goal on sustainable consumption and production, the target on decoupling economic growth from environmental degradation was placed under goal 8, which addresses economic growth.

Development of the OWG outcome

The first draft presented by the co-chairs contained nineteen 'focal areas':

1   Poverty eradication
2   Food security and nutrition
3   Health and population dynamics
4   Education
5   Gender equality
6   Water and sanitation
7   Energy
8   Economic growth
9   Industrialization
10   Infrastructure
11   Employment and decent work for all
12   Promoting equality
13   Sustainable cities and human settlements
14   Sustainable consumption and production
15   Climate
16   Marine resources, oceans and seas
17   Ecosystems and biodiversity
18   Means of implementation
19   Peaceful and nonviolent societies, capable institutions.

(Focal area 19 merged human rights)

The nineteen focal areas shared some similarities with the twelve illustrative goals proposed by the High-Level Panel. But there were also differences. The panel's proposal contained two goals dedicated to 'peace and security' issues (Goals 10 and 11), which for many delegations were outside the scope of the OWG, dealing only with economic, social and environment. The co-chairs' draft, in contrast, merged human rights and peaceful societies under focal area 19. In addition, the twelve illustrative goals omitted basic development issues such as industrialization and infrastructure, issues that African delegations in particular emphasized.

In the OWG, new proposals kept coming from all sources. Governments, UN agencies, NGOs and many others wanted their favorite issues to be part of the new framework. The OWG had to make a choice and control the volume of proposals, which was becoming unmanageable. For example, if a target proposed was not universally applicable, it would not be incorporated in the text.

Whereas some delegations were proposing additional language, others were seeking to reduce the text. A considerable number of delegations wanted no more than twelve SDGs and urged the OWG to adopt a model similar to that proposed by the HLP. In the subsequent three months, the OWG made sustained efforts to reduce the number of goals. Various alternative approaches were tested, but none attracted the necessary consensus.

Sustainable development is not business as usual

Ambassador Kamau regularly reminded delegations that "sustainable development is not business as usual" and encouraged them to step beyond their comfort zones in the search for agreement.

The following sections illustrate with four of the SDGs discussed in the OWG the efforts made by negotiators to find common ground and to develop an OWG outcome that would be truly transformative.

FIGURE 2.2 Paula Caballero Gomez from Colombia with Victor Muñoz Tuesta from Peru explaining interlinkages

Photo by IISD/ENB (www.iisd.ca/sdgs/owg7/images/8Jan/8_IMG_5389_FR.jpg)

SDG 1 – End poverty in all its forms

From the start, no one questioned that the first goal should deal with poverty eradication. Delegations had to decide whether to go for a minimalist approach or to create a goal that would be multidimensional. Member states overwhelming supported an ambitious goal. This was apparent in the language eventually selected: 'End poverty in all its forms'. As the discussion evolved, it became clear that the targets needed to address poverty beyond economic terms.

The targets under SDG 1 sought to address structural issues such as social protection floors, ensuring equal rights for men and women to own land, access to microfinance and increasing resilience to climate change.

Moreover, the overall commitment to eradicate poverty was treated not only as a stand-alone goal, but also as an overarching objective for the entire SDG agenda. Thus, every goal will seek to eradicate poverty.

BOX 2.3 GOAL 1: END POVERTY IN ALL ITS FORMS EVERYWHERE

1.1 By 2030, eradicate extreme poverty for all people everywhere, currently measured as people living on less than US$1.25 a day.

1.2 By 2030, reduce at least by half the proportion of men, women and children of all ages living in poverty in all its dimensions according to national definitions.

1.3 Implement nationally appropriate social protection systems and measures for all, including floors, and by 2030 achieve substantial coverage of the poor and the vulnerable.

1.4 By 2030, ensure that all men and women, in particular the poor and the vulnerable, have equal rights to economic resources, as well as access to basic services, ownership and control over land and other forms of property, inheritance, natural resources, appropriate new technology and financial services, including microfinance.

1.5 By 2030, build the resilience of the poor and those in vulnerable situations and reduce their exposure and vulnerability to climate-related extreme events and other economic, social and environmental shocks and disasters.

1.a Ensure significant mobilization of resources from a variety of sources, including through enhanced development cooperation, in order to provide adequate and predictable means for developing countries, in particular Least Developed Countries, to implement programmes and policies to end poverty in all its dimensions.

1.b Create sound policy frameworks at the national, regional and international levels, based on pro-poor and gender-sensitive development strategies, to support accelerated investment in poverty eradication actions.

(UN, 2015a)

SDG 5 – Gender equality and women's empowerment

There was widespread support for a stand-alone goal on gender equality and women's empowerment and also for the inclusion of this issue in other goals, such as those relating to economic growth, health and poverty. The SDG framework addresses women's empowerment in a holistic way: it requests that girls have equal access to education, it supports women as mothers and it requests that women have equal economic opportunities. Moreover, delegations overwhelmingly supported the target on ending discrimination against women. There were calls for gender-disaggregated data as a crucial measurement of progress.

Nevertheless, there were substantive difficulties regarding the ambition of this goal. One of the major controversies was a proposed reference to women's reproductive health and reproductive rights. The first draft distributed by the co-chairs did not include this term because of strong opposition on the part of a number of states. On the other hand, a group of some fifty delegations argued that, without ambitious goals and targets on women, the entire agenda would be jeopardized. Major groups and other stakeholders supported these calls.

Language on reproductive health and rights continued to be controversial throughout the OWG and beyond. These divergent views aroused from differing ethical and religious perspectives. The language that was finally agreed to for target 5.6 was one of the last trade-offs negotiated in the final hours of the OWG.

Another target that took persuasion was 5.3: Eliminate all harmful practices, such as child marriage, early forced marriage and female genital mutilation. Several delegations opposed 5.3, arguing, for example, that the definition of 'child' varied from one country to another. The co-chairs forcefully challenged those delegations who opposed this target and succeeded in retaining it in the final text.

BOX 2.4 GOAL 5: ACHIEVE GENDER EQUALITY AND EMPOWER ALL WOMEN AND GIRLS

5.1 End all forms of discrimination against all women and girls everywhere.

5.2 Eliminate all forms of violence against all women and girls in the public and private spheres, including trafficking and sexual and other types of exploitation.

5.3 Eliminate all harmful practices, such as child, early and forced marriage and female genital mutilation.

5.4 Recognize and value unpaid care and domestic work through the provision of public services, infrastructure and social protection policies and the promotion of shared responsibility within the household and the family as nationally appropriate.

5.5 Ensure women's full and effective participation and equal opportunities for leadership at all levels of decision making in political, economic and public life.

5.6 Ensure universal access to sexual and reproductive health and reproductive rights as agreed in accordance with the Programme of Action of the International Conference on Population and Development and the Beijing Platform for Action and the outcome documents of their review conferences.

5.a Undertake reforms to give women equal rights to economic resources, as well as access to ownership and control over land and other forms of property, financial services, inheritance and natural resources, in accordance with national laws.

5.b Enhance the use of enabling technology, in particular information and communications technology, to promote the empowerment of women.

5.c Adopt and strengthen sound policies and enforceable legislation for the promotion of gender equality and the empowerment of all women and girls at all levels.

(UN, 2015b)

SDG 13 – The rise of the climate goal in the last sessions

During the first phase of the OWG's work, delegations did not look for a stand-alone goal on climate change but were content for this issue to be mainstreamed across the agenda. A main consideration was that, given the complex negotiations underway in the UNFCCC, it would not be helpful to include a stand-alone goal in the OWG outcome.

However, the co-chairs believed that in the interest of overall credibility and demonstrating that it was responsive to twenty-first-century challenges, the new framework would have to include a stand-alone goal on climate change. MGoS in the room and in capitals pressed their delegations to include a stand-alone goal in the SDG framework. The LDCs began to press for a stand-alone goal. AOSIS also came on board in this respect. Eventually it was agreed by all that there would be a stand-alone goal.

Looking back, having a stand-alone goal on climate change is of important value. It has integrated climate change into the mainstream sustainable development agenda.

BOX 2.5 GOAL 13: TAKE URGENT ACTION TO COMBAT CLIMATE CHANGE AND ITS IMPACTS*

13.1 Strengthen resilience and adaptive capacity to climate-related hazards and natural disasters in all countries.

13.2 Integrate climate change measures into national policies, strategies and planning.

13.3 Improve education, awareness raising and human and institutional capacity on climate change mitigation, adaptation, impact reduction and early warning.

13.a Implement the commitment undertaken by developed-country parties to the United Nations Framework Convention on Climate Change to a Goal of mobilizing jointly US$100 billion annually by 2020 from all sources to address the needs of developing countries in the context of meaningful mitigation actions and transparency on implementation and fully operationalize the Green Climate Fund through its capitalization as soon as possible.

13.b Promote mechanisms for raising capacity for effective climate change–related planning and management in Least Developed Countries and Small Island Developing States, including focusing on women, youth and local and marginalized communities.

(UN, 2015c)

*Acknowledging that the United Nations Framework Convention on Climate Change is the primary international, intergovernmental forum for negotiating the global response to climate change.

SDG 16 – Peaceful and inclusive societies

In the discussion about whether there should be a stand-alone goal on peaceful and inclusive societies, there were different starting points. Some leading G77 members pointed out that the Rio+20 outcome had made no reference to peace and security and maintained, therefore, that these issues fell outside the OWG's mandate. Some recalled that, although the Millennium Declaration had contained seventeen references to peace, not one had made it into the MDGs. Other G77 members, however, supported the inclusion of a stand-alone goal. Many WEOG members emphasized the links between peace and development and recalled also that the HLP had two stand-alone goals: one on peaceful societies and the other on governance and institutions.

With strong views being expressed on all sides of this debate, considerable opposition to Goal 16 remained until the last hours of the OWG. In the interest of reaching consensus, a proposed reference in the title to the rule of law was deleted, though a mention survived in the third target. Ultimately, despite the many difficulties, agreement was reached on Goal 16, possibly the most sensitive and controversial of all.

BOX 2.6 GOAL 16: PROMOTE PEACEFUL AND INCLUSIVE SOCIETIES FOR SUSTAINABLE DEVELOPMENT, PROVIDE ACCESS TO JUSTICE FOR ALL AND BUILD EFFECTIVE, ACCOUNTABLE AND INCLUSIVE INSTITUTIONS AT ALL LEVELS

16.1 Significantly reduce all forms of violence and related death rates everywhere.

16.2 End abuse, exploitation, trafficking and all forms of violence against and torture of children.

16.3 Promote the rule of law at the national and international levels and ensure equal access to justice for all.

16.4 By 2030, significantly reduce illicit financial and arms flows, strengthen the recovery and return of stolen assets and combat all forms of organized crime.

16.5 Substantially reduce corruption and bribery in all their forms.

16.6 Develop effective, accountable and transparent institutions at all levels.

16.7 Ensure responsive, inclusive, participatory and representative decision making at all levels.

16.8 Broaden and strengthen the participation of developing countries in the institutions of global governance.

16.9 By 2030, provide legal identity for all, including birth registration.

16.10 Ensure public access to information and protect fundamental freedoms, in accordance with national legislation and international agreements.

16.a Strengthen relevant national institutions, including through international cooperation, for building capacity at all levels, in particular in developing countries, to prevent violence and combat terrorism and crime.

16.b Promote and enforce nondiscriminatory laws and policies for sustainable development.

(UN, 2015d)

SDG 17 – Means of implementation: revitalize global partnership for sustainable development

Goal 17 stands out from all the other SDGs. In what proved to be a long and fraught negotiation, the G77 and China sought a stand-alone goal on means of implementation and global partnership. They also consistently requested that each goal have

FIGURE 2.3 Left to right: Oana Rebedea, Romania, consulting with Felix Dodds, Global Research Institute at University of North Carolina and a senior fellow at the Tellus Institute, discussing the work around SDG 16 for the Friends of Governance for Sustainable Development

Photo by IISD/ENB (www.iisd.ca/post2015/in7–8/images/22jul/Romania.jpg)

its own means of implementation (MOI). WEOG countries did not want to have a specific MOI for each goal.

Adding to the polarization of the debate, the Rio+20 outcome had established an Intergovernmental Committee of Experts on Sustainable Development Finance, with the objective of creating a sustainable development financing strategy. Most WEOG countries felt that, given that parallel process, it was inappropriate to discuss means of implementation in the OWG.

However, the united front presented at all stages by the G77 and China on this issue ultimately left the co-chairs with little room to maneuver. A stand-alone goal and MOI targets in all the goals were incorporated into the final text. Nevertheless, some of these targets lack specificity.

Some of the most important achievements of this goal include the reference in target 17.6 of a Technology Facilitation Mechanism. G77 countries had been advocating for the creation of such a platform that would allow them to access new technologies that would enable them to accelerate progress.

BOX 2.7 GOAL 17: STRENGTHEN THE MEANS OF IMPLEMENTATION AND REVITALIZE THE GLOBAL PARTNERSHIP FOR SUSTAINABLE DEVELOPMENT

Finance

17.1 Strengthen domestic resource mobilization, including through international support to developing countries, to improve domestic capacity for tax and other revenue collection.

17.2 Developed countries to implement fully their official development assistance commitments, including the commitment by many developed countries to achieve the target of 0.7 per cent of gross national income for official development assistance (ODA/GNI) to developing countries and 0.15 to 0.20 per cent of ODA/GNI to Least Developed Countries; ODA providers are encouraged to consider setting a target to provide at least 0.20 per cent of ODA/GNI to Least Developed Countries.

17.3 Mobilize additional financial resources for developing countries from multiple sources.

17.4 Assist developing countries in attaining long-term debt sustainability through coordinated policies aimed at fostering debt financing, debt relief and debt restructuring, as appropriate, and address the external debt of highly indebted poor countries to reduce debt distress.

17.5 Adopt and implement investment promotion regimes for Least Developed Countries.

Technology

17.6 Enhance North-South, South-South and triangular regional and international cooperation on and access to science, technology and innovation and enhance knowledge sharing on mutually agreed terms, including through improved coordination among existing mechanisms, in particular at the United Nations level, and through a global Technology Facilitation Mechanism.

17.7 Promote the development, transfer, dissemination and diffusion of environmentally sound technologies to developing countries on favorable terms, including on concessional and preferential terms, as mutually agreed.

17.8 Fully operationalize the technology bank and science, technology and innovation capacity-building mechanism for Least Developed Countries by 2017 and enhance the use of enabling technology, in particular information and communications technology.

Capacity-building

17.9 Enhance international support for implementing effective and targeted capacity-building in developing countries to support national plans to implement all the Sustainable Development Goals, including through North-South, South-South and triangular cooperation.

Trade

17.10 Promote a universal, rules-based, open, nondiscriminatory and equitable multilateral trading system under the World Trade Organization, including through the conclusion of negotiations under its Doha Development Agenda.

17.11 Significantly increase the exports of developing countries, in particular with a view to doubling the Least Developed Countries' share of global exports by 2020.

17.12 Realize timely implementation of duty-free and quota-free market access on a lasting basis for all Least Developed Countries, consistent with World Trade Organization decisions, including by ensuring that preferential rules of origin applicable to imports from Least Developed Countries are transparent and simple and contribute to facilitating market access.

Systemic issues

Policy and institutional coherence

17.13 Enhance global macroeconomic stability, including through policy coordination and policy coherence.

17.14 Enhance policy coherence for sustainable development.

17.15 Respect each country's policy space and leadership to establish and implement policies for poverty eradication and sustainable development.

Multistakeholder partnerships

17.16 Enhance the Global Partnership for Sustainable Development, complemented by multistakeholder partnerships that mobilize and share knowledge, expertise, technology and financial resources, to support the achievement of the Sustainable Development Goals in all countries, in particular developing countries.

17.17 Encourage and promote effective public, public-private and civil society partnerships, building on the experience and resourcing strategies of partnerships.

Data, monitoring and accountability

17.18 By 2020, enhance capacity-building support to developing countries, including for Least Developed Countries and Small Island Developing States, to increase significantly the availability of high-quality, timely and reliable data disaggregated by income, gender, age, race, ethnicity, migratory status, disability, geographic location and other characteristics relevant in national contexts.

17.19 By 2030, build on existing initiatives to develop measurements of progress on sustainable development that complement gross domestic product and support statistical capacity building in developing countries.

(UN, 2015e)

The final hours: 19 July 2014 – the roulette ruse

The deadline for completion of the OWG's work was on Friday, 18 July. An all-night session proved necessary in order to reach final agreement. Around 1 p.m. on Saturday, 19 July, after forty-eight hours of nonstop work, the sleep-deprived and exhausted co-chairs opened the final meeting. The hundreds of delegates in the room were equally exhausted.

When Ambassador Kamau opened the meeting, not knowing how it was likely to go, he emphasized to delegations the very delicate balance achieved in this final version of the text. He admitted that it would have been virtually impossible to achieve the balance in any other way.

FIGURE 2.4   Photo of the co-chairs with their teams and the UN Secretariat discussing during the final hours of negotiations, 19 July 2014

Photo by IISD/ENB (www.iisd.ca/sdgs/owg13/images/18jul/East%20River.jpg)

Although there was some restlessness over a number of issues, overall delegations accepted that the document, though not perfect, had indeed achieved the right balance. Among dissenting notes, the G77 regretted that 'foreign occupation' had been omitted from Goal 16 (though there was a reference in the text's preamble). In addition, a number of countries sought to reopen target 5.6 (sexual and reproductive rights); it seemed, however, that their primary aim was to place their concerns on record.

The co-chairs gaveled the text through, and the agreement thereby reached on seventeen Sustainable Development Goals and 169 targets to be proposed to the GA was warmly applauded. Deep appreciation was expressed to the two co-chairs. The Kenyan and Hungarian Ambassadors were also warmly applauded (and their staff, Tobias Owgeno, Evans Maturu, Zsofia Tomaj and Anna Reich).

As the OWG drew to an end, one delegate remarked that 'the end of this journey is the beginning of the next'. The OWG had ended, but wider negotiations would have to begin shortly on the overall post-2015 development agenda.

We the peoples

The OWG involved exceptionally close collaboration between member states and MGoS. The process truly changed the way in which member states engage with stakeholders on issues of such importance for the future of humanity. Breaking new ground in the quality of this engagement, the co-chairs instituted a practice whereby delegations would be invited to meet with stakeholders and UN agencies each morning during the OWG sessions (at 9 a.m. for an hour prior to the session beginning at 10 a.m.).

MGoS also approached these negotiations with a high degree of commitment and ambition. Many of them presented detailed proposals that aimed to bring about real qualitative improvement in the outcome toward which delegations were working.

Sustainable development solutions network

In August 2012, launching his initiative for a Sustainable Development Solutions Network (SDSN), UN Secretary-General Ban Ki-moon said:

> The Sustainable Development Solutions Network will be an innovative way to draw upon worldwide expertise in the campuses, universities, scientific research centers and business technology divisions around the world.
>
> *(Ki-moon, 2012)*

Its objective, he made clear, would be to work with MGoS, UN agencies and other international organizations to identify and share the best pathways to achieve sustainable development. The SDSN director was Jeffrey Sachs, who was also director of the Earth Institute and special advisor to the Secretary General on the Millennium Development Goals.

Special event on MDGs

Arising from Rio+20, the President of the General Assembly (PGA) convened a special event (SE) in September 2013 to review the progress made in implementing the MDGs. The preparation of this one-day event, which was held in the UNGA on 25 September 2013, was entrusted to the Permanent Representatives (PRs) of Ireland and South Africa. Appointed as co-facilitators early in 2013, Ambassador Anne Anderson of Ireland and Ambassador Kingsley Mamabolo of South Africa had the task of brokering agreement on the modalities for the special event and of leading the negotiations to agree to an outcome document. On the completion of Ambassador Anderson's posting to the UN in late July 2013, her successor, Ambassador David Donoghue, was appointed to succeed her as co-facilitator. Benefiting from a smaller drafting group of key delegations, which the co-facilitators were able to assemble for the end game, the negotiations on an outcome document reached a successful conclusion shortly before the special event.

The purpose of the special event was to take stock of the progress made in implementing the MDGs, but at the same time to look ahead to the negotiations that would be needed to devise a successor framework. Some important markers were laid down in the outcome document.

First, Heads of State and Government (HOSG) underlined the urgency of achieving the MDGs in full by 2015. Although significant and substantial advances had been made in this regard, the unevenness and gaps in achievement were of concern, and immense challenges remained. Second, the document recognized that "those who have been left behind" among and within developing countries required the most urgent attention and support. It highlighted the special challenges faced by groups such as LDCs, LLDCs, SIDS, African countries, conflict and post-conflict countries and people living under foreign occupation. Describing actions they would take to accelerate progress, particularly in relation to the most off-track MDGs, HOSG emphasized the importance of approaches that would have a cross-cutting and multiplier effect. They also gave special prominence to gender equality and the empowerment of women and girls.

Third, anticipating the substance of what would become goal 16 in the 2030 Agenda, they reaffirmed the importance of promoting human rights, good governance, the rule of law, transparency and accountability at all levels. Fourth, they underlined their determination to "craft a strong post-2015 development agenda", which would build on the foundations laid by the MDGs, complete the unfinished business and respond to new challenges.

Fifth, regarding the sensitive issue of "common but differentiated responsibilities" (a Rio principle that Western Europe and Other Group [WEOG] states saw as applicable only to environmental policy but which the G77 plus China insisted was relevant to sustainable development in the broadest sense), HOSG reaffirmed all the principles of the Rio Declaration on Environment and Development, "including inter alia, the principle of common but differentiated responsibilities, as set out in Principle 7 thereof". This reversion to previously agreed-upon language was a difficult task that was achieved only in the final stages of the negotiations on the outcome document.

Sixth, HOSG underscored "the central imperative of poverty eradication". Recognizing the intrinsic interlinkage between this and sustainable development, they envisaged working toward a single framework and set of goals that would be universal in nature and applicable to all countries while taking into account differing national circumstances and respecting national policies and priorities. This framework should also promote peace and security, democratic governance, the rule of law, gender equality and human rights for all.

Finally, HOSG decided to launch a process of intergovernmental negotiations at the beginning of UN General Assembly (UNGA) 69 which would lead to the adoption of the post-2015 development agenda. They urged the completion by September 2014 of the various processes mandated by Rio+20, and as an input to the negotiations at the beginning of UNGA they called on the UN Secretary General to synthesize the full range of inputs then available and to present a synthesis report before the end of 2014. Noting that the final phase of the negotiations would culminate in a summit at HOSG level in September 2015 to adopt the post-2015 development agenda, they asked the PGA to convene intergovernmental consultations to achieve agreement on organizational modalities for the summit.

Thematic consultations

The United Nations Development Group (UNDG)[1] organized a set of eleven thematic consultations on conflict and fragility; education; environmental sustainability; governance; growth and employment; health; hunger, food and nutrition; inequalities; population dynamics; and energy and water. These consultations were hosted, in many cases, by two governments – one developed and one developing – and were supported by the relevant UN agencies and programs (see Table 2.2). Each thematic consultation held at least one meeting but also utilized the Web for online discussions around 'think papers' that had been produced by experts from the UNDG. This made the process very open and inclusive, which stakeholders responded to very well.

The outputs from these thematic consultations were fed into the High-Level Panel's deliberations and to the UN Secretary General's synthesis report. Beyond the substance, there were three overall key messages:

1 The issues covered by the MDGs were still fundamental.
2 The MDGs need to be adapted to take into account advances in measurement and social media, the need for qualitative results and the demand for policy coherence between issues.
3 There was a strong call for an expanded development agenda that would reflect strengthened public accountability, equity and human rights and would remodel itself to respond to new realities, including the ongoing jobs crisis, good governance, growing and moving populations, resource scarcity and environmental degradation, and peace and security (UN, 2014a).

Again, as the input from consultations grew, it was becoming clearer that an "MDG+" agenda would not address the concerns and challenges of 2015.

TABLE 2.2 Thematic consultations lead UN agencies and programs and governments

Theme	Leading agencies	Host government
Inequalities	UNICEF/UN WOMEN	Denmark
Health	WHO & UNICEF	Sweden and Botswana
Education	UNDP/OHCHR	Canada
Growth and employment	UNDP/ILO	Japan
Environmental sustainability	UNEP & UNDP	France
Food security and nutrition	FAO/WFP	Spain
Governance	UNDP/OHCHR	Germany
Conflict, Violence and Disaster	UNDP/PBSO/UNICEF/ UNISDR	Finland
Population dynamics	UNFPA/UN HABITAT/ UN DESA/IOM	Switzerland
Water	UN WATER & UNICEF	Jordan, Liberia, Mozambique, the Netherlands and Switzerland
Energy	UN ENERGY	Mexico, Norway and Tanzania

One critical problem of the thematic consultations and the national consultations that followed was that they happened in parallel and did not feed into each other. The thematic consultation outputs, however, did feed into the issue briefs produced by the UN for preparation for the SDG OWG.

National consultations

The national consultations were the weakest of the outreach processes because the timelines did not work to ensure effective input to the thematic consultations and then into the High-Level Panel. Nearly 100 countries carried out national consultations; UNDP supported 88 of these consultations facilitated by UN country teams. The teams worked with a wide range of stakeholders, including governments, NGOs, the private sector, media, universities and think tanks.

Although the usefulness of the national consultations was questioned by some, they did, however, enable a national dialogue that could be developed with the same groups during the implementation stage. There was some expectation that the national processes would feed into governments' positions in New York during the OWG process. In retrospect, in most cases there is little evidence to suggest that country missions in New York took up, or were even aware of, outcomes from the national consultations. Overall, the consultations did support the need for a more transformative agenda – one that addressed the new challenges faced by people. Slowly the development community started to realize that the agenda they were defending was no longer adequate and did not address the requirement that Rio+20 had put on the 2015 outcome: that the new goals and targets had to be universal and address not just development, but sustainable development.

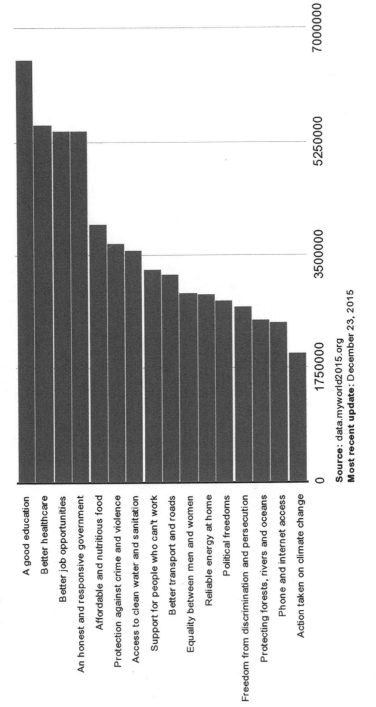

9,716,636 votes for All Countries & Groups / All Genders / All Education Levels / Age Group (All Age Groups)

A good education
Better healthcare
Better job opportunities
An honest and responsive government
Affordable and nutritious food
Protection against crime and violence
Access to clean water and sanitation
Support for people who can't work
Better transport and roads
Equality between men and women
Reliable energy at home
Political freedoms
Freedom from discrimination and persecution
Protecting forests, rivers and oceans
Phone and internet access
Action taken on climate change

0   1750000   3500000   5250000   7000000

Source: data.myworld2015.org
Most recent update: December 23, 2015

FIGURE 2.5   The My World Survey results

The world we want

With Rio+20, the UN tried to utilize social media as a platform to engage citizens, but it wasn't until the post-2015 process that real advancements were made. The input of citizens to the post-2015 process included a global online conversation through the website www.worldwewant2015.org. Social media were used as a platform to convey the views of citizens across the world.

Over 7 million people took part in the My World survey up to the end of 2014. This enabled individuals to rank their own priorities. The survey asked people to vote for six out of sixteen priority areas for development and showed real-time results in an interactive graph on its website. The My World initiative was developed through a partnership between the United Nations Development Program, the UN Millennium Campaign, the Overseas Development Institute and the World Wide Web Foundation, with support from over 230 partners worldwide. This helped the initiative reach out to communities and constituents across the planet. However, one serious problem was how it represented the world's population: 70 percent of those responding had come from only five countries (MDF, 2016, p. 18).

Another major criticism of the My World survey was that there were no real advocates for the outcomes within the negotiating chamber. The UN did pass on the outputs to the UN Task Team, but these were seldom picked up by stakeholders in their lobbying of member states.

The survey did give some room for activist NGOs to flood it. One example was that of the World Society for Animal Protection (WSPA, now World Animal Protection) who managed to persuade their members around the world to add 'Animal Protection' in the line 'Other' in the survey. This at one point brought animal protection second only to health. A few reports of the My World campaign would show this information, but they were slowly deleted from further analysis, and the explanation was that the seventeenth priority was being used as a "campaigning tool".

UN global compact consultations

The Global Compact is a voluntary initiative involving the corporate sector. Its signatories are committed to aligning their operations and strategies with ten Global Compact principles on human rights, labor, environment and anticorruption. Civil society and other nonbusiness organizations can also participate through a number of Global Compact engagement mechanisms, including policy dialogues, learning, local networks and partnership projects.

The Global Compact was invited by the UN Secretary General to assess and report on the views of business leaders on global sustainability priorities. It carried out a number of consultations to gather the views of the corporate sector. It published a report to the UN Secretary General, entitled, 'Corporate Sustainability and the United Nations Post-2015 Development Agenda', which called for a greater role and sought a set of goals and targets to extend and amplify the MDGs.

Financing for (sustainable) development

As mentioned in Chapter 1 the history of financing sustainable development goes back to the original Rio Earth Summit (1992) when it was estimated by the UN secretariat that to implement Agenda 21 it would require US$625 billion and that US$125 billion would be transferred from developed to developing countries primarily through Official Development Assistance (ODA). In 1992 ODA was at around US$52 billion from OECD countries and, in fact, fell in the period 1992 to 2000, only rising back to 1992 levels by 2002. At the five-year review of Agenda 21 in 1997 member states recognized there was a serious problem in financing sustainable development, and there was an attempt to set up an intergovernmental panel to:

- Review quality and quantity of ODA.
- Assess the impact of Foreign Direct Investment (FDI), currency specula-
  tion, privatization, structural adjustment and debt.
- Mobilize domestic resources for a transition to sustainable development.
- Find new financial mechanisms.

(Bramble, 2000)

At the same time the UN General Assembly (UNGA) adopted the Agenda for Development, and in December 1997, the UNGA adopted Resolution 52/179, which agreed to set up an ad hoc working group under the UNGA to help mobilize financial resources to fully implement the outcomes not only from the 1992 Rio Conference but all the major conferences of the 1990s.

This outcome was reflected in the 1999 UNGA Resolution 54/196, which agreed to a process that would be the first Financing for Development Conference that was held in Monterrey in March 2002. This was to try and ensure coherence with the World Summit on Sustainable Development (WSSD), which would happen in September 2002. The UN Secretary General appointed the same Secretary General for both conferences: Nitin Desai. Nitin had been Maurice Strong's deputy for the 1992 Earth Summit and the first under-Secretary General for the Department for Policy Coordination and Sustainable Development, which was merged with the Department for Economic and Social Information and Policy Analysis and the Department for Development Support and Management Services to become the Department for Economic and Social Affairs (DESA).

The Monterrey Consensus was adopted at the conference and embraced six areas:

- Mobilizing domestic financial resources for development.
- Mobilizing international resources for development: foreign direct investment and other private flows.
- Looking at international trade as an engine for development.
- Increasing international financial and technical cooperation for development.
- Addressing external debt.
- Addressing systemic issues: enhancing the coherence and consistency of the international monetary, financial and trading systems in support of development.

In 2008, there was a follow-up conference in Doha, Qatar, during the financial crisis. It reviewed the implementation of the Monterrey Consensus and had two key messages:

1   A strong commitment to continue funding ODA.
2   A decision to host a UN conference at the highest level on the impact of the current financial and economic crisis on development.

Intergovernmental Committee of Experts on Sustainable Development Finance (ICESDF)

One of the key outcomes from Rio+20 was the establishment of the Intergovernmental Committee of Experts on Sustainable Development Finance (ICESDF). Rio+20 had recognized that there would need to be significant mobilization of resources to enable developing countries to develop more sustainably and to achieve the yet-to-be-agreed-upon SDGs.

The committee would be tasked with identifying 'the mobilization of resources from a variety of sources and the effective use of financing, in order to give strong support to developing countries in their efforts to promote sustainable development' (UNDSD, 2013).

The ICESDF was established through the UN General Assembly decision A67/559. Unlike the SDG process, there was little competition for the thirty expert places for the ICESDF. It elected as its co-chairs H.E. Ambassador Pertti Majanen from Finland and Mr. Mansur Muhtar from Nigeria (see Box 2.8).

BOX 2.8 MEMBERS OF THE INTERGOVERNMENTAL COMMITTEE OF EXPERTS ON SUSTAINABLE DEVELOPMENT FINANCE

African Group: André Lohayo Djamba (Democratic Republic of the Congo), Admasu Nebebe (Ethiopia), Karamokoba Camara (Guinea), Ahmed Jehani (Libya), Joseph Enyimu (Uganda), Mansur Muhtar (Nigeria), Lydia Greyling (South Africa).

Asia-Pacific Group: Zou Ji (China), Khalid Al Khudairy (Saudi Arabia), Takeshi Ohsuga (Japan), Mohammad Reza Farzin (Islamic Republic of Iran), Sung Moon Up (Republic of Korea), Lukita Dinarsyah (Indonesia), Rajasree Ray (India).

Latin American and Caribbean Group: Gaston Lasarte (Uruguay), Saúl Weisleder (Costa Rica), Dulce María Buergo Rodríguez (Cuba), Chet Neymour (Bahamas), Reginald Darius (Saint Lucia), Samuel Moncada (Venezuela).

Western European and Others Group (WEOG): Nathan Dal Bon (Australia), Pertti Majanen (Finland), Anthony Requin (France), Norbert Kloppenburg (Germany), Liz Ditchburn (United Kingdom of Great Britain and Northern Ireland).

Eastern European Group: Emiliya Kraeva (Bulgaria), Tõnis Saar (Estonia), Viktor Zagrekov (Russian Federation), Dragan Županjevac (Serbia), František Ružička (Slovakia).

The thirty experts were selected by their regional groups. These experts unfortunately were from the more traditional 'development discourse'. They didn't include any of the major think tanks on sustainable development finance nor from key stakeholders who were working on innovative sustainable development financial options. Particularly missing was anyone who had experience from the finance sector.

The exceptions were from developing countries: Lydia Greyling (South Africa), who had worked on climate change financing; Zou Ji (China), who worked in the area of climate and energy financing; Rajasree Ray (India), a climate financing expert; and from the Eastern European Group Tõnis Saar (Estonia), who had been working on environmental auditing. All the Western and other group representatives were drawn from the development ministries.

There was considerable criticism from some sectors of the NGOs and other stakeholders that the committee had become more of a preparatory committee for the traditional 'Financing for Development' process than what it had been set up to do. In a sister publication to this book, *From Rio+20 to a New Development Agenda*, which mapped out the journey to Rio+20, it suggested the ICESDF would be judged on whether it had a set of recommendations that included:

1   identifying the external mobilization of financial resources for sustainable development;
2   identifying innovative mechanisms for financing the protection of the global environment;
3   developing a matrix of policy options and financial instruments for countries to use depending on their level of development.

(Dodds et al., 2014)

It could be argued it did none of this, and in addition, unlike the SDG OWG, its meetings were closed to stakeholders. It had five meetings: the first two were held in 2013 and the remaining three in 2014. The report, published on August 8 as an outcome document (ICESDF, 2014), significantly showed the development bias of its members, who were led by the United Kingdom and Germany. It did not fully embrace the new ideas around sustainable development finance. Nevertheless, as a document to prepare an agenda for a third Conference on Financing for Development, it successfully put forward a narrative that would be picked up by the Addis Conference.

Particular areas where it fell short concerning sustainable development finance were:

- Proposing any regulations to ensure that Foreign Direct Investment does not negatively affect sustainable development.
- Any recognition that FDI is focused primarily at a few middle income countries so is not likely be effective for LDCs.
- No real depth in how to enable capital markets to help deliver finance for sustainable development.
- No action on how Sovereign Wealth Funds could have the Santiago Principles amended to invest in sustainable development.

- No date for environment, social and governance reporting to be mandatory for companies listed on stock exchanges.
- Only a passing reference to how cooperatives or mutual funds can be utilized for sustainable development.
- No attempt to have international financial institutions audited against the SDGs to ensure their actions do not go against what will be agreed in 2015 – a do-no-damage clause.
- No mention of what role green banks can have to promote sustainable development despite examples in places like the United Kingdom and Australia.
- No suggestions on international liability for actions taken within national boundaries that have environmental impacts beyond national jurisdictions.
- No recommendation for an introduction of a financial transaction tax.
- No reform of credit rating agencies requiring them to build in sustainability criteria.

The UN system task team

The 2010 High-Level Plenary Meeting of the UNGA on the progress toward the MDGs requested the UN Secretary General to:

> report annually on progress in the implementation of the Millennium Development Goals until 2015 and to make recommendations in his annual reports, as appropriate, for further steps to advance the United Nations development agenda beyond 2015.
>
> *(UN, 2010)*

The initial responses to this were given in the Secretary General's report in August 2011, note 4. He established the UN System Task Team 5 on the Post-2015 UN Development Agenda to coordinate system-wide preparations for the agenda. It would be co-chaired by United Nations Department of Economic and Social Affairs (UNDESA) and UNDP, and its terms of reference included not only outreach within the UN family, but also to other stakeholders to develop a 'system-wide vision and road map on the post-2015 UN development agenda' (UN, 2011).

The task team was established parallel to the process around Rio+20, but it was becoming increasingly obvious that an MDG+ agenda would not address the challenges that member states and stakeholders were trying to get to grips with.

In its June 2012 report it called for:

- A vision for the future that rests on the core values of human rights, equality and sustainability.
- An agenda format based on concrete end goals and targets, one of the key strengths of the MDG framework should be retained, but reorganized along four key dimensions of a more holistic approach: (1) inclusive social

development; (2) inclusive economic development; (3) environmental sustainability; and (4) peace and security. This focused approach is consistent with the principles of the Millennium Declaration which set out a vision of freedom from want and fear for present and future generations and builds on the three pillars of sustainable development.

- To realize the future we want for all, a high degree of policy coherence at the global, regional, national and sub-national levels will be required. The core set of "development enablers" can be identified as a guide for such policy coherence without making the post-2015 UN development agenda a prescriptive one. In setting the agenda, it should be recognized that there are no blueprints and that one size does not fit all. Hence, the agenda should leave ample space for national policy design and adaptation to local settings, but be guided by the overall vision and its underlying principles.

- The post-2015 UN development agenda should be conceived as a truly global agenda with shared responsibilities for all countries. Accordingly, the global partnership for development would also need to be redefined towards a more balanced approach among all development partners that will enable the transformative change needed for a rights-based, equitable and sustainable process of global development. This would also involve reforms of mechanisms of global governance.

- It is still too early to define concrete goals and targets for the post-2015 UN development agenda. Various processes will need to run their course first. The outcome of and follow-up to the Rio+20 Conference on Sustainable Development will provide critical guidance and the proposed vision and framework for the post-2015 agenda must be fully aligned with that outcome. Also, broad and inclusive consultation processes on the vision for the post-2015 agenda are still ongoing and will be essential in shaping a shared vision.

(UN, 2012b)

The task team would play an important role in producing twenty-nine issue briefs (April 2013–March 2014) for the SDG OWG. The technical support team (TST) that was constructed under the task team would involve many of the staff who would shortly be engaged in the thematic consultations. These briefs had a vital role in what would become the SDG OWG outcome. They would also frame the eleven thematic areas around which the global consultations were organized. These areas included 'non-MDG' issues like energy, inequality, conflict, violence and disaster and population dynamics (MDF, 2016, p. 19).

As the input process finished and before the formal negotiations started, it is worth looking at an overview of where we have come from and what would now take place. Figure 2.6 gives a clear picture of what an enormous process agreeing to the SDGs was.

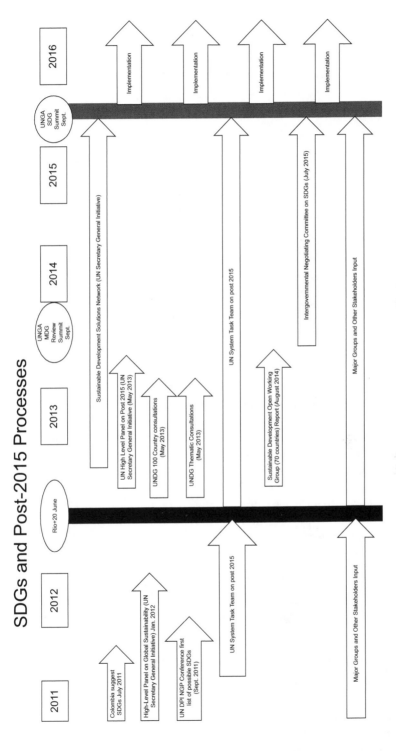

SDGs and Post-2015 Processes

| 2011 | 2012 | | 2013 | 2014 | | 2015 | 2016 |

Rio+20 June

UNGA MDG Review Summit Sept.

UNGA SDG Summit Sept.

Colombia suggest SDGs July 2011

High-Level Panel on Global Sustainability (UN Secretary General Initiative) Jan. 2012

UN DPI NGP Conference first list of possible SDGs (Sept. 2011)

Sustainable Development Solutions Network (UN Secretary General Initiative)

UN High Level Panel on Post 2015 (UN Secretary General Initiative (May 2013)

UNDG 100 Country consultations (May 2013)

UNDG Thematic Consultations (May 2013)

Implementation

UN System Task Team on post 2015

UN System Task Team on post 2015

Sustainable Development Open Working Group (70 countries) Report (August 2014)

Intergovernmental Negotiating Committee on SDGs (July 2015)

Implementation

Major Groups and Other Stakeholders Input

Major Groups and Other Stakeholders Input

Implementation

Implementation

FIGURES 2.6   SDGs and post–2015 processes

Informal alliances: why are they important and how did they shape the process?

Parallel to the formal process are a number of informal processes – often not obvious unless you know about them or are engaged in them. These fall into three broad areas. The first is that member states that are interested in a particular area create a 'friends' group; this enables them to have informal conversations across political groupings and also enables better understanding of a particular issue than can be obtained just from the negotiations. Often these groups will bring in outside experts for meetings or workshops. The second one is where a stakeholder group itself organizes an informal workshop and invites stakeholders to attend; the final one is where a UN agency or program organizes an informal briefing or workshop on a particular issue.

These meetings play an important role and help overcome differences, often building trust between delegates outside of the traditional negotiating alliances that tend to dominate official spaces. They can be held at an Ambassador level or at a working level. One of the limiting factors is that they are not open, but often if stakeholders are engaged firmly in a particular issue and are talking regularly with relevant delegates, it is not difficult to get invited or to present a paper.

Some of the most influential 'friends' groups are discussed in the following sections.

Friends of Water

The Group of Friends of Water was established by the initiative of the UN Permanent Mission of Tajikistan in 2010. It initially was a platform for the implementation of the United Nations General Assembly Resolution 64/198: "Midterm comprehensive review of the implementation of the International Decade for Action, 'Water for Life', 2005–2015". In 2012, the steering committee of the Group of Friends of Water was established with the participation of Finland, Tajikistan, Thailand and Hungary; it has thirty-nine members (Friends of Water, 2013).

At the 6th World Water Forum in Marseille, the group endorsed the idea of a Sustainable Development Goal on water to be adopted at Rio+20. They continued to hold meetings and support this through the 2015 process and successfully advocated for a target on sanitation.

Friends of Sustainable Energy for All

In September 2011, the UN Secretary General launched the Sustainable Energy for All (SE4ALL) initiative with three core objectives to be attained by 2030:

- Universal access to modern energy services.
- Doubling the rate of improvement in energy efficiency.
- Doubling the share of renewable energy in the global energy mix.

The initiative was co-chaired by Charles Holliday, the then chairman of Bank of America, and Kandeh Yumkella, who was then chair of UN Energy and director general of the United Nations Industrial Development Organization.

As in many other UN processes, "a group of friends" was established to support the initiative. The co-chairs were the Danish, Norwegian and Pakistan Ambassadors. They jointly hosted meetings with member states to keep them interested in the issue, gave regular reports on what the initiative was accomplishing and the steps it was taking to build relationships, in particular within the MGoS.

As the SDG process was underway, the need for a goal on energy became increasingly apparent, and the friends continued a high level of engagement among member states to ensure that the SDGs would include an energy goal. This was very important among G77 members, which comprised both energy producers and energy-impoverished member states. The momentum created for Rio+20 was carried through the negotiations on the SDGs. The friends group worked with SE4ALL, suggesting language for the SDGs that closely reflected the objectives of SE4ALL and had universal support among member states. The language of the SDG 7 is "Ensure access to affordable, reliable, sustainable and modern energy for all".

Friends of Governance for Sustainable Development

The Friends Group on Governance for Sustainable Development was originally set up for the Rio+20 negotiations and co-chaired by the Ambassadors of Kenya, Mexico and Indonesia. It was a major discussion place for the Institutional Framework for Sustainable Development – one of the major themes of Rio+20 – looking to explore options around the replacement of the UN Commission on Sustainable Development and how to approach strengthening UNEP. However, in the aftermath of Rio+20 it ceased to be active

As the SDG Open Working Group began, a wide range of states recognized the need for a place to discuss 'governance for sustainable development' outside of the formal sessions.

Toward the end of the Open Working Group, terms of reference for the group were developed and the leadership was taken up by three co-chairs: the Ambassadors of Mexico (Ambassador Jorge Montano), Republic of Korea (Ambassador Choonghee Hahn) and Romania (Ambassador Simona-Mirela Miculescu), with another dozen countries as the core group. Article 19 acted as the secretariat.

> The main objective of the Friends group is to create that informal space for governments to have discussions among themselves, backed up by expert papers when requested, issues relating to good governance and Institutional Framework for Sustainable Development (IFSD) in relation to the development and implementation of the post 2015 development agenda.
>
> *(Friends of Governance for Sustainable Development, 2014)*

The work of the friends group focused on Goal 16, but also looked forward to the work on indicators, institutional reform and implementation at the global, regional and national level. One of the issues it raised, which would be reflected in 'Transforming Our World', would be the increased role that parliaments should play.

Friends of SDGs

The friends of the SDGs came together ahead of the Rio+20 Conference. It was a diverse group of countries that supported the SDG proposal from the early days. The group started as a very informal platform to push the SDG process in the lead-up to the Rio+20 Conference. However, the group expanded and kept meeting throughout the three-year negotiation process. This group kept advocating for an ambitious and transformative agenda. The SDG friends included Paula Caballero and Marcela Ordoñez from Colombia, Kitty van der Heijden and Peter van der Vliet of Netherlands, Farrukh Khan of Pakistan, Jimena Leiva of Guatemala, Victor Muñoz of Peru, Majid Hasan Alsuwaidi of UAE, Yeshey Dorji of Bhutan, Franz Perrez of Switzerland, Damaso Luna of Mexico, Marianne Loe of Norway, Michael Gerber of Switzerland and many others.

Friends of Food and Nutrition Security

The Ambassador of the Netherlands convened the Friends of Food and Nutrition Security, and this group was active throughout the process. Although the group did not come together to make formal language proposals into the process, it did act as an important space to gather governments – and sometimes other stakeholders – to deepen understanding around key aspects of this issue and helped to ensure that there was a groundswell of political support for the eventual SDG 2. It was within this group that FAO, IFAD and WFP were able to introduce their thinking on the possible content of a goal built around sustainable agriculture, food security and nutrition – all of the elements that eventually found their way into the final set of SDGs. The group also became a venue to explore the interlinkages between SDG 2 (End hunger, achieve food security and improved nutrition) and promoting sustainability and the other goals, as well as emerging partnerships with nonstate actors.

Friends of Children

More than thirty states formed a Group of Friends for Children and the Sustainable Development Goals. This group of friends was an advocacy platform for a cross-regional coalition of member states that would champion the rights of children and issues related to them during negotiations on the new SDG framework and the framework for financing for development. The group had the following objectives:

- Advocate the inclusion of child-related goals and targets that were proposed in the OWG report.
- Advocate investing in children as a basis for sustainable development during the negotiations before and at the International Conference on Financing for Development in Addis Ababa in July.
- Build coalitions of key partners not only from among member states, but from civil society, academic institutions and businesses.
- Create a sense of ownership for children's rights and interests.

The group considered it very essential that children remain at the center of the post-2015 development agenda and that child-related issues were addressed in an integrated and comprehensive manner across all goals and targets. The group argued that the Declaration of the Post-2015 Development Agenda should include a suitable reference to the needs and interests of children.

Friends of Rule of Law

The group of Friends of the Rule of Law has been coordinated by Austria since 2006. It aims to promote cooperation and system-wide coherence in the UN's rule of law activities. It has also tried to enhance the engagement of member states, as well as the UN as a whole, for rule of law in various intergovernmental fora of the UN, such as the General Assembly (in particular the 6th Committee). The group comprises close to fifty members and was particularly active during the SGD OWG, as well as in the negotiations for the Agenda 2030. Its efforts to highlight that development depends on the rule of law throughout the negotiations on the Sustainable Development Goals (through joint statements and letters) garnered the support of a large cross-regional group – even beyond the group of friends – and was instrumental in achieving a strong Goal 16, including a reference to the rule of law.

World Resource Institute retreats

The "offline" discussions facilitated by the World Resource Institute (WRI) under the umbrella of the "Independent Research Forum on a Post-2015 Development Agenda" (IRF, 2015), offered member states the space to brainstorm and imagine how to design the SDGs.

IRF2015 held over seven retreats, inviting more than forty member states and NGOs. In these meetings, delegations discussed a number of key issues, for example: How would universality and differentiation be addressed? What kind of targets lead to concrete and measurable actions? How would interlinkages and synergies between the goals be addressed? These retreats became a safe space of interaction and experimental learning that had to occur outside the walls of the UN.

As example, given the strong and opposing views on the subject of means of implementation and global partnership, WRI with the IRF2015 organized a number of meetings on this issue. The discussion focused on what could be the new and transformative components of Goal 17. These retreats were held at Chatam House and allowed delegations to speak more frankly with each other. These retreats built trust among delegations on many divisive topics.

Stakeholder preparation and influence in the policy definition process

In 1992, the Earth Summit agreed on nine chapters of Agenda 21 on the rights and responsibilities for nine sectors of society, called Major Groups. These Major Groups were, over the period since 1992, more and more integrated into the decision-making process at the UN sustainable development meetings, in particular, around the CSD. This engagement with stakeholders became central to Rio+20 (2012a) and continued in the SDG OWG, but then broadened out to include 'other stakeholders' for the 2015 negotiations. This included stakeholders such as the disabled, older people and volunteers in particular. Some organizations or coalitions of stakeholders tried to present themselves as 'stakeholders', but it was clear they were in most cases just a subset of one or two of the Major Groups.

With such a large number of stakeholders engaging in the process, grouping them made it easier for member states to understand the weight of what was being proposed. If industry representatives could agree a particular issue should be taken up, then it made it clear that it had substantive weight and this applied to the other Major Groups. If a number of the Major Groups could agree among themselves on a particular issue, then this gave even greater weight to it being considered by member states.

Stakeholder influence was greatest at the beginning of the process when member states were in 'listening mode' and reduced as it got closer to the end of the negotiations in August 2015. Although an example of never giving up would be on the Friday of the first week of the last negotiating session, a group of NGOs and the youth caucus managed to at last persuade member states to add to 'Transforming Our World: The 2030 Agenda for Sustainable Development:

> . . . including by addressing growing anti-microbial resistance . . .
>
> *(UN, 2015)*

This had been something that a number of organizations tried to have a target on in the 2014 SDG OWG negotiations without success. It's a good example of never giving up and promoting your ideas until the gavel goes down on the final agreement.

BOX 2.9 MAJOR GROUP ORGANIZING PARTNERS AND OTHER STAKEHOLDERS

The role of the Major Group organizing partners (OPs) was to reach out within their sector and help prepare common views where possible. The OPs are listed next.

Major Groups coordinating organizations

Business and industry

- Louise Kantrow, PhD: Permanent Representative to the United Nations for the International Chamber of Commerce (ICC)
- Igor Runov: Under-Secretary General International Road Transport Union (IRU)
- John Drexhage: Consultant International Council on Mining and Metals (ICMM)

Children and youth

- Sarah Haynes: Restless Development (2014–16) supported by Miriam Freudenberg and Joke Lannoye
- Stephanie Beecroft European Youth Forum (2014–16) supported by Joan Conca Domenech
- Tahere Siisiialafia Pacific Youth Council (2014–16) supported by Inangaro Vakaafi and Tarusila Bradburgh
- Aashish Khullar Children and Youth International (2015–17) supported by Lloyd Russell-Moyle and Luciano Filho

Farmers

- Ms. Luisa Volpe: World Farmers Organization (WFO)
- Mr. Carlos Marentes: Equipo Técnico de la Región Norte América/North American Region Technical Team: La Via Campesina – International Peasant Movement
- Ms. Jessica L. Roe: La Via Campesina – International Peasant Movement
- Mr. Drew Black: Canadian Federation of Agriculture

Indigenous peoples

- Ms. Galina Angarova: Tebtebba – Indigenous Peoples' International Centre for Policy Research and Education
- Mr. Roberto Borrero (Taino): UN Programs Consultant, International Indian Treaty Council (IITC)

Local authorities

- Mr. Yunus Arikan: ICLEI – Local Governments for Sustainability
- Ms. Natalene Poisson: United Cities and Local Governments (UCLG)
- Secretary General: Network of Regional Governments for Sustainable Development

Non-governmental organizations

- Mr. Jeffery Huffines: CIVICUS: World Alliance for Citizen Participation
- Ms. Leida Rijnhout : European Environmental Bureau (EEB)
- Mr. Philipp Schönrock: Centro De Pensamiento Estrategico Internacional (CEPEI)

Science and technology community

- Dr. Lucilla Spini: International Council for Science
- Mr. Reginald Vachon: World Federation of Engineering Organizations (WFEO)
- Ms. Heide Hackmann, PhD: International Social Science Council

Women

- Ms. Sascha Gabizon: Women International for a Common Future
- Ms. Isis Alvarez: Global Forest Coalition
- Ms. Eleanor Blomstrom: Women's Environment and Development Organization

Workers and trade unions

- Mr. Matt Simonds: International Trade Unions Confederation (ITUC)
- Ms. Laura Martin: Sustainlabour

Other stakeholders

Educational and academic entities

- Camila Croso: Global Campaign for Education

Persons with disabilities

- Vladimir Cuk and Orsolya Bartha: International Disability Alliance
- Priscille Geiser and Elizabeth Lockwood: International Disability and Development Consortium

Volunteer groups

- Mwangi Waituru: VSO International
- Adjmal Duloo: International Forum for Volunteering in Development

Older persons

- Bethany Brown: HelpAge
- Frances Zainoeddin: Gray Panthers

Global networks

- Naiara Costa: Beyond 2015
- John Romano: TAP

Beyond 2015 Coalition

The Beyond 2015 Coalition was created in 2010. Its objective was to build a global civil society movement focusing "on the new global development framework to replace the Millennium Development Goals after 2015" (Beyond 2015, 2010).

It had two goals:

- A global, overarching, cross-thematic framework to succeed the Millennium Development Goals, reflecting Beyond 2015's policy positions.
- A participatory and inclusive process to develop this framework, responsive to the voices of those directly affected by poverty and injustice.

When it was set up it was criticized because of 'initial dominance by Northern NGOs, particularly from the UK' (Beyond 2015, 2015, p. 9) and in particular the big UK development NGOs. This later changed, and a much better balance between northern and southern civil society organizations was achieved.

Beyond 2015 had initially focused on the High-Level Panel with its input and then focused on the SDG OWG when it became the main negotiating forum. It found the space it was coming into dominated by a different organizing principle, that of the Major Groups. As was reflected in their 2015 evaluation of the Beyond 2015 campaign from a quote by a member of Beyond 2015:

> The platform for engagement offered by the UN Major Groups at the early stages of the post Rio+20 follow up processes was saturated by the Rio+20 actors and sustainable development constituencies, and was not adapting quickly enough to accommodate the required convergence of the development and sustainable development tracks into the single Post-2015 process.
>
> *(Beyond 2015, 2015, p. 18)*

This was a real problem throughout the 2015 process, and as one member of the UN staff underlined:

> There was too much complexity involved in separating the identity between Beyond 2015 and the NGO Major Group. We couldn't understand why a campaign of NGOs couldn't work with the NGO Major Group. For us it was very frustrating and we perceived that it went in detriment to everybody's effective engagement in the process.
>
> *(Beyond 2015, 2015, p. 21)*

The coalition operated at all levels from national events and lobbying to regional and global ones. This was a real attempt to ensure that voices could be heard from the grassroots to the negotiating table.

The coalition claims a number of successes:

- A strong commitment toward the universal, integral and interlinked nature of the new agenda, as well as to a high level of ambition.
- The principles of "leaving no one behind" and of "no target can be considered met until it is met for all social and economic groups". The latter could only survive political negotiation with the rewording "all segments of society".

- Anchorage in human rights. Several references were either not strong enough or watered down during the negotiations. However, all in all, Beyond 2015 is satisfied and very proud of having firmly advocated for this from the early stages of the process, engaging with the UN Secretary General High Level Panel of Eminent Persons for post-2015. The inclusion of a human rights perspective in a "sustainable development" agenda was one of the major political challenges of the process. The consultant recommends the deeper analysis of human rights commitments, prepared by the Center for Economic and Social Rights (CESR).
- Individual Sustainable Development Goals (SDGs) on gender, inequality, sustainable consumption and production, climate, and peaceful and inclusive societies.
- Protection of the planet as an overarching principle.
- Affordable, reliable and sustainable energy, instead of just "modern energy".
- Sustained, inclusive and sustainable economic growth, instead of only "growth".
- Commitment to develop broader measures of progress to complement gross domestic product (GDP).
- Within means of implementation, labor and child rights protection and environmental and health standards.
- A Technology Facilitation Mechanism (TFM) based on multistakeholder collaboration between member states, civil society, the private sector, the scientific community, UN entities and other stakeholders (Beyond 2015, 2015, p. 23).

As the process for implementation moved back to the national level, the work undertaken by Beyond 2015 could offer in some countries established platforms to engage in the national follow-up.

Communitas coalition

Communitas is the coalition for sustainable cities and regions in the new UN Development Agenda. It played a vital role in the securing of Goal 11: 'Make cities and human settlements inclusive, safe, resilient and sustainable'. The Communitas Coalition was formed with a management board of local and subnational governments (ICLEI and the Network for Sustainable Development), the Tellus Institute and UN Habitat. Its advisory board was extensive and brought together all the major stakeholders interested in human settlements. Its main purpose was to secure an urban goal and relevant targets. It organized workshops on particular issues that had become a problem in the negotiations, such as rural-urban linkages. By doing so it offered a safe space for member states, the UN agencies and programs and stakeholders to address problems and seek solutions for the negotiations.

Stakeholder events to influence the process

Numerous events were held to influence the process. The next sections discuss a couple that had some impact.

Nexus Conference 2014

The Water Institute at the University of North Carolina at Chapel Hill and collaborators hosted the Nexus 2014: Water, Food, Climate and Energy Conference on 5–8 March 2014 to examine the nexus approach in the context of input to the SDGs. The conference brought together member state negotiators, scientists and practitioners working in government, and MGoS to focus on the questions of how and why the nexus approach is, and can be, used on international and local levels. It produced the 'Building Integrated Approaches into the Sustainable Development Goals Declaration' (The Water Institute, 2014). The declaration made suggestions on different goals and targets to ensure a more integrated approach between the four sectors:

> An integrative approach is a valuable strategic tool for operationalizing the goals and targets of the Sustainable Development Goals and the post-2015 development agenda. Constructing integrated goals and targets presents challenges but also clear opportunities for policy makers.
>
> *(The Water Institute, 2014)*

65th UN DPI NGO Conference

This was the second UN DPI NGO Conference that was organized in the new way to enable stakeholders to provide input to intergovernmental processes. The first had helped frame the SDG discussions in 2011, being the first meeting to come out with suggested SDGs and targets. Over 2,000 attended the 2014 UN DPI NGO Conference, and it was chaired by Jeffery Huffines from CIVICUS and one of the organizing partners for the NGO Major Group.

The declaration focused on what they hoped would be the outcome document that heads of state would address in 2015, what was missing in the SDGs and what should be considered in the follow-up process. It highlighted that the document should have a:

> Rigorous human rights-based accountability systems, based on compulsory reporting, must be established at both the domestic and international levels as part of an effective system of accountability.
>
> *(UNDPI, 2014)*

Note

1 United Nations Development Group: Food and Agriculture Organization of the United Nations (FAO), International Fund for Agricultural Development (IFAD), International Labour Organization (ILO), International Telecommunications Union (ITU), Office of the High Commissioner for Human Rights (OHCHR), Office of the Special Adviser on Africa (OSAA), Office of the Special Representative of the Secretary-General for Children and Armed Conflict (OSRSG-CAC), United Nations Economic and Social Commission for Western Asia (UN-ESCWA), United Nations Human Settlements Programme

(UNHabitat), Office of the High Representative for the Least Developed Countries (UN-OHRLLS), Landlocked Developing Countries & Small Island Developing Countries, United Nations Entity for Gender Equality and the Empowerment of Women (N-Women), Joint United Nations Programme on HIV/AIDS (UNAIDS), United Nations Conference on Trade and Development (UNCTAD), United Nations Department of Economic and Social Affairs (UNDESA), United Nations Development Programme (UNDP), United Nations Economic Commission for Africa (UNECA), United Nations Economic Commission for Europe (UNECE), United Nations Economic Commission for Latin America and the Caribbean (UNECLAC), United Nations Environment Programme (UNEP), United Nations Economic and Social Commission for Asia and the Pacific (UNESCAP), United Nations Educational, Scientific and Cultural Organization (UNESCO), United Nations Population Fund (UNFPA), United Nations High Commissioner for Refugees (UNHCR), United Nations Children's Fund (UNICEF), United Nations Industrial Development Organization (UNIDO), United Nations Office on Drugs and Crime UNODC), United Nations Office for Project Services (UNOPS), United Nations World Tourism Organization (UNWTO), World Food Programme (WFP), World Health Organization (WHO), World Meteorological Organization (WMO), Observers: Director, Office of the Deputy Secretary General (DSG), Office for the Coordination of Humanitarian Affairs (OCHA), Office of the Spokesperson for the Secretary-General, United Nations Department of Political Affairs (UNDPA), United Nations Department of Public Information (UNDPI), United Nations Fund for International Partnerships (UNFIP), World Bank.

References

Beyond 2015 (2010) Objectives and guiding principles of Beyond 2015. Information from web site. Available online at: www.beyond2015.org/objectives-and-guiding-principles-beyond-2015

Beyond 2015 (2015) Beyond 2015 campaign final evaluation. Available online at: http://beyond2015.org/final-evaluation-beyond-2015

Bramble, B. (2000) *Financial Resources for the Transition to Sustainable Development in Earth Summit 2002*, edited by Dodds, F., Earthscan, London.

Dodds, F., Laguna-Celis, J. and Thompson, L. (2014) *From Rio+20 to a New Development Agenda*, Routledge, New York.

Friends of Governance for Sustainable Development (2014) Terms of reference. Available online at: http://friendsofgovernance.org/index.php/about-us/

Friends of Water (2013) Reporting on progress from the Group of Friends of Water. Available online at: www.un.org/waterforlifedecade/friends_of_water.shtml

Intergovernmental Committee of Experts on Sustainable Development Financing (2014) Report of the Intergovernmental Committee of Experts on Sustainable Development Financing. Available online at: https://sustainabledevelopment.un.org/content/documents/4588FINAL percent20REPORT percent20ICESDF.pdf

Ki-moon, B. (2012) United Nations Secretary-General announces new sustainable development initiative. UN Press Release. Available online at: www.un.org/millenniumgoals/pdf/SDSN percent20FINAL percent20release_9Aug.pdf

MDF (2016) Outcome evaluation report: Building the Post 2015 development agenda – open and inclusive consultations for the United Nations Development Group, page 18, Ede, MDF.

Sachs, J. (2016) Implementing the Paris Climate Agreement, Horizons Winter Journal, Available online at: www.cirsd.org/publications/magazines_article_view_short/english/128

United Nations, Agenda 21 Chapter 2 24 to 32. UN. New York. Available online at https://sustainabledevelopment.un.org/content/documents/Agenda21.pdf

United Nations (1992a) Agenda 21, New York. Available online at: https://sustainable development.un.org/content/documents/Agenda21.pdf

United Nations (2012b) High-level panel of eminent persons on the post-2015 development agenda framing questions. Available online at: www.un.org/sg/management/pdf/HLP_Framing_Questions.pdf

United Nations (2014a) OWG, session 7, meeting 3. Available online at: https://sustainabledevelopment.un.org/index.php?page=view&nr=872&type=12&menu=1807&template=1042&play=607

United Nations (2014b) OWG, session 9. Available online at: https://sustainabledevelopment.un.org/processes/post2015/owg/session9

United Nations (2014c) OWG, session 9, meeting 1. Available online at: https://sustainabledevelopment.un.org/index.php?page=view&nr=872&type=12&menu=1807&template=1042&play=492

United Nations (2015) Transforming our world: The 2030 agenda for sustainable development. Available online at: https://sustainabledevelopment.un.org/post2015/transformingourworld

United Nations (2015d) Highlights from the conference. Available online at: www.un.org/esa/ffd/ffd3/special/highlights-from-the-conference.html

United Nations (2015e) Pope Francis address in the General Assembly. Available online at: http://webtv.un.org/search/address-by-his-holiness-pope-francis-general-assembly-3rd-plenary-meeting-70th-session/4509290546001?term=pope%20francis

UNDPI (2014) 2015 and beyond: The 65th UN DPI NGO conference – our action agenda. Available online at: http://outreach.un.org/ngorelations/files/2014/09/Conference-Outcome-Document_opt.pdf

United Nations Division on Sustainable Development (2013) Sustainable development knowledge platform. Available online at: https://sustainabledevelopment.un.org/index.php?menu=1558

The Water Institute (2014) *Building Integrated Approaches into the Sustainable Development Goals*, Chapel Hill, The Water Institute. Available online at: http://nexusconference.web.unc.edu/files/2014/08/nexus-declaration.pdf

3

THE BIG YEAR

The preparatory process

Introduction

The journey of rebirth for sustainable development that had started at the UN General Assembly in September 2007 with Brazilian President Lula da Silva's call for Rio+20 gained further momentum through promotion of the Sustainable Development Goals (SDGs) by some key countries. This process developed through the Rio+20, through the HLP report, through the special event outcome in September 2013, though the OWG-SDG outcome in July 2014, through the SG synthesis report in December 2014 and through discussion in a wide range of meetings, workshops and side events and papers. It would now culminate in a set of intergovernmental negotiations in the GA.

Moving forward from the OWG

Following agreement on the OWG outcome, the Kenyan and Hungarian co-facilitators forwarded this document to the PGA. In conformity with the Rio+20 mandate, they presented it as the proposal of the OWG for Sustainable Development Goals, which they were forwarding to the General Assembly for consideration and appropriate action.

The G77 and China requested that this proposal be adopted as "the basis for integrating the SDGs into the post 2015 agenda". They argued that, although not all goals and targets had inspired equal enthusiasm among delegations, the seventeen SDGs and 169 targets were being accepted by all as a package, and any attempt to reopen individual goals or targets could lead to very protracted and difficult negotiations. The G77's emphatic approach was a little surprising given the reservations expressed by members of the group in the final stages of the OWG process about various aspects of the document. A further G77 concern may have been to embed the OWG outcome firmly as an integral part of the forthcoming intergovernmental negotiations in advance of the appearance of the 'synthesis report' which the Secretary General had been asked to prepare under Resolution 6/68. Fresh from the battles over Goal 16 and other controversial parts of the OWG outcome, some G77 members may have been apprehensive that the Secretary General's report might seek to reopen some of these issues in ways with which they would not be comfortable, and that this could end up upsetting a political balance that had been carefully achieved in the OWG outcome.

WEOG members (WEOG is being used in this chapter as shorthand for developed countries in a broad sense), on the other hand, did not see the OWG outcome as the final word in terms of defining the goals and targets for the new agenda. They also felt that space had to be left for other inputs, including the SG's synthesis report. They therefore preferred a more tentative description of the status of the OWG outcome.

Informal contacts took place over a few weeks, with the PGA involving himself personally. The compromise formulation agreed on was that the OWG outcome would be the "main basis for integrating sustainable development goals into the post-2015 development agenda". This appeared in a GA resolution (68/309) in September 2014, which welcomed the OWG report, decided that the proposal of the OWG "shall be the main basis for integrating SDGs into the post-2015 development agenda (UN, 2014a) and recognized at the same time that "other inputs will also be considered" (UN, 2014b).

In October 2014, the President of the UNGA, Sam Kutesa, appointed Ambassador David Donoghue of Ireland and Ambassador Macharia Kamau as co-facilitators to "lead open, inclusive and transparent consultations on the post-2015 development agenda, including the organization and modalities for the intergovernmental negotiations and the remaining issues related to the summit for the adoption of the post 2015 development agenda". A lot of expectations rested on the shoulders of the two co-facilitators. They began work immediately, convening in November–December 2014 a series of informal consultations at which they set out their own hopes for the negotiations and invited member states to share their perspectives.

Informal consultations on modalities

Given the fractious atmosphere in the final stages of the OWG's work and the testy exchanges in early September over the status of the outcome document, the mood in the opening sessions was surprisingly constructive. Confrontations that had been feared over issues such as Goal 16 or means of implementation did not materialize. And, although there were bumps along the way, this positive and forward-looking dynamic was largely sustained over the subsequent nine months.

There was, perhaps, a recognition of the enormity of what was at stake and, in particular, of the price of failure. There was a sense that, with a summit fixed for September 2015 and only a few months available in which to craft a post-2015 agenda that would live up to the hopes and ambitions of millions of ordinary citizens around the globe, no time could be wasted. Although new issues and challenges surfaced along the way and a handful of core difficulties remained stubbornly to the end, it was reassuring nevertheless that delegations largely resisted the temptation to reopen compromises that had been reached during the OWG phase.

The heavy emphasis of the G77 on the sanctity of the OWG outcome led to other groups accepting in due course that there was no prospect of securing substantive changes to the goals and targets proposed in that process. There was a sense all round that if any serious attempt were made to reopen a substantial issue, the entire edifice of what the OWG had agreed to could be imperiled. With that recognition, it became easier to concentrate the attention of negotiators on several other key difficulties affecting the future agenda and on how these could be overcome.

The informal sessions in November gave member states an opportunity to address both the content of the agreement they would be working toward and the structure and modalities of the Intergovernmental Negotiations (IGN).

In terms of content, the co-facilitators emphasized from the outset the historic nature of the task ahead and the expectations attached worldwide to this process. It was clear that delegations were in full agreement; all spoke of the enormous responsibility that would weigh on the negotiators.

In terms of modalities, it became clear that many member states valued the relative informality and flexibility of the OWG working methods and wished to retain these to the extent possible during the IGN. The fact that all 193 member states were involved in the IGN meant, of course, that it was not practical to continue the much smaller OWG's division of participants into troika arrangements (which had had a cross-regional dimension and had been found very useful). But, bearing in mind the importance of the post-2015 agenda for all member states, it was tacitly accepted that individual member states should be able to complement the positions presented by regional groups in the negotiations.

Member states spoke freely, both on substance and on procedure, and, while regional groups took the floor regularly, they did so in a way that did not constrain their individual members. There were, it is true, key moments during the negotiations when the regional groups played a pivotal role in defining the parameters for making progress or in brokering solutions to an impasse. Examples included the reaching of a final agreement on the modalities or the handling of discussions relating to the financing for development process; regional groups were also decisive in the end game in July 2015. On the whole, however, the negotiations were characterized by an easy succession of interventions from groups and individual member states which progressively built consensus and prepared the way for eventual agreement.

In light of the wide variety of comments made by delegations during the opening informal meetings, the Co-Facilitators circulated in early December a proposal on modalities. This covered the scope envisaged for the negotiations, the organizational arrangements and working methods and dates for the individual sessions.

On scope, the proposal listed what had emerged as common ground among member states. Reflecting the content envisaged for the document which would issue from the summit in September 2015, the negotiations would have four substantive components: (i) an opening political declaration, (ii) Sustainable Development Goals and targets, (iii) means of implementation and global partnership for sustainable development, and (iv) follow-up and review.

In their formulation of (ii), the Co-Facilitators were deliberately minimalist, avoiding any qualifying language that might appear to preempt the negotiations (e.g., "completion" or "finalization" of the goals and targets). With regard to (iv), the formulation "follow-up and review" was used in deference to G77 sensitivities about the connotations of language such as 'accountability' or 'monitoring'.

In suggesting dates for the IGN sessions and proposing an overall 'roadmap' for the negotiations, the Co-Facilitators took account of the dates already agreed to for the parallel Financing for Development process (which was already underway and was due to be completed in June, ahead of the Addis Ababa summit in July). Back-to-back arrangements, designed in particular to help member states with limited resources to handle the demands of both processes, proved possible in several instances.

The 'roadmap' proposed a rhythm of, on average, one four-day session per month from January to May inclusive. (More frequent meetings were initially contemplated, but these fell victim to budgetary considerations as well as to concerns on the part of some member states that too much time for the negotiations could ultimately be counterproductive). A June session would utilize part of the meeting of the High-Level Political Forum (HLPF) scheduled for that month. In July there would be a two-week session immediately following the Addis Ababa summit. The intention, the Co-Facilitators made clear, was to complete the negotiations by 31 July.

The roadmap envisaged that the January session would carry out an initial 'taking stock' of the negotiations as a whole and the issues they would cover. This would be followed in February by a focus on the declaration; in March by a discussion of goals, targets and indicators; in April by a discussion of means of implementation and the Global Partnership for Sustainable Development; in May by a discussion of the follow-up and review arrangements; and in June by negotiations on a first draft of the outcome document. The July session would be devoted to completing negotiations on the draft outcome document, particularly in the aftermath of the Addis Ababa conference. The sequence proposed for these topics reflected a number of tactical judgments on the part of the CoF (who, for example, saw merit in deferring by a month or two what was likely to be a difficult engagement on goals and targets).

In the course of four intensive meetings in December 2014 (3, 10, 11 and 16 December), agreement was reached on the full set of modalities for the IGN. On the proposal of the CoF, much of the final meeting was devoted to informal consultation among several key players – notably the European Union and the G77 – to resolve a number of contentious points. Although protracted standoffs on procedural issues are not unusual in negotiations of this kind, in this instance a conciliatory and pragmatic approach was displayed on all sides; negotiators were no doubt conscious of the need to resolve these matters rapidly if the negotiations were to begin on schedule in January.

The G77 had pressed initially for a General Assembly resolution to give effect to whatever agreement was reached on modalities. WEOG and others resisted this, however, as they feared that work on a resolution (possibly with lengthy preambular material) might be time consuming and distracting. As a compromise, the CoF proposed the more informal expedient of a GA decision. This was agreed, and drafts of two decisions, on modalities and dates, respectively, were circulated. The terms of these were agreed on 16 December, and the two decisions were adopted by the GA on 14 January 2015.

The participants

The series of monthly negotiation sessions, which began in January 2015, were held in a number of large conference rooms in the UN complex (generally in the basement area). With delegates attending in large numbers, both from missions and from capitals, and with the Major Groups and Other Stakeholders (MGoS) also heavily represented throughout, the rooms were invariably packed to full capacity. Attendances of upwards of 400 were the norm. This was a reflection of the extraordinary importance of these negotiations, affecting as they did the direct interests of every UN member state, large or small. Member states frequently attended at the Permanent Representative (PR) level, with the numbers rising as the negotiations moved toward the end game. Many sent ministerial or other high-level representatives from capital to individual sessions.

An inclusive process

The preparation of the 2030 Agenda – in effect a blueprint for the development of humanity and the planet over the next fifteen years – had been envisaged all along as an inclusive process, one in which the voices of a wide range of stakeholders and interest groups would be clearly heard. Unsurprisingly, the level of MGoS interest in the negotiations remained intense throughout the seven months.

During each monthly session, a diverse set of representatives of the MGoS followed developments closely from the upper tier of the conference room. Since the Earth Summit in 1992, it was recognized that achieving sustainable development would require the active participation of all sectors of society and all types of people. To facilitate this, nine sectors of society were identified as the main channels through which broad participation would be facilitated in UN activities related to sustainable development, officially known as the "MGoS". The broad and active range of stakeholders provided a large volume of written contributions both before and during the negotiations. They also mixed freely and informally with delegates on the margins of the negotiations.

Building on very positive practices which had been developed during the OWG phase, the CoF instituted a set of arrangements for structured interaction with the MGoS during each monthly session. Typically, these involved reserving a three-hour period, usually a morning in mid-week, when member state delegates would have a structured 'interactive dialogue' on the issues of the week with the MGoS.

In an organizational innovation, this dialogue took place in the main part of the conference room, with participants from both sides seated alongside each other and nameplates dispensed with for added informality. The MGoS would select their own representatives beforehand for each dialogue, and these would make short opening presentations. The secretariat in turn would have invited individual member states in advance to respond.

In contrast to the somewhat meager turnout of member state representatives for the early-morning discussions with MGoS held during the OWG phase, there was a far higher level of member state representation at these dialogues. The CoF chaired these sessions and intervened frequently to guide the discussion or seek clarification or amplification of points made. Overall, these monthly structured dialogues proved highly popular with MGoS and member states alike and, by providing an opportunity for both sides to explore issues jointly in a relaxed environment, contributed significantly to the ultimate success of the negotiations. They also regularly generated fresh insights or striking concepts and formulations, some of which were drawn on by the CoF when preparing their successive drafts of the outcome document.

The role of the co-facilitators

There was a general welcome for the appointment of the Ambassadors of Ireland and Kenya as co-facilitators for the negotiations on the post-2015 development agenda. In addition to his profound expertise on global development issues, his involvement in major negotiation processes in this field and his extensive experience of the UN, Ambassador Macharia Kamau of Kenya had been a highly effective co-chairman, with Hungary's Ambassador Csaba Kőrösi, of the OWG. He therefore provided direct continuity from this critical precursor to the intergovernmental negotiations on the post-2015 development agenda. Ambassador David Donoghue of Ireland, for his part, had co-facilitated with South Africa (Ambassador Kingsley Mamabolo) the special event on the MDGs which was held in the General Assembly in September 2013 and which, following closely on the Rio+20 conference, supplied important impetus for the post-2015 process. He also brought development expertise and extensive negotiating experience to the table.

Ambassadors Kamau and Donoghue were assisted by small but highly efficient teams. The Irish team, led by DPR Tim Mawe, consisted of John Gilroy, Michael McManus, Christina McElwaine and Jeanne Spillane. The Kenyan team consisted of Evans Maturu and Arthur Andambi. A DESA team was led by Nikhil Seth with very able assistance from David O'Connor and others.

Ambassadors Kamau and Donoghue set about their task with strong motivation and determination to deliver the result expected of them. While the contribution made by a co-facilitator to a negotiation process is in principle weaker than that of a co-chairman, in practice this distinction proved irrelevant. The CoF managed to build confidence from the outset, to win respect on all sides and to assert quiet but firm control over the process. This required a steady hand and good judgment at all times.

Critical to success was reaching clear agreements with each other on how each successive challenge of the negotiations, whether procedural or substantive, would be handled. This close partnership became even more important as the steadily greater challenges of the final weeks of negotiations were reached. Chairing the meetings alternately and sharing the tasks of introducing and summing up the discussions, the CoF took pains to demonstrate at every juncture the strength of their partnership and also of their resolve to bring the agreement to fruition on time. This focus and single-mindedness was commented on frequently by delegations and helped over time to build the authority of the CoF and to ensure cross-regional support for their leadership.

A test of their authority was the extent to which the CoF would succeed in "holding the pen" when it came to the drafting of the outcome document. While it was accepted that the CoF would provide a "zero draft" of this document, this could not be taken to mean that all regional groups would be content for the CoF to remain in charge of the drafting process until the final product was achieved. In earlier large negotiations there had been a tendency on the part of some groups to ask in the later stages that the draft be projected onto a screen, along with all amendments proposed, and to insist on a collective drafting exercise from that point on which would involve line-by-line negotiation. This generally had the effect of complicating and protracting the process of reaching agreement on a text.

In the IGN the CoF circulated on 1 June an initial "zero draft" which they had prepared. In keeping with the working methods used in the OWG, they used the negotiation sessions in June and July to gather comments on successive versions of this draft which they presented, to the point where a sixth and final version was adopted by acclamation on 2 August. It was a textbook example of the CoF retaining the pen from beginning to end. At no point did member states propose any other arrangement for finalizing the document. Although many obstacles arose in the final drafting stages, no outside mediation was required to overcome these; they were resolved in the course of detailed negotiations among member states, sometimes in smaller groups that were instituted under the authority of the CoF. At the end, member states thanked the CoF warmly for the firm leadership they had shown throughout this process.

19–21 January: the substantive negotiations begin

Marking the solemnity of the occasion and the historic nature of the challenge that lay ahead, the Secretary General of the UN and the President of the General Assembly were in attendance for the opening of the substantive phase of the negotiations on 19 January. The SG in his remarks emphasized that

> the world is watching and expectations are high, and we must demonstrate that we are determined to work together to build a better life and a brighter future for the most vulnerable, their children and their grandchildren . . . to build a better world, based on solidarity, trust and mutual responsibility.
>
> (UN, 2015a)

The PGA's remarks focused on the people-centered nature of the new agenda, calling for it to:

> be responsive to and meet people's needs and aspirations. It should preserve our planet for the present and future generations.
>
> *(UNPGA, 2015)*

The President of Economic and Social Council (ECOSOC) and the two CoF also delivered strong messages of encouragement.

In addition, a number of leading academics and development experts made presentations to stimulate discussion under the different headings (goals and targets, the declaration, means of implementation and the global partnership and follow-up and review).

Reflecting the close coordination with the FfD negotiations that had been agreed to, statements were made by the CoF of those negotiations, the Ambassadors of Norway and Guyana. (A pattern of mutual briefings continued for the remainder of each set of negotiations; there was also a very effective joint process in April/ May that achieved important results.) To mark the linkage to the climate change negotiations, a briefing by the Peruvian Minister for the Environment on COP 20 in Lima was planned, but the Minister could not attend.

The three-day session proceeded to take stock in overall terms of the work to be done and the possible shape and content of the post-2015 development agenda. There was broad agreement that the new agenda should be universal, ambitious, transformative and inclusive and should complete the unfinished business of the MDGs. It was also agreed that the OWG outcome would be the main basis for integrating the SDGs into the new agenda. While the EU, Canada and other OWG states gave the SG's synthesis report strong support, G77 countries were more equivocal, seeing this as a useful resource but not as the basis for the IGN.

Member states exchanged views on what the CoF had suggested might be the four main components of the outcome document for the September summit: a declaration; the goals and targets; the means of implementation and the global partnership; and the arrangements for follow-up and review. Over the three days, upwards of 200 statements were delivered. A number of distinguished outside experts contributed. In the first of the monthly dialogues, MGoS representatives voiced their hopes for the negotiations.

Overall, the atmosphere was very positive; the CoF were encouraged by the constructive engagement shown and by the readiness of delegations to move beyond procedural debate and into substance. The issues that attracted greatest interest at this stage were the content envisaged for the declaration, the process for the development of global indicators to accompany the targets and what should be done if a 'technical proofing' of the targets (which had been commissioned following the December session) revealed a need to adjust some targets.

In terms of the declaration, it was generally agreed that this should be concise, visionary and inspirational. Many views were expressed about specific themes and references it should include. Various documents were proposed as source material, from the Millennium Declaration to the Rio+20 outcome document, the outcome document of the special event on the MDGs that was held in September 2013, the "chapeau" section of the OWG report (of particular importance to the G77) and the SG's synthesis report (emphasized by WEOG states). Several member states emphasized the need for language that could communicate the new agenda easily to the general public. In this regard, however, differences emerged over the utility of the six 'essential elements' contained in the SG's synthesis report: dignity, people, planet, prosperity, justice and partnership. Some WEOG states saw these as a useful communication and framing tool; however, some G77 felt that they encouraged silo thinking and they therefore advocated caution (with a complaint made by one or two that the six essential elements did not adequately reflect the breadth and depth of the SDGs).

Many member states highlighted the special needs and circumstances of different regions. Cases were made in particular for the needs of the members of the Caribbean Community and Common Market (CARICOM), Small Island Developing States (SIDS), the Alliance of Small Island States (AOSIS), the Least Developed Countries (LDCs) and the Landlocked Developing Countries (LLDCs) to be explicitly highlighted and addressed in the outcome document.

17–20 February: framing the declaration

The initial discussion of the declaration at the January stock-taking meeting was deepened and extended in a four-day session dedicated to this subject from 17–20 February.

On 2 February, the CoF had circulated an 'elements' paper to stimulate this discussion. They had also asked member states to address a number of questions regarding the key messages on vision, common principles and transformative approaches that might be contained in a declaration.

Almost one hundred statements were made by regional groups, by groups of member states congregating around specific issues and by individual member states over the first day-and-a-half in response to these questions and the 'elements' paper. In addition, there had already been in advance of the session a huge flow of written contributions on the declaration from member states and from MGoS.

In order to move the process forward and to identify clearly where convergence might be found, the CoF circulated a further 'discussion paper' to delegates on the morning of 19 February. Reactions to this took up the remaining day and a half of the February session.

The 'elements' paper was essentially a series of bullet points grouped under six headings:

- A collective vision of the road to 2030.
- What we must do to get there.
- How we will do this.

- Follow-up and review.
- Our commitment.
- A final call to action.

(UN, 2015b)

The 'discussion paper' went further. In a relatively detailed fashion, it captured many of the points made in the opening statements and, although not offering a developed text at this stage, provided member states with an example of the scope, form and potential size of a declaration. The paper indicated a desire to keep the declaration to three pages for it to remain effective. In saying this, the CoF were deliberately signaling that they envisaged, and were strongly recommending, a concise declaration. Many member states warmly welcomed the discussion paper as a confidence booster for the process. Many also expressed full confidence in the ability of the CoF to, as one delegate put it, "provide a compelling narrative that inspires action".

From the outset, and responding to the many calls for an easily communicable agenda, the CoF envisaged a short preface to the declaration which would explain succinctly the nature and purpose of the goals and targets. Drafting of this text, however, did not begin until much later in the process.

Overall, reaction to the papers of 2 and 19 February was very positive. Both served their purpose in focusing interventions during the opening days and enabling points of convergence and difference to be identified over the final days of the session. Although certain controversial issues were not as prominent as might have been expected, others were highlighted repeatedly. In the end, the great majority of the membership appeared to agree that the declaration should break from the traditional structure and language used in UN documents of this kind, should communicate clearly the core messages at the heart of the post-2015 development agenda and serve as an inspiring call to action. Group after group echoed the view that the declaration should be concise, visionary, ambitious, actionable, communicable and simple. (Capturing the attention of many, one member state called for the declaration to be understandable to a 13-year-old and suggested that it be proofread by a young person). And, although groups insisted on references to hallowed texts from previous UN conferences, a quiet consensus emerged that these could ultimately take the form of footnote references.

There was also a strong view across the membership that the declaration should prioritize action to address the needs of the poorest and most marginalized people. The multidimensionality of poverty and the cross-cutting importance of achieving gender equality and women's empowerment were further themes. There was also general approval for the idea that no target should be considered met unless it was met for all social and economic groups and that "nobody should be left behind". On the latter point, however, one G77 member suggested that this principle tended to distract attention from "those who are too far ahead" and felt that the principle of equality had to be given greater recognition.

Picking up on a theme from the January meeting, delegates considered in some detail the six "essential elements" put forward in the Secretary General's synthesis report and the extent to which these could serve as a structural principle for the declaration. There were sharp divergences on this point, with WEOG states welcoming the six elements as a good basis for discussion and the G77 distinctly more hostile to them. One leading G77 member favored dropping "dignity" and "justice" and settling instead for "four Ps": people, planet, prosperity and partnership. If a common view could be distilled from the discussion, it was probably that, although the approach proposed in the synthesis report was attractive in some respects, the selection of elements was not ideal and could not in itself attract consensus.

More generally, there was a clear aversion across regional groups to any approach that might appear to organize the seventeen SDGs in "clusters". There were concerns that any such approach could restore the "silo" thinking, which the new agenda would be seeking to transcend, and could jeopardize the careful political balance between the views and interests of diverse regions that had been achieved in the OWG outcome.

Divisions emerged over the prominence that should be given in the declaration to human rights, the rule of law and good governance. Prefiguring one of the more contentious points that dogged the final days of the negotiations in late July, some G77 members warned that they could not accept references to "all" human rights.

As in January, there were multiple calls for references to the special situations of particular groups of countries (e.g., the LDCs, LLDCs, SIDS and Africa) and also to the needs of vulnerable communities such as migrants and indigenous peoples.

Overall, the CoF were content with the progress made on the declaration during the February session and the constructive spirit in which the majority of member states intervened on this. They felt that they had been provided with ample guidance and direction from which to prepare a first draft of the declaration, which they would include within a "zero draft" of the overall outcome document to issue by the end of May.

23–27 March: coming to grips with goals, targets and indicators

On goals and targets, the substantive negotiations had opened in January with a number of WEOG states favoring some presentational repackaging of the seventeen goals to assist in communicating the latter to a wide audience. Only a very small number of member states sought an actual reduction in the number of goals. They did so in muted terms, however, and ceased to press the point when it became clear that, for differing reasons, the overwhelming majority of delegations (including WEOG members) would not countenance any reduction or repackaging.

The 169 targets were a different matter. It was generally recognized that, in the rush to complete the OWG outcome document within a tight deadline, a number of targets had been drafted in terms that were technically deficient or incomplete or which did not take account of all relevant international agreements. As it had not been possible to provide all necessary numerical values within the time available, a number of targets still contained "x" references. Others were closer to general policy objectives, less amenable to precise measurement and arguably more appropriate for the declaration. Others were more appropriate to the indicator level. There was a case to be made for technical modification of the targets which would improve and strengthen them but would not reopen them in a substantive sense or upset the delicate political balances which underlay many of them. This, of course, in itself involved fine judgments, and, although WEOG states could generally accept the distinction and were open to technical refinement of this kind, the G77 viewed any such efforts with suspicion and, at key junctures in the negotiations, flatly opposed them.

As for indicators, work had been initiated by the UN Statistical Commission, sometime before the IGN began on a set of draft global indicators to help member states monitor their progress in implementing the goals and targets. While recognizing its essentially technical nature, member states showed keen interest in this work. They regarded global indicators as an integral part of the agenda and, while accepting that these would not be negotiated within the IGN, wanted nonetheless regular opportunities to consider the progress being made and offer political guidance.

At the December 2014 meeting, which agreed upon the modalities for the negotiations, the CoF noted that the work of preparing global indicators would require detailed input from the individual agencies and entities represented on the UN's technical support team. To provide this, the latter would have to review each target to check that it was fit for purpose (in the sense of specific, action-oriented and measurable) and that all relevant international agreements had been taken into account in formulating it. The CoF proposed, therefore, that the UN Statistical Commission (UNSC) be asked, as part of its work on global indicators, to refer the targets to the UN's technical support team for appraisal from this perspective – and from this perspective only. This was agreed, and the CoF communicated with the chair of the Statistical Commission in these terms.

In the January session, some continuing G77 caution on this issue was evident. Many reiterated the importance of not reopening the OWG outcome; some could countenance minor "tweaking" of targets but wanted clear criteria for this to be followed. In the February session, Stefan Schweinfest, the director of the UN Statistical Division, updated member states on the indicators work, making clear that the Commission regarded any possible adjustment of the targets as a political matter falling within the responsibility of member states.

In the course of January and February, the UN system devoted a great deal of effort on the work involved in a technical review of the targets. All relevant UN agencies provided detailed observations which, in most instances, adhered to the strict criteria set by the CoF. In light of this, and with the assistance of the secretariat, a document was prepared which the CoF conveyed to member states, under a cover letter setting out the rationale involved. This document contained proposals for technical amendments to nineteen targets.

The stage was set, accordingly, for a March negotiation session with a detailed focus on goals, targets and indicators. This was always likely to be a difficult and divisive week, given the strength of feeling on these various topics. The CoF made

FIGURE 3.1 Co-facilitators Ambassador David Donoghue (Ireland, left) and Ambassador Macharia Kamau (Kenya, right) confer with Amina J. Mohammed, UN Secretary-General's Special Advisor on post-2015 development planning

Photo by IISD/ENB (www.iisd.ca/post2015/in3/images/24mar/IMG_1331.JPG)

clear at the outset that member states would be free to raise any issues they wanted, whether in relation to goals, targets or indicators; there were no taboo areas. In the event, however, the mood was pragmatic and constructive and, although there were several clear areas of contention, tangible progress was made over the few days.

The issue of the number of goals was effectively considered resolved. On targets, the G77 questioned the exercise that had been carried out by the UN system and were not willing to engage in detailed consideration of the individual proposals for amendments. Other groups, however, fully approved of the exercise. And a small number of member states wanted it to go further and involve a wider range of amendments. All agreed that more time was needed to reflect on the issues involved and to consult with their capitals. The CoF managed to keep their document in play, securing agreement that, in consultation with the secretariat, they would produce a revised version which would explain in greater detail the rationale behind the proposed changes, with the latter to be confined to populating the 'x' values and ensuring consistency with international agreements.

With regard to the indicators, the CoF had circulated on 18 March a preliminary report they had requested from the Statistical Commission on the process it was using to develop a global indicator framework. The Commission had earlier sought submissions from a wide range of UN agencies on what should be included within this framework. To facilitate this input from the UN system and also contributions from MGoS, an Interagency and Expert Group on SDGs Indicators (IAEG-SDG) had been set up. The Commission's report included (a) provisional indicators compiled by the Commission from the submissions received and (b) an initial assessment by national statistical offices of these provisional indicators.

The chair of the Commission, John Pullinger (Chief Executive of the UK Statistics Authority), introduced this report at the outset of the March meeting. He outlined the Commission's approach, including the UNSC roadmap for the months ahead, the establishment of the IAEG-SDG and the criteria to be used for the development of global indicators.

Arising from this briefing, there was broad agreement that this work should not be rushed, and it was again accepted that the draft global indicators should not be negotiated within the IGN. The "roadmap", or agreed timetable, for the Commission's work was considered the most appropriate way to move them forward; member states would, however, have the benefit of periodic progress reports in the IGN from the Commission, and these would help them to give broad political guidance for the work. After the March meeting, the CoF wrote to the chair of the Commission to confirm the support of member states for the roadmap, to invite the Commission to provide a further update at the May session and to encourage the Commission to involve MGoS in its preparation of the indicators.

Among other issues handled by the March meeting, member states endorsed a proposal from the CoF for a joint meeting of the Financing for Development and IGN tracks in April. They considered also the organizational arrangements for that meeting, agreeing (though with some G77 resistance) to a proposal to curtail it by one day in order to allow delegates to attend a previously planned ECOSOC meeting with the Bretton Woods institutions.

A further item of business entrusted to the IGN was the definition of themes for the six 'interactive dialogues' planned for the September summit. While the modalities for the summit had been painstakingly agreed in the course of 2014 in a separate process co-facilitated by Ib Petersen, Permanent Representative of Denmark, and Robert Guba Aisi, Permanent Representative of Papua New Guinea (PNG), this issue had deliberately been left over for resolution in the IGN, as it was not considered sensible to settle these topics so far ahead of the summit.

Accordingly, the CoF presented a paper with six proposed themes to the March session. Member states made some suggestions for changes and other themes or topics which they wished to see included, and the CoF agreed to revise their proposal in the light of these inputs. In early May they circulated a revised paper and followed up on this with informal consultations convened at expert level which sought to resolve major difficulties.

As part of the May negotiations, an afternoon session on 22 May finally brought agreement on the set of themes. These were (i) Ending poverty and hunger; (ii) Tackling inequalities, empowering women and girls and leaving no one behind; (iii) Fostering sustainable economic growth, transformation and promoting sustainable consumption and production; (iv) Protecting our planet and combating climate change; (v) Building effective, accountable and inclusive institutions to achieve sustainable development; and (vi) Delivering on a revitalized global partnership.

There were last-minute complications due to the prolonged refusal of one G77 member to accept a formulation that most of its G77 colleagues had already accepted. With the entire package of compromises on the themes at risk, the impasse was only overcome when the CoF persuaded the delegation in question that its concern could be met not within the list of titles (which was duly forwarded to the PGA) but within a less formal list of subthemes.

21–24 April: joint consideration of Means of Implementation and the global partnership

The decision to hold a joint session of the IGN and the FfD process in April and a breakthrough agreement that was in due course reached in one area (technology facilitation) arising from this had an important impact on the IGN and contributed significantly to its ultimate success.

From the outset, there had been deep and painful divisions between the major blocs over the degree of interdependence between the two processes. Although the G77 position was not monolithic and there were important differences of emphasis among key players, the broad G77 view was that, because sufficient means of implementation and a credible global partnership would be critical to the success of the post-2015 agenda, these were legitimate subjects of interest within the IGN and could not be considered only in the FfD process. Goal 17 and the means of implementation related targets were of fundamental importance to them. They saw the FfD as complementing and supporting the work on the post-2015 agenda; however, for them its scope went beyond financing the SDGs. Anything not addressed in Addis Ababa should, in the G77 view, be addressed in the IGN.

WEOG states, for their part, feared that the G77 would seek to exploit the two processes tactically and, in effect, to hold an IGN agreement hostage to securing

FIGURE 3.2 Participants listening to post-2015 co-facilitator Ambassador David Donoghue, Permanent Representative of Ireland

Photo by IISD/ENB (www.iisd.ca/post2015/in4/images/21apr/DSC_3388.jpg)

what they would consider adequate means of implementation. While accepting that Goal 17 and the means of implementation related targets would be part of the new agenda (though for a while they toyed with presentational variants), WEOG states maintained that the FfD process was the appropriate place for detailed consideration of the means of implementation and a global partnership. The outcome of the Addis Ababa conference in July should, in their view, constitute the means of implementation component of the post-2015 agenda.

Nobody disagreed, however, with the need to ensure maximum coherence and complementarity between both processes. As it was clear that certain issues could reasonably be regarded as appropriate to both, the CoF proposed a joint session in April, back to back with the FfD session from 13–17 April.

With all four CoF seated together at the podium throughout, this session helped to clarify the relationship between the two tracks and to defuse tensions between them. The engagement of all four CoF in a joint manner sent a strong signal to delegates on coherence. It also served to strengthen the working relationship between all four and to give the CoF a clearer sense of the shared challenges they faced in the months ahead. The session was co-chaired by Ambassadors Donoghue and Kamau, with the FfD CoF making opening and closing statements and a number of other interventions. The session opened with addresses by all four CoF, who called for the level of ambition in the SDGs to be matched by an equally high level of ambition in the FfD track. Delegates participated constructively, and the session was not marred by the procedural wrangling that had stalled progress in the opening days of the FfD meeting the previous week.

There were, however, fundamental differences on substance. One key issue was how the future Addis Ababa outcome would be integrated within the post-2015 agenda. Although a number of options were aired, no agreement was reached on how to proceed in this respect. It was clear that this was in part due to a G77 concern to leave their options open in the event of an Addis Ababa outcome that was less than optimal from their perspective. WEOG states insisted that the Addis Ababa outcome should be framed as the comprehensive means of implementation pillar of the post-2015 agenda, encompassing all financial and nonfinancial means of implementation. They were opposed to duplicative means of implementation negotiations in the IGN and made clear that they would be unwilling to reopen in the IGN issues that had been settled in Addis Ababa.

Summing up the discussion on coherence, the four CoF observed that all member states recognized that the two processes were distinct but that they were also synergistic and mutually reinforcing. They made clear their view that member states should aim for a presentation of commitments in the Addis Ababa outcome which could be fitted neatly into the post-2015 outcome document. Two tendencies were noted in the debate: while some member states were clear that there should be no further negotiations on means of implementation commitments after Addis Ababa, others did not want to see Addis Ababa as the last word on MoI for the new agenda. The CoF saw a risk of losing a lot of the ambition for the FfD outcome if it was understood that there could be continuing negotiations on MoI after Addis Ababa.

A further topic of common interest that was discussed during the joint session in April was the follow-up and review arrangements, which would be needed to monitor implementation of the MoI commitments. It was generally recognized that a weakness of the Monterrey process had been its failure to define a follow-up and review framework. There were divergent views, however, on whether a separate mechanism should be created to monitor the MoI commitments under the new agenda.

The WEOG states favored a single overarching monitoring and review framework for the entire post-2015 agenda, covering all aspects of the goals and targets and all MoI. The G77, on the other hand, wanted a distinct framework, under the authority of the General Assembly, which would track implementation of the MoI commitments. Again, the G77 did not present a united front; several key members could accept a single framework. The CoF summed up this debate by suggesting that, although there could be scope to make specific arrangements covering individual aspects, the approach of a single overarching framework should still be followed.

Other subjects of interest to both tracks included the scope for transformational "deliverables" at the Addis Ababa summit (e.g., major initiatives in the fields of health, education or infrastructure) which would be commensurate with the level of ambition shown in the SDGs.

A further issue of common interest was the long-standing proposal for a Technology Facilitation Mechanism. A full day was devoted to consideration of this and other science, technology and innovation issues. Ambassador Paul Seger of Switzerland and Ambassador Guilherme de Aguiar Patriota, the Deputy Permanent Representative of Brazil, addressed the session as co-moderators of the UNGA structured dialogues on technology. From their addresses and a question-and-answer session that followed, as well as in the statements made later, a clear divide emerged between WEOG and G77 countries. The G77 wanted a discussion in the IGN – with extra time to be allocated to this if necessary – of concrete deliverables in relation to the functions and administrative arrangements of a Technology Facilitation Mechanism. WEOG states, on the other hand, were ready to engage in further consideration of the proposal – but only as part of broader discussions about science, technology and innovation issues in the FfD context. The United States and Japan, traditionally skeptical about a Technology Facilitation Mechanism (TFM), reiterated their long-standing views.

However, the close attention paid to this issue in the joint session, coupled with the desire of a number of key players to move toward agreement in this area, created a helpful dynamic. The mood of the discussion was positive and constructive. An earlier French nonpaper had identified some ways in which progress could be made, and it was clear that member states felt an agreement on TFM was within reach.

Having noted various concrete ideas that had arisen in the discussion (such as a global forum on technology and innovation for sustainable development or a global technology partnership – or multiple partnerships – to address the technology needs of different countries or regions and around different goals), the four CoF proposed that the idea of a TFM, on which there were still divergences, should be taken forward as a "joint endeavor" of both the post-2015 and FfD tracks. Adequate time would be given to this issue during the next FfD session. This discussion would be chaired by the CoF.

It was also privately accepted that the TFM would be included in the Addis Ababa outcome document along with other technology and MoI issues. With the blessing of the four CoF, informal contacts were undertaken by Brazil and Switzerland with key players to see whether progress could be made in a format outside both tracks.

TFM was duly discussed in a joint session on 15 May which formed part of the FfD's May meeting. Arising from this, the four CoF on 18 May circulated a joint 'food for thought' paper (UN, 2015c) which laid out what would ultimately go on to constitute the TFM established in the Addis Ababa outcome and launched at the September summit. It identified the main areas of the mechanism as an online knowledge hub and information-sharing platform; a forum on science, technology and innovation for the SDGs; a UN system interagency working group on science, technology and innovation (STI) for the SDGs; and a coordinated STI capacity-building program.

18–22 May: the follow-up and review framework

The fifth round of the intergovernmental negotiations, and the last to focus on a specific component of the new agenda, took place from 18–22 May. It was devoted largely to the arrangements needed for follow-up and review of implementation. However, time was also provided for an update from the Statistical Commission on its preparation of global indicators, for discussion of a revised targets proposal and, as previously noted, for finalization of the themes for the "interactive dialogues" at the September summit.

A four-page discussion paper on a follow-up and review framework, with two annexes, had been circulated by the CoF prior to the meeting. Building on member states' comments at the January and April meetings, this invited delegates to respond to a number of questions posed about the nature of the arrangements required.

In the discussion beginning on 18 May, it was clear that there was broad agreement among member states on a number of principles that should underpin the framework. It should be universal; voluntary; nationally owned; evidence and data-based; multistakeholder in nature; inclusive; transparent; "positive but not punitive"; "and lean but not mean" (in the words of one G77 member), i.e., promoting exchanges of best practice and experience, using existing mechanisms and not over-burdening countries. It was also agreed that follow-up and review should take place at the global, regional and national levels. The HLPF, furthermore, should be the main platform for follow-up and review at the global level.

Issues of terminology resurfaced, with WEOG states repeating their preference for the formulation "monitoring and accountability" and the G77 insisting on "follow-up and review".

A number of delegations suggested that the level of planning for the framework should be limited to broad principles, with details to be elaborated in other fora in the months following the September summit.

On the issue of whether there should be a separate mechanism for follow-up and review of MoI commitments, the divisions that had emerged in April were again in evidence: WEOG states favored a single overarching framework for the entire post-2015 agenda, whereas the G77 favored two separate but coherent processes. It was tacitly accepted that this issue would probably have to await resolution at the Addis Ababa summit.

The CoF summed up in a tentative way the main points they had noted from the discussion; these impressions were subsequently circulated in writing. They said that they were reassured to see that all shared the conviction that implementation of the SDGs would depend on a well-functioning and effective review framework. It was accepted that the HLPF would be the main platform at the global level. Member states generally concurred, furthermore, on the actions they wished the HLPF to perform. It should keep track of progress in implementing the SDGs and identify shortcomings and gaps. It should make recommendations on what countries would need to do to stay on track as well as on the global partnership and MoI. And it should also discuss new and emerging issues. It would have to address major challenges such as how to ensure the measurability of targets and indicators. One delegation had described it as "the crown of a network of accountability mechanisms"; a mapping of such mechanisms had been requested, and the CoF had asked the secretariat to prepare such a document.

Many member states, the CoF continued, also envisaged that thematic reviews of progress could be conducted in various platforms throughout the UN system, feeding into the HLPF. ECOSOC and the General Assembly would have a key role in this regard. The CoF would need guidance from member states on how tasks should be shared between the HLPF and ECOSOC. ECOSOC, they noted, had undergone a major reform two years previously. The creation of the HLPF – meeting under both the General Assembly and ECOSOC – was part of this endeavor. But it was important to keep in mind that ECOSOC had been in a constant state of reform virtually since its inception. These reforms were not cast in stone, even though they had to be built on.

Further discussion, the CoF noted, would be required on a number of points. There was some divergence on how to follow up and review the commitments relating to MoI and financing for development: whether there should be a single overarching framework or separate mechanisms. Addis Ababa would need to define ways of following up on the MoI. But ultimately the follow-up work on MoIs would also feed into the work of the HLPF.

The CoF would need to clarify other aspects specifically related to the HLPF. What should be the key outcomes of its work? It was already mandated to adopt a negotiated ministerial declaration. Some delegations had suggested that it should also generate reports on global progress. One had observed that a "review" would in itself trigger a need for "follow-up".

Clarification of the differences between the HLPF when it met every year under the auspices of ECOSOC and when it met every four years under the auspices of the GA would also be required. It should not be overburdened – and particularly when it met at the head of state or government level.

A further issue was what the HLPF should do when it met in 2016, or more generally during the first cycle leading to its next meeting under the auspices of the GA. Some had suggested that it should focus in 2016 on how countries were adjusting their national frameworks to respond to the SDGs and what kinds of strategies they were putting in place. The importance of national ownership had been underscored, as well as the need to take into account countries' priorities and specific situations. Some had suggested that the HLPF in 2017 could review the SDGs, which had absorbed the agendas of the MDGs, and provide time, therefore, for countries to integrate the other SDGs into their systems.

Other questions about the role of the HLPF needed to be considered. There was a certain urgency in terms of defining the HLPF's working methods. Consideration might also be given to the idea of the HLPF meeting perhaps twice a year. There might also be a need to consider whether there were tasks that the HLPF could delegate to other platforms. This would apply in particular to the thematic reviews, which could be done in other governing bodies and possibly culminate in a discussion at the HLPF. In addition, member states might consider whether, given the volume of activities which they wished to transfer to the HLPF, some activities on other tracks should be discontinued so as to free up time and resources. It could not be the case that the UN intergovernmental system continually added processes without letting some of them go.

A further idea was that country reviews could be discussed at the regional level. Some member states, indeed, wanted all country reviews to take place at the regional level. Others felt that this would not be possible in all regions. It would, of course, be difficult to imagine a HLPF without country reviews.

The Global Sustainable Development Report (GSDR), the CoF went on, would play a critical role in supporting the HLPF. Some considered that it should support thematic reviews, building on the work of the UN system, other sources and scientific evidence.

Member states had spoken of the "vertical" and "horizontal" dimensions of a follow-up and review framework. The former involved reviews at local, national, regional and global levels. All seemed to agree with this kind of architecture and wanted to ensure coherence and linkages between the various levels, without at the same time being too prescriptive. The "horizontal" dimension, on the other hand, related to the interplay between governments and MGoS. There was broad agreement that reviews should be inclusive and participatory – at all levels. Some had mentioned the need to hold nonstate actors accountable for their own actions, including through reporting by the private sector. The UN system would also need to report on its support for member states in their implementation of the new agenda.

A further point on which the CoF sought the views of member states was whether there should be two separate secretariats for ECOSOC and the HLPF or an integrated one.

Finally, with an eye to their impending preparation of the "zero draft" for the outcome document, the CoF indicated that a judgment would have to be made as to how much of the detail of the follow-up and review framework should be included in that document and how much left over for other fora to determine over the coming months (bearing in mind also the overlap between some of the proposals made and the mandates of other UN bodies).

The May session dealt also with indicators and targets. With regard to the indicators, the chair of the Statistical Commission briefed delegates on the progress that the Commission was making. He said also that the IAEG-SDGs would meet for the first time on 1–2 June. General satisfaction was expressed at the state of the work, and it was agreed that Mr. Pullinger would be asked to give a further update in June (however, this took place in July). The question of how to provide for ongoing political oversight of this work, notably after the IGN had concluded, was also considered.

On the proposed 'tweaking' of some targets, the CoF had circulated a revised paper on 7 May. This included a clearer rationale for the changes suggested. It also proposed a refinement to one additional target (14c) to ensure consistency with international agreements. Target 14c proved over time to be the most contentious of the proposed changes. Many member states made clear that they were unhappy with an outcome from the OWG which they considered was in contravention of the UN Convention on the Law of the Sea (UNCLOS). A small number of countries, however, took a different view and saw the OWG language in this respect as an opportunity to gain leverage in wider discussions on Law of the Sea issues. The CoF also proposed to include references to humanitarian assistance in two targets in order to emphasize the importance of this issue. One or two of the changes suggested earlier had been adjusted slightly in the light of comments received from the UN system.

In the discussion, the G77 made clear that they remained flatly opposed to any reopening of the political balance achieved in the OWG outcome and could not accept any of the proposed revisions. Not even addressing the "x" values was acceptable, it seemed; the CARICOM and AOSIS representatives were particularly adamant in this regard. WEOG countries, for their part, were strongly supportive of the "tweaking" exercise, though they had some suggestions for further refinement and expressed full confidence in the CoF to continue this work.

The CoF made clear that there would be no further "tweaking" of targets beyond the work done in this revised paper. Summing up, they indicated that they would take account of this discussion in framing the relevant section of the "zero draft".

1 June: tabling of the "zero draft"

With the sequence of monthly issue-based meetings completed, the CoF turned their attention to finalization of the "zero draft" of the outcome document for September. They had promised this for the end of May or beginning of June and they duly delivered it on 1 June.

The work of preparing the draft declaration, a key component of the overall "zero draft", was intense and at times grueling. The biggest challenge was to compile a text which would be equal to the ambition of the SDGs themselves and would meet the various criteria that had been set. It would need to be framed in visionary and inspiring terms and be easily understood by ordinary citizens around the world. Yet, detracting somewhat from this goal of communicability, it would also need to reference key UN and other agreements cherished by one or other regional group, include some technical and legal clarifications and contain elements to reassure individual constituencies. It would have to be concise; yet the ground it would potentially have to cover was vast. Not only were the goals and targets themselves, individually and collectively, of profound importance to the membership – and, accordingly, a rich source of inspiration for the declaration – but there were many additional themes and concepts that member states wished to see included. In some cases, these were themes and concepts that had not received sufficiently clear treatment in the OWG outcome; in other cases, they had not featured at all in the latter document.

From the very beginning of the negotiations, member states on all sides had indicated the kind of declaration they wished to see and had set out in detail the content they envisaged for it. The January session was devoted almost entirely to this subject. Alongside the copious suggestions from member states, provided over a period of many months, were a constant stream of inputs from MGoS, UN bodies and many other organizations. These frequently took the form of fully developed draft declarations. The CoF also had the benefit of the monthly interactions with the MGoS and other stakeholders, a further valuable source of comment and advice. In short, there was an abundance of material available to the two Ambassadors as they set about crafting this critically important component of the new agenda. The challenge was how to select from this and to come up with a text with the requisite qualities of succinctness, balance and readability.

In other parts of the "zero draft", there were other big challenges requiring careful tactical consideration. One was how the CoFs' proposed changes to some targets would be handled, given the deep divisions among member states on this subject. Another was how to treat the issue of MoI and the global partnership, with work continuing in the Financing for Development track and the prospects for a successful Addis Ababa summit very uncertain at that stage. A third was the balance to be struck in the section on follow-up and review between the rigorous and systematic approach favored by one set of member states and the less constraining model preferred by another, with a heavy emphasis on voluntary involvement and differing national circumstances and capacities.

Among the many challenges faced in preparing the draft declaration were the relative weighting to be given to particular international agreements and sets of principles, what reference should be made to the principle of "common but differentiated responsibilities" (given the diametrically opposed positions of the G77 and WEOG on this) and how particular human rights and nondiscrimination references should be worded. A basic difficulty was the extent to which individual goals and targets should be selected for special attention in the declaration; this helped with general presentation and communication of the agenda, but was arguably at odds with the integrated and indivisible nature of the goals and targets.

Over a ten-day period in May, the two Ambassadors had a round of intensive consultations, sometimes alone and sometimes with their supporting teams. Out of this came a "zero draft" of the entire outcome document, running to forty-four pages, which was circulated to all member states on 1 June under a cover letter from the CoF. Three annexes were attached to it: (i) the paper proposing revisions to twenty-one targets, unchanged from the May meeting and "strongly recommended" by the CoF to member states; (ii) the "food for thought" paper on a Technology Facilitation Mechanism, which had previously been circulated on 18 May and was now provided again as "a basis for continued discussion"; and (iii) the "chapeau" of the OWG report, attached "for reference" and without comment. The first of these annexes reflected a decision by the CoF to keep the proposed revisions in play with a view to eventual agreement on them (or at least some of them), even if they were contested as of now by a significant section of the membership. The second and third reproduced known documents, but their inclusion in annex form would have provided some comfort to the latter. (The G77 objective, in fact, was to secure squarely within the agenda the verbatim reproduction of the entire OWG report, i.e., including "chapeau" and reservations; WEOG's response to this was to point out that HOSG could hardly be expected to endorse at the September summit reservations that individual member states had entered in the final stage of the OWG; the CoFs' own approach was to hope that the issues covered in the "chapeau" would be absorbed over time into the outcome document, so that eventually there would be no justification for retaining any reference to the "chapeau", let alone the reservations.)

The "zero draft" opened with a draft declaration entitled 'Transforming our World by 2030 – a New Agenda for Global Action'. This came to eight pages, including a half-page preamble. The preamble contained a deliberate echo of the 'four Ps' but added a fifth: peace. Emphasizing the resolve of world leaders to implement the new agenda, it pledged that "no one will be left behind" (a motif with which in the meantime the entire 2030 Agenda has become synonymous). To assist in communicating the agenda to a vast global audience, it sought to capture the essence and scope of the agenda in nine bullet points.

The declaration itself amplified many of the points made in the preamble. It noted key texts and principles. The common but differentiated responsibilities (CBDR) reference was practically identical to one that had appeared in the outcome document of the special event on the MDGs held in September 2013. It observed the huge challenges of today's world and set out a vision of how the new SDGs could overcome these. It went on to describe some of the key approaches and aims of the new agenda, such as universality, human rights, gender equality, peaceful societies, environmental degradation, climate change and the integrated nature of the agenda. On implementation, it envisaged welcoming and endorsing the future Addis Ababa outcome; it also considered selected MoI and the global partnership. It ended with a rousing call for action to "change the world", recalling the circumstances in which the UN came to be founded seventy years ago and enjoining leaders and peoples, and in particular today's youth, to set out together on "the road to 2030".

The next section of the "zero draft" introduced the goals and targets (noting also the work underway on global indicators). The seventeen goals and 169 targets were then listed. The subsequent section dealt with MoI and the global partnership, prefaced with a caveat that this was placeholder language pending the outcome of the Addis Ababa summit. This section also reiterated the MoI-related targets. Then came a section dealing with follow-up and review (with an illustrative attachment). And finally, the three annexes as mentioned earlier.

In the days and weeks that followed its circulation, the "zero draft" received a warm welcome from the membership. The vision and tone of the draft declaration, and the effort clearly made to find inspiring language going beyond traditional UN formulations, were particularly praised. There was strong appreciation also for the focus in the declaration on poverty eradication and on the principle of "leaving nobody behind".

The Co-Facilitators had a round of meetings with regional groups to explain their approach on particular issues and to seek buy-in. The G77, not surprisingly, sought stronger references to CBDR and the Rio+20 outcome document. WEOG concerns about the language on MoI were answered with a strengthened assurance that the Addis Ababa outcome would replace this. The CoF stressed their hope that delegations would not seek to add too much to the declaration, which all member states wanted to be concise.

On 4 June the Secretary General hosted a cross-regional meeting of key Ambassadors who were uniformly supportive of the "zero draft" and saw it as a good basis for further work in the IGN. At the same time, concerns were expressed about difficulties that were being encountered in the FfD process and that were raising questions about the prospects for agreement at the Addis Ababa summit. There was a general recognition that an unsatisfactory outcome in Addis Ababa, whether a complete breakdown of the negotiations or a weak agreement, could sour the atmosphere in the continuing IGN negotiations and threaten its chances of success.

In the course of June, the "zero draft" also drew very positive responses from MGoS, UN agencies and other stakeholders. Many lobbied the CoF for further refinements, seeking either to strengthen existing references or to have new issues inserted. One of the more striking proposals was one for the revision of four targets so as to add references to ending modern slavery and human trafficking (in addition to child labor and the exploitation of migrant labor). This was mediated to the CoF from His Holiness Pope Francis. In the final version of the outcome document, these references were included.

22–25 June: member states react formally to the "zero draft"

The June session gave member states an opportunity to react more formally to the "zero draft". Warm support was voiced on all sides, though various proposals were made for specific amendments and improvements. The CoF pressed delegations to be specific in their comments and to make textual recommendations where possible; the time for general statements of position was now over – the group had entered the drafting stage.

The most detailed comments related to the draft declaration and its preamble. The main faultlines of the debate were as follows: (i) some dissatisfaction with an appearance of selectivity in the preamble and declaration ("cherry-picking" of the goals and targets); (ii) G77 unhappiness with the proposed CBDR reference; (iii) continuing G77 opposition to revision of the targets (though with some willingness on the part of key G77 players – for the first time – to engage on the detail of individual changes); and (iv) the detail of the follow-up and review section (with the G77 considering the draft as it stood too prescriptive and others either welcoming it or seeking to strengthen it further).

Many G77 countries questioned the added value of the nine bullet points in the preamble. They were concerned that this amounted to repackaging the SDGs and they therefore favored deletion of the bullet points. Once again, however, the G77 reaction was not monolithic; some individual G77 members expressed varying degrees of support for the intention behind the bullet points and proposed various options for editing these. WEOG countries, for their part, were strongly supportive of them as a communications tool and suggested their retention but with amendments. There was widespread support for the "five Ps" approach.

On the draft declaration as such, most welcomed its readability, comprehensiveness and succinctness as well as its uplifting tone. Many member states, however, felt that it could be shortened, perhaps to as little as two to three pages. WEOG countries supported the idea of a succinct summary of the agenda, but also had some worries about what might appear to be selective clustering of the goals.

With regard to the CBDR reference, it was not yet possible to bridge the traditional G77/WEOG divide. Whether and how to address this principle was mentioned frequently during the week, but there was overall no narrowing of well-known differences. Battlelines were by now fully drawn up, with leading G77 players insisting that this principle is a fundamental underpinning for sustainable development and WEOG retorting that its validity extends only to environmental degradation. There were several vehement exchanges on this subject across the floor of the negotiations. There was also a classic stand-off over a proposed reference to the right to development.

WEOG countries wished to see the human rights and gender equality references strengthened. Emphasizing the importance of the rule of law, justice and good governance for sustainable development, they wanted to see these given more prominence in the declaration. Several of them also wanted a reference to sexual and reproductive health and reproductive rights (SRHR) in the declaration. The African Group, in contrast, felt that human rights were overemphasized in the declaration.

A reference in the draft declaration to peoples living under foreign occupation – which had already been contentious in the FfD negotiations – was challenged by Israel and other WEOG countries. (Subsequently tentative agreement was reached in meetings with the PGA that this issue would be dealt with in the IGN only and not in FfD; it proved eventually to be the last hurdle to be overcome before the completed outcome document was adopted on 2 August.)

Many delegations across the regions wanted to have the migration references in the declaration recognize the positive effects of migration on development. There were strong calls from a number of countries for the role of national parliaments to be highlighted. There were also calls for the role of the UN system in supporting the implementation of the goals and targets to be given more attention. Support for a clear reference to UN reform came from both G77 and WEOG members.

Referring to a paragraph in the declaration that combined references to cultural diversity and to sport, a number of delegations sought an expanded reference to sport, and language for a stand-alone paragraph was suggested.

When the negotiations reached the other parts of the "zero draft" of the outcome document, member states reacted along largely predictable lines to the treatment of the targets. The G77 reiterated their opposition to any technical revision of the targets, though individual members indicated some openness on this point. Conversely, WEOG members were very supportive of the changes proposed by the CoF – and, helpfully, did not call for revisions to any targets beyond the twenty-one concerned. Regarding the x values that had yet to be filled in, one WEOG member suggested that, rather than populating these with specific numbers, the phrase "substantially increase" might be inserted.

There was a similar stand-off over the issue of whether the "chapeau" of the OWG outcome, with accompanying reservations, should be included in the outcome document. The G77 demanded this; WEOG members opposed it.

With regard to indicators, although a Statistical Commission briefing that had originally been envisaged was postponed to the July session, various delegations expressed support for the work of the Commission and the Interagency and Expert Group. Some G77 members sought clarity on the arrangements to ensure intergovernmental oversight of this process.

Because the FfD negotiations in preparation for the Addis Ababa conference had not yet been completed, the debate on MoI was relatively short. WEOG members maintained that, with those negotiations still in progress, it was not necessary to engage on the placeholder material in the "zero draft". They again insisted that the Addis Ababa outcome would be the MoI pillar of the post-2015 agenda. The G77, on the other hand, stuck to their view that the Addis Ababa outcome should seek not to replace MoI, which had already been agreed to, but merely to complement them. The language on MoI in the "zero draft" should not be seen purely as placeholder language; it was in itself a good basis for further negotiation. G77 members suggested that the MoI-related targets together with the Addis Ababa outcome could constitute the MoI for the post-2015 agenda. With regard to how to integrate the Addis Ababa outcome into the September document, it suggested that a short paragraph endorsing the outcome and annexing the text might suffice. It saw no need for a substantive renegotiation of this section of the "zero draft".

Some WEOG countries advised against duplication of the SDGs and targets in two different parts of the "zero draft".

There was agreement that a paragraph on the Technology Facilitation Mechanism, which had been negotiated in the FfD track, could be included in this section of the draft.

One leading G77 member indicated that they would need to determine whether there were MoI gaps after the FfD negotiations had been completed; if so, work would have to be done in the IGN to see how these gaps could be closed. The LDCs warned that if the Addis Ababa outcome did not meet their expectations, they would have to "come back to post-2015 to seek more".

With regard to the follow-up and review arrangements, there was wide support for the role envisaged for the HLPF and also for the general principles (though a few minor additions and suggestions were made). However, although its members were supportive on individual aspects of the proposed framework, the G77 complained that the "zero draft" was too prescriptive in its approach to national and regional review and proposed that the follow-up and review arrangements should focus on the honoring of ODA commitments, on technology transfer and on capacity building. The concerns about an overly prescriptive approach found echoes with some WEOG members. Several LLDCs welcomed the proposal for the Secretary General to provide guidelines for national reviews. Some leading G77 members made strong interventions in support of national reporting on implementation of the agenda.

A small number of G77 members insisted that religious and moral values to which they attached importance would have to take precedence in the principles underpinning the follow-up and review framework. WEOG states, for their part, were very supportive of the proposed framework, particularly of the multilevel approach, of the flexibility envisaged and of the inclusion of MGoS. WEOG members also called for more specifics on how follow-up would operate at the three levels.

Most member states also supported the idea of building on existing systems and avoiding duplication. Some also called for a clearer explanation of the importance and benefits of follow-up, a strengthening of the language on data collection and inclusion of the role of the UN system.

At the conclusion of the meeting, the CoF indicated that they would produce and circulate a revised version of the "zero draft" in the coming weeks. Although there was still a long way to go, the differences were not insurmountable. They both expressed confidence that the final text of the outcome document would be agreed by the deadline of 31 July.

Privately, they were relieved that the "zero draft" had passed muster as a solid basis for the remaining work. The declaration had gone down reasonably well. It had been a gamble to propose a preamble, to assist in communicating the agenda, but this appeared to have paid off; one group had sought its deletion, but others had rallied to the idea. On specific challenges, the CoF had managed to keep the proposed target revisions on the table; there was also a prospect that G77 calls for full integration of the "chapeau" might ease as work continued on the declaration; and, although the follow-up and review section was under fire for being too prescriptive, many of its detailed recommendations had attracted support.

In the days after the June meeting, the CoF and their teams went back to work to revise the "zero draft" in the light of everything they had heard. The UN Secretariat provided valuable support, technical and substantive, during this period. Member states, UN agencies, MGoS and many others sent a constant stream of requests and suggestions, particularly for the declaration. Lobbying from all quarters was intense and unremitting as the negotiations entered their end game.

Ultimately, the hard choices had to be made by the two CoF themselves. In what was probably the most difficult and lonely phase of the negotiations, Ambassadors Donoghue and Kamau went into conclave to draw up what they sensed would be close enough to the final version of the document. In a number of lengthy private meetings, variously in the Kenyan or Irish Missions or in the Irish residence, they labored intensively over every aspect of the draft. As had been the case throughout the process, but was never truer than now, they knew that the first and most important precondition for success in these negotiations was agreement between themselves. If they could agree on text between themselves and hold firm to that and defend it to all comers, they would keep confidence in the process alive and would have a good chance of steering the negotiations over the line. If they could not agree, the doubts and unease that this would instill in negotiators could jeopardize the entire process.

As the end game arrived, of course, the stakes were rising, "red lines" were multiplying and the room for maneuver was narrowing. However, the two CoF made enormous efforts to square the circle on major points of contention in the draft, of which there were perhaps two dozen. In some cases, they could identify relatively quickly compromise solutions which might work, albeit with pain on all sides. In many others, however, where the gaps seemed fundamentally unbridgeable, it was a case of seeking solutions involving verbal ingenuity and a degree of constructive ambiguity. Inevitably, as the CoF faced up to the toughest decisions, linkages and potential trade-offs arose between a number of the issues.

The 2015 meeting of the High-Level Political Forum took place in early July. While its focus was linked closely to the ongoing negotiations, the meeting could have in practice little concrete impact. Both CoF played an active role in various panels and events over the course of the forum and worked closely with the ECOSOC President. However, with the IGN ongoing, Addis Ababa unresolved and much work yet to be progressed specifically on the follow-up and review component, the HLPF discussions were necessarily tentative.

8 July: the second version is circulated

On 8 July the CoF issued their revised version of the outcome document, described – with studied optimism – as the "final draft". The key changes were as follows.

First, the title was altered slightly; it now read 'Transforming Our World: the 2030 Agenda for Global Action'. This was done so as to hint at what could eventually be a shorthand description for the new framework (the 2030 Agenda).

Second, the preamble was extended to a full page, spelling out more fully and more clearly the key objectives of the agenda under each of the five headings (people, planet, prosperity, peace and partnership).

Third, in the declaration proper some important additions were made. In the introduction, a reference was added to "the dignity of the human person" (borrowing from a recent papal encyclical). To bring out more clearly the universal scope of the agenda, as well as its relevance for the most vulnerable and marginalized, a key passage was amplified so that it read: "We wish to see the goals and targets met for all nations and peoples and for all economic and social groupings. And we will endeavour to reach the furthest behind first". Several other passages were strengthened in the same direction. There was also some re-ordering and regrouping of elements in the declaration.

A section setting out "Our vision" was extended so as to reflect all three dimensions of sustainable development. A presentational distinction was made between key texts underpinning the new agenda and the outcomes of several major conferences which had helped to shape it. A section describing "Our world today" was expanded to highlight the opportunities available today as well as the challenges. Deleting an earlier reference to the "growing migration challenge" (which had been misunderstood by some member states), the CoF provided a dedicated paragraph later in the declaration which presented the migration issue in fuller and more balanced terms. Various references to the environmental dimension were strengthened. A paragraph dealing with culture and sport was divided into two separate references.

Across the whole declaration, there was a deliberate balancing of amendments sought by the various regional groups. For example, a list of grounds on which there could be no discrimination was brought into conformity with standard international agreements by adding at the end the phrase "or other status". This point had been insisted on by WEOG states but was resisted by many G77 members. Conversely, some small changes were made that WEOG would resist but would be important for G77 members; an example was a reference in a paragraph on the economic dimension to "progressive policies aimed at redistribution". Difficult decisions had to be taken by the CoF on references sought by individual groups of member states to, for example, the role of the family or to sanction regimes. Whether elements in the "zero draft" that had been strongly favored or resisted by one or another group should remain in the new version was also the subject of intensive discussion between the CoF. They worked at all times with one goal clearly in mind: how to fashion a document which, with various balancing elements and trade-offs, would build support in key constituencies and ultimately attract the consensus needed to deliver the new agenda.

On the targets, the CoF took the bold decision to promote almost all of the proposed revisions (nineteen out of twenty-one) from annex status into the actual list of targets. This was consistent with their earlier "strong recommendation" of the proposed revisions when circulating the "zero draft" on 1 June. It was also an attempt to engage all sides in a detailed consideration of the substance of what was involved, moving beyond the issue of principle (inviolability of the OWG outcome) which had to date inhibited this discussion. Ultimately it would be for the member states to decide collectively whether or not they wanted the proposed changes or whether, for example, some would be acceptable but not others. The CoF saw it as their duty to launch this substantive consideration. They kept the proposed change to target 14c in the annex for "further consideration by member states"; although this proposal had been hotly contested by a small number of delegations, the point at issue was essentially one of legal interpretation and the proposal, therefore, was in a different category from all the others.

The MoI chapter was revised to take account of the latest draft of the outcome document for the Addis Ababa conference (which would begin a few days later).

Finally, the follow-up and review section was adjusted slightly in the direction of G77 concerns, bringing out more clearly the voluntary nature of these processes and national ownership of them. The reference to the work being done on global indicators was moved to this section.

The reaction from member states to this new version of the outcome document was very positive. Regional groups saw it as fair and balanced and as a further improvement on the "zero draft", even if – from their particular perspectives – they had individual concerns that they would still wish to pursue. The fact that the new draft had been circulated well in advance of the July session, giving sufficient time for capitals to absorb it, went down well. MGoS also gave the new text a general welcome.

20–24 July: the final phase begins

The finale of the negotiations on the outcome document for the September summit was reached on 20 July. Delegations assembled in New York for the opening week of a final fortnight of negotiations. The CoF's intention, proclaimed consistently over the preceding months, was to have the outcome document fully agreed by 31 July. There was a palpable sense of excitement and tension as the session opened on 20 July.

G77 negotiators returning from Addis Ababa (where the conference had concluded only four days previously) were in a somewhat disgruntled mood. Overall they were not particularly satisfied with the agreement reached on financing for development. The outcome on tax had been particularly disappointing and frustrating from their point of view. Even if they could work with the outcome and would hope to build on it over time, they maintained that insufficient attention had been paid to their concerns. They did not, however, allow this resentment to overshadow unduly the work of finalizing the outcome document for September. It was clear that, although on the one hand they would not accept any fulsome references in that document to the Addis Ababa outcome, they were not, on the other hand, going to hold this final phase of the IGN hostage to an attempt to renegotiate what had been agreed to in Addis Ababa. They approached the end game in a generally constructive frame of mind, as did all other regional groups. Although there had been some speculation earlier that the G77 might seek to delay reaching agreement until early or even mid-September (in the hope of extracting further concessions – or at least of being seen in their capitals to have kept up a fight to the end), it was clear in the final fortnight that they were as committed as all others to reaching agreement on schedule.

Opening the session on 20 July, the CoF stressed the historic juncture now reached in the process, the limited time left for agreement and the need for flexibility and compromise on all sides in these final days. They made clear that they did not envisage major amendments being made to the 8 July draft. Delegations should concentrate on the three or four final points of divergence. Indicating that they would work through each of the main components in sequence and that evening sessions would be provided for if necessary, the CoF encouraged regional groups to interact freely with each other across the floor in the search of agreement. The time for lengthy presentation of positions was over; the focus now had to be purely on textual issues. No delegation would get everything that it wanted; people would have to be willing to come out of their comfort zones; compromises, sometimes painful ones, would have to be made across the floor. But the CoF were confident that agreement would be reached – and on time.

Numerous MGoS representatives were present for the final phase. With delegations now embarking on detailed textual work, the format for the participation of the MGoS was modified at the latter's request: replacing the single longer meeting which had formed part of each monthly session to date, the CoF invited a small number of representatives to comment briefly at the end of each day on issues arising in the negotiations. In the final week (28 July), the CoF themselves held a longer session with Major Group representatives to give the latter an opportunity for input. As the negotiations moved into the final days, MGoS representatives were able to mingle freely with delegates in the room, contributing informally on all of the issues still under discussion. They were present during the night-long session from Friday 31 July to 1 August – and were there in large numbers as the agreement was finally gaveled through on the afternoon of Sunday 2 August. Unusually, the G77 did not seek to exclude them in the final, fraught days of the process, as would have almost invariably been the case in earlier large negotiations of this kind.

The key issues to be resolved in the week of 20–24 July were the following (in order of their appearance in the draft): first, the final shape of the preamble; second, whether there should be a CBDR reference in the declaration; third, a number of other contentious elements in the declaration (some human rights references, the family reference, the absence of a paragraph on sanctions and 'foreign occupation'); fourth, how the proposed target revisions should be handled; fifth, how to refer to the Addis Ababa outcome; sixth, the reference to climate change and the COP 21 negotiations; seventh, the detail of the follow-up and review section; and eighth, whether the text of the OWG report's "chapeau", and reservations, should be included.

FIGURE 3.3   Co-facilitators Ambassador David Donoghue (Ireland) and Ambassador Macharia Kamau (Kenya) consulting with their teams after Wednesday's session (29 July)

Photo by IISD/ENB (www.iisd.ca/post2015/in7–8/images/29jul/dais4-tn.jpg)

On the first of these, the G77 reiterated their opposition to having a preamble at all but showed some openness to working on the draft provided. Other regional groups were very supportive of the draft, though some individual delegations preferred a shorter text which would avoid any appearance of selectivity in summarizing the scope of the agenda. On CBDR, there were familiar rehearsals of position (with India and Japan prominent on opposite sides of this debate) but no consensus was achieved. On other elements in the declaration, the family reference was challenged by many WEOG speakers; Cuba and other G77 states lamented the absence of a sanctions reference, and there were some hostile exchanges over the foreign occupation issue. Little progress was made on any of these points. On foreign occupation, the United States and Israel had indicated privately their unhappiness at having any such reference in the text; it was agreed nevertheless that, as in the FfD negotiations, informal contacts would be pursued with the Palestinians with a view to reaching agreed language in this respect.

With regard to the targets, the CoF's decision to import into the list nineteen of the twenty-one revisions they had earlier proposed surprised many. The G77 reiterated its opposition in principle to this exercise and, disappointingly, barely engaged on the substance involved. Groups such as CARICOM did engage on a number of the individual proposals (such as the proposal to replace the x's with numerical values) – but did so only by way of explanation for their continuing opposition to the exercise. The LLDCs, however, broke ranks with the rest of the G77 by calling for the inclusion of references to LLDCs in a series of targets – targets which, in fact, were largely outside the group of twenty or so under discussion. The CoF's decision to leave the proposed revision to target 14c in an annex drew predictable ire from SIDS, the EU and many others. However, following some informal group consultations for which the CoF had called, compromise language emerged which was ultimately acceptable to all member states. This language was incorporated into the next draft of the outcome document. The addition made by the CoF to target 8.7 (relating to human trafficking and modern slavery) attracted no particular comment.

On MoI, delegations debated the significance of the Addis Ababa outcome, though it was tacitly accepted by all that there would be no reopening of content. The discussion focused on how to define the relationship between the Addis Ababa Action Agenda (AAAA) and the 2030 Agenda. The CoF had privately considered a number of options beforehand which would have involved reproducing in some form within the 2030 Agenda the most relevant parts of the Addis Ababa outcome. A variant considered at one point, but not finally pursued, was that in advance of Addis Ababa a summary text might have been negotiated in the FfD track, alongside the main Addis Ababa text, which could then have been incorporated directly into the September outcome document.

Three broad positions emerged in the debate on how to reflect the Addis Ababa outcome. At one end of the spectrum, the G77 did not want the latter to be included even in an annex. They preferred to focus on Goal 17 and the MoI-related targets (and had no difficulty with the latter appearing twice in the document). At the other end was the US delegation, which sought deletion of the MoI-related targets and called for full incorporation of the Addis Ababa outcome into the September outcome document. It pointed out that the Addis Ababa Action Agenda had been finely negotiated over many months, whereas the MoI-related targets had been drafted more loosely. How were the inconsistencies between both to be addressed? Which document would prevail? Between these two poles of the debate, the EU called for the Addis Ababa outcome to be annexed and for the MoI-related targets to be included in the MoI chapter but dropped from the list of goals and targets.

On the follow-up and review component, the reworking to accommodate some G77 concerns was welcomed by the G77, along with Australia and others, but criticized by the EU. At the same time, it was becoming clear that this component was well on its way to gaining consensus and that no major fresh changes would be required; the pendulum had swung back and forth between rival sets of desiderata but was now settling slowly in the middle.

Delegations remained divided along predictable lines on the question of whether the "chapeau" in the OWG report should be included, annexed or omitted altogether from the outcome document. While almost all of its content had by now been addressed either in the declaration or in other parts of the draft, the G77 remained attached to the "chapeau", partly, it seemed, because it contained two CBDR references and partly because it addressed one or two issues (such as Mother Earth and respect for different models of development), which had not yet been included in the draft outcome document.

By the afternoon of Friday 24 July, the CoF decided that a new draft responding to a number of concerns raised during the week would issue over the weekend. They announced this and said that the negotiations would reconvene on Monday 27 July at 3 p.m. (allowing time for group coordination meetings on the new draft). Overall, the CoF felt privately that not as much progress had been made as they would have liked. Their concluding presentations were generally upbeat but included a despondent note about groups remaining entrenched and not showing the flexibility needed at this late stage of the negotiations.

Over the weekend, the CoF and their teams consulted intensively together on a redraft of the document. The two Ambassadors had two lengthy sessions in which they went over each line of the document, weighing what could be done to accommodate the conflicting concerns of groups and individual delegations. These consultations were perhaps the most difficult of all, as the CoF worked to bridge gaps which, with all sides jostling for advantage in this final phase of the negotiations and tension rising all round, were becoming almost impossible to bridge. Even as the two co-facilitators toiled in the July heat to square circles and agree to a new version of the text, they were receiving last-minute entreaties and wish lists from a range of delegations. MGoS were also assiduous. The pressures were considerable. Nevertheless, the two Ambassadors were able to agree finally with each other on the following main changes.

First, the preamble. Responding to concerns from some member states that the five Ps as they stood would perpetuate silo thinking, the CoF decided to capture more clearly under each of these headings the three dimensions of sustainable development. They would also flag more clearly the interconnections and the integrated nature of the new goals and targets.

Second, the declaration. A reference to unilateral sanctions on regimes would be added, as would an extra sentence in the climate change paragraph containing a CBDR reference (to mark its optional status, this would be proposed "for consideration"). To remove any ambiguity about the primacy of sustainable development as the concept underlying the new goals, an earlier reference to "new global goals for the sustainable development of humanity and of our planet" would be altered to read "new global Sustainable Development Goals". The phrase "and for all economic and social groupings" would be deleted; some G77 members had objected strongly to this for reasons which were not explicitly stated but which were linked to their policies on lesbian, gay, bisexual, and transgender (LGBT) issues. However, some alternative formulation to signal the need for category-specific monitoring of implementation would be needed.

A section on "shared principles and commitments" would reunite foundational texts and the outcomes of relevant UN conferences. One challenge for the CoF was to agree to prioritization for the former in a way that would command consensus across all groups. Another was the placement of the CBDR reference within the section.

In other parts of the declaration, a reference to national sovereignty over wealth and natural resources would be added. The references bearing on human rights would in some instances be weakened slightly and in others strengthened. (Examples of the former included a qualifier on the pre-eminence of international law, the inclusion of 'culture' as a qualifier in relation to the goals and targets and a qualifier reference to national legislation when referring to the participation of stakeholders in implementation.) The gender equality references would be improved. A reference to eradicating forced labor and human trafficking and eliminating the worst forms of child labor would be added. Various elements of the declaration would be rearranged, many paragraphs and individual formulations strengthened and additional points proposed by delegations that the CoF considered reasonable would be taken on board. In the MoI section, the global partnership paragraph would be given more prominence, a reference to the Technology Facilitation Mechanism would be added and the reference to the Addis Ababa outcome would be strengthened. The role of the UN system in supporting achievement of the new goals would also be highlighted. In the follow-up and review section, a fuller reference would be made to the data challenge.

Third, in the MoI/global partnership part of the document, the listing of the MoI targets would be dropped but the general material here expanded and strengthened. The follow-up and review section would be revised slightly to include some additional guiding principles and to strengthen – largely in the direction of WEOG concerns – the elements relating to the national, regional and global levels.

Fourth, the proposed target revisions would be returned to the annex, the "chapeau" would remain in the annex and the Addis Ababa outcome would not be included as an annex but would be referenced through a footnote.

A third version of the outcome document – which, again with determined optimism, was called the "draft for adoption" – incorporated these various changes and was circulated by the CoF late on the evening of Sunday 26 July. With only five days to go to the deadline of 31 July, the CoF asked in a cover letter that group arrangements be used to the maximum extent possible during the coming days to articulate the views of member states. On the basis of successive consideration of the various components, they would be aiming to secure ad referendum agreement on the various components as they proceeded. Provision would be made for a number of "informal informal" evening sessions so as to ensure that the negotiations were completed on schedule.

27–31 July: the end game

Negotiations resumed on the afternoon of Monday 27 July on the basis of the new draft. Regional groups and individual member states delivered statements on the declaration until 9 p.m. Most put forward specific language proposals on further issues they wished to see addressed. There were contributions on the overall thrust and balance of the text, with some expressing concern that, with successive additions, its value in terms of communicating the agenda to a wider audience was being eroded. WEOG countries voiced unhappiness at the presence of the CBDR and sanctions references and at the dilution of some key human rights references.

On the preamble, some member states – from both the G77 and WEOG camps – were worried that it also was being expanded to a point where it would no longer be useful as a communications tool. The CoF had prepared on a contingency basis a shorter and leaner version of the preamble, paring this down to essentials and sharpening the presentation. The CoF decided to test this option informally on a number of key players. It was very well received. They later decided that this would be proposed to the wider membership; it duly appeared in the next draft of the document and in due course was approved, without alteration, as the final version of the preamble.

During the Monday debate, African and Arab members of the G77 began to take up very conservative positions on a range of human rights and gender equality issues. For their part, WEOG countries registered various concerns about the MoI section of the declaration and the MoI chapter of the overall document.

On Tuesday and Wednesday, the focus shifted from the declaration to the other components. It was at this point that the G77 finally began to relent in their formal opposition to the proposed target revisions – after they had been subjected to some relatively pointed questioning from the CoF. Thereafter, the LLDCs and SIDS requested changes that would increase the focus of certain targets on these 'countries in special situations'. Their proposals were, however, directly opposed by the chair of the Least Developed Countries. Over the next few days, a confrontation developed between the LDC and SIDS leaderships over the issue of whether the SIDS should receive special mention within a target dealing with climate financing. This had been agreed to in the final stages of the OWG's work but had not been given formal effect. The SIDS wished this omission to be corrected in the finalized version of the targets. The LDC leadership was unwilling to concede the point, complaining that LDCs were the most disadvantaged group of all and that it would be unfair to give SIDS a specific mention in this target. This stand-off was to persist for the remainder of the negotiations, despite repeated efforts by the CoF to broker an agreement between the respective chairs.

With regard to inclusion of the OWG "chapeau", cracks began to appear in the G77 position and the indications were that a footnote reference to it would ultimately be acceptable as a compromise solution.

On MoI, some leading G77 players hinted at possible compromises that would address the WEOG concerns. However, the EU and others were heavily critical of proposals to have merely a footnote reference to the Addis Ababa outcome.

On follow-up and review, the revisions that the CoF had made to address some WEOG concerns were not challenged with any great intensity, though a number of further changes were sought.

By Wednesday afternoon (29 July), the negotiations were adjourned. Time was needed for the CoF to prepare a new version of the outcome document, which would take account of the multiplicity of comments and competing perspectives and seek to narrow further the distance between key groups on the remaining points of contention. The Ambassadors worked together in the Irish Mission, hammering out compromises and trade-offs and drawing also on the vital supportive work done by their two teams. By midnight they had agreed on practically all of the changes required. On the following morning (Thursday 30 July), they held a meeting with representatives of the main players to get a sense of the latter's thinking on key points such as the preamble (the shortened version of which was provided to all present). Following a further meeting between the CoF and their teams, a few final changes were agreed.

This fourth version of the outcome document, bearing the title "Text for adoption" (in a further deliberate signal that the negotiators were almost there), was circulated to delegations on the afternoon of 30 July. It contained some critical changes. First, two options for the preamble were provided: the earlier version (now even fuller with new elements sought by delegations) and the new much shorter version. Second, some sequencing changes had been made to the declaration which had the effect of streamlining it and improving its overall balance and readability. Third, on CBDR, although there was still a stand-alone reference in the declaration's section on shared principles and commitments, an additional paragraph now appeared immediately after this which highlighted the values and principles of the Millennium Declaration. Fourth, the family reference was dropped, as was the 'culture' qualifier (both problematic from a human rights perspective). A creative formulation was found to deal with G77 sensitivities relating to ICPD review conferences. Fifth, many of the MoI paragraphs in the declaration were transferred into the MoI component and aligned with the Addis Ababa outcome where possible. And sixth, a dozen or so target revisions which the CoF felt had attracted broad support were included in the list of targets.

Shortly before 8 p.m. on Thursday evening, the negotiations resumed. Member states gave their views on the new draft until 10 p.m. and then again on the following morning (Friday 31 July) from 10 a.m. to 2 p.m. The two Ambassador and their teams then moved to the Irish Mission to work on a further version, responding to points made and seeking to bridge the remaining gaps. The major issues to be resolved at this stage included the continuing impasse over CBDR, how the ambitions for the COP 21 conference should be described, the references being sought to foreign occupation and to sanctions and various human rights references on which there was a continuing gulf between some G77 states and WEOG countries (in particular LGBT-related but also touching on migration issues).

By 7 p.m. on Friday evening, this new fifth version was agreed to, entitled the "Finalised text for adoption", and was circulated to member states. At a brief meeting with representatives of the main regional groups, the Ambassadors went through the key changes and issues.

At 9 p.m. the plenary was reconvened. The room was packed, with many member states now fielding Ambassadors as well as experts in these final stages. MGoS were also present in large numbers. There was a strong sense of excitement and of anticipation as what would prove to be a long night got underway.

Friday night and Saturday

The deadline set by the CoF months earlier for agreement had been Friday 31 July. As a result, delegations met in almost continuous session from 9 p.m. on Friday evening until the moment of approval of the finally agreed document was reached in the late afternoon of Sunday 2 August. Negotiators who had already been working intensively for agreement since 20 July would have very little sleep over these final two days.

On Friday evening, the CoF heard a long series of statements from the main regional groups and others on the latest draft. There were over thirty interventions. At 5.30 a.m., at a time when heads were nodding more in sleep than in agreement, the final speaker was heard. The CoF decided to suspend proceedings to allow delegates to get a few hours' rest. They were also conscious that the negotiations in plenary had run their course and that a different approach would be needed the following day to try to achieve agreement on the major outstanding issues.

Formally the plenary was to reassemble around noon on Saturday (1 August). In the event, resumption of the plenary was postponed as the focus shifted to various informal formats which met throughout the day on specific issues, in particular climate issues, foreign occupation and the link to FfD. Early on Saturday morning, the two Ambassadors and their teams met to consider various 'tweaks' that could be made to the latest draft in response to the interventions by groups and individual member states during the night. The CoF then met on their own to agree to the way forward for the remainder of the negotiations. Identifying which issues were of crucial importance for the individual groups and which might be tradeable, they explored ways in which each group could feel that it had gained and lost in equal measure.

In the light of this, the two CoF arranged a series of meetings with key players. One was with the G77, EU and United States where they outlined what they saw as the major stumbling blocks. They encouraged the representatives of the different groups to work together to reach a compromise on these key issues. But they also made very clear that, if compromise language was not provided to the CoF by a certain point later in the day, they would go ahead and make the call themselves when producing a final take-it-or-leave-it version of the outcome document. A similar meeting was held with the other groups (LDCs, LLDCs, SIDS, etc.), and a further meeting was held with all of these representatives plus a number of WEOG members.

The two Ambassadors encouraged the LDC and SIDS chairs to resolve their differences bilaterally over the issue of including a reference to the SIDS in target 13b. They also chaired a cross-regional meeting of delegates who at this point had been working on the climate change paragraph in the declaration for over four days. This proved a crucial meeting; shortly afterward a compromise text for this paragraph was agreed upon.

Helpful contacts took place between the United States and South Africa (for the G77) on the vexed issue of how the Addis Ababa outcome should be reflected. Informal contacts on a foreign occupation reference continued between the key delegations involved.

Throughout the day and the previous night, the negotiators had been working in less than ideal circumstances. The UN complex of buildings is not well equipped for prolonged negotiations over a weekend, and there had probably never been a negotiation process quite on this scale. Hundreds of delegates, MGoS representatives and others were present in the wider conference area over the weekend. Because the UN canteen and cafes were closed, supplies of food had to be brought in from outside. Dispensing machines for soft drinks rapidly ran out of stock, not helped by the soaring July temperatures outside. The cooling systems of conference and meeting rooms were overburdened and regularly broke down. All in all, the physical conditions were not easy. It was clear, however, that people were determined to push these negotiations through to a conclusion, however long it took and despite the uncomfortable circumstances.

The CoF decided that they would prepare a final version of the outcome document for circulation in mid-evening, which would take account of whatever degree of agreement had been achieved by then in the various informal formats on key outstanding issues. The intention was to pressure delegations into reaching compromises on these issues sooner rather than later. If no agreement was reported on a particular issue, the CoF would make their own judgment on how the issue should be handled and that would go into the final version.

In the late afternoon delegations were told that there would be no further plenary on Saturday and that member states would instead reconvene at 10 a.m. on Sunday morning. (One reason why the CoF decided to proceed in this manner was that they recognized that it could be counterproductive if delegations were to work through the night for a second night in succession; mounting fatigue would not improve the chances of agreement.) Meanwhile, the CoF met to consider a draft of the final version that their teams had put together based on the comments received in the Friday night session and on the CoFs' discussions earlier that day.

At this point, key compromise language on foreign occupation, on water and sanitation and on climate change was supplied by those states that had been working informally on these issues. The CoF also made crucial calls themselves on a number of issues. Picking up on a phrase used by a G77 delegate at an earlier meeting, they would use the term "segments of society" – instead of the contested "economic and social groupings" – in the key section of the declaration on "leaving nobody behind". They would replace a paragraph on nondiscrimination with agreed Rio+20 language on this issue. They would adhere to the OWG language in relation to all the targets where the LLDCs and SIDS had sought changes (largely due to the LDCs chair's continuing opposition).

By midnight, it was clear that agreements on the relationship between the Addis Ababa outcome and the agenda on specific targets and on the MoI component had not yet been achieved and were not imminent. The CoF decided, therefore, not to wait any longer but to circulate their revised version, which was entitled simply "The 2030 Agenda for Sustainable Development". This included language of their own related to some of the unresolved issues.

Sunday 2 August

A 10 a.m. deadline for the gaveling-through of the outcome document had been set by the CoF more for tactical reasons of their own than in any serious expectation that the document would be ready at that point. The pressure worked, however. Key deals were made one after another in the early part of Sunday morning. The United States, which had secured tentative G77 support for two target revisions relating to biodiversity, accepted the CBDR reference that the CoF had originally proposed. It also accepted the proposed unilateral sanctions reference and a proposed mention of the right to development. The G77, for its part, agreed to language with the United States on the Addis Ababa outcome and slight adjustments to the paragraphs on debt and on international financial institutions.

The LDCs accepted the inclusion of LLDCs in target 7b – but only if a further addition was made to limit the scope of the LLDC amendments. On the other hand, no agreement was reached between the LDCs and SIDs in relation to target 13b. This remained unchanged in the text adopted on 2 August but was subsequently addressed as a technical correction by the secretariat in the outcome document adopted by the GA.

There was also a disagreement between, on the one hand, a number of countries (such as Mexico, Philippines and Bangladesh) who wanted to insert "migration status" into a list of grounds for nondiscrimination in para 19 of the declaration and, on the other, a number of groups (first the EU, then the African and Arab groups) who, for different reasons, would not accept any amendment to this paragraph.

Intensive negotiation on a whole range of issues took place in the late morning among key players who were gathered in informal consultation in the corridor outside the ECOSOC chamber. Significant difficulties continued to arise in relation to the formulation of various references affecting human rights and nondiscrimination. The LDCs/LLDCs issue was also a source of continuing tension, both between the groups concerned and more widely. The two CoF moved among the various clusters of delegates, working at feverish pace to defuse these problems and create a basis for agreement on the final text in plenary.

Around 1 p.m., just as it appeared that all the major issues either had been resolved or were very close to resolution, a fresh and somewhat unexpected difficulty arose. In the final version of the document that they had circulated at midnight the previous night, the CoF had inserted language on foreign occupation which had been agreed to among the three delegations most directly concerned (United States, Israel and Palestinians). Early on Sunday morning a number of G77 members objected to the formulation in question (which contained the phrase "people living under occupation and colonial rule"). Argentina felt that the use of the singular term "people" would have the effect of excluding others such as the people of the Falklands. The Arab group, led by Egypt, followed with objections of their own on similar grounds. Egypt pushed for "people" instead of "peoples" and also sought other amendments. Argentina and Egypt pointed out that "peoples" had been used in the Rio+20 declaration.

The plenary was briefly reconvened, the key changes sought by these countries were read out and the plenary was again suspended so that efforts could be made to find a compromise solution. High-level contact was undertaken between the United States, Israel and the Palestinians to try to resolve the problem. Several hours went by while various key individuals were sought. The long delay made other delegations restive and jittery. All other points in the text were deemed to have been resolved, and there were fears that the fragile consensus that had been built over the previous couple of days might not survive a prolonged impasse on this issue.

Finally, around 4.30 p.m., the two CoF received word that agreement had been reached between those directly concerned on a revised foreign occupation reference which would include the word "peoples" but in return soften a reference to the international community's commitment to removing obstacles to self-determination.

This break-through gave the two Ambassadors the green light to convene a plenary straight away for adoption of the document and of the new 2030 Agenda. They were far from certain, of course, that this would go through smoothly. Adoption could only be by consensus, and there was plenty of scope for one or other dissatisfied group or individual member state to lodge procedural objections of some kind in order to thwart adoption. But the CoF sensed that, after many hours of delay and uncertainty, the vast majority of delegates wanted to close the deal and bring this agreement home.

To mark the keen personal interest of the Secretary General in the proceedings, the SG's chef de cabinet, Susana Malcorra, joined the CoF on the podium for this final session. Messages of encouragement had also been received from the President of the General Assembly. Amina Mohammed, the SG's special representative for the post-2015 development agenda (and a figure of pivotal importance behind the scenes in guiding and supporting the process as well as in her worldwide public diplomacy for the new agenda), was also on the podium.

As delegates took their seats, Ambassador Kamau was introduced to Sofia Colombano, the young daughter of Joe Colombano, a key assistant to Amina. Responding spontaneously to the sense of occasion, and in recognition of the profound importance of the new agenda for Sofia's generation, Ambassador Kamau came onto the podium with Sofia in his arms. This was a poignant reminder of what was at stake in this final session.

The two CoF got down to business straight away, with Ambassador Kamau in the chair. Their intention was to reach the point of gaveling as quickly as possible. They would first, however, have to gauge the mood of the major blocs and see whether a critical mass of support existed for the text which they had circulated at midnight on Saturday, updated with the various agreements on points of detail which had been reached in the course of Sunday.

The first group to take the floor was the G77 and China, represented by the PR of South Africa. In an intervention that was brief and to the point, Ambassador Kingsley Mamabolo made clear that the group he represented was ready to join consensus on the text circulated by the CoF the previous evening. This was a pivotal moment: endorsement at the outset by 134 of the UN's 193 member states – and without reservation of any kind. This had an important stabilizing effect and raised the prospects for a positive conclusion to this final session.

The second intervention was from the EU, no less clear and powerful in its impact: the EU would be joining consensus on this text. There followed interventions from various other regional groups and a number of individual member states, all signalling that they could accept the text. Within half an hour or so, the CoF felt that a moment was approaching where they could lift the gavel (partly, it must be said, to forestall one or two member states who had requested the floor and whose previous form would not inspire confidence that they would be supportive). They were conscious, however, that, if they miscalculated in picking the moment to gavel, they could potentially open a hornet's nest of procedural complications with the capacity to derail the final session.

At a certain point, Ambassador Donoghue handed the gavel to Ambassador Kamau and they raised it together, bringing it down to conclude what had been the most significant and far-reaching negotiation process at the UN for many years. This was greeted by tumultuous applause around the conference room. Exhausted delegates and MGoS representatives, who had had barely more than a few hours' sleep over the previous three days, stood to express their delight and relief that this agreement – for which many of them had worked hard not just in recent months but over several years – had now been achieved. It was a truly historic, and unforgettable, moment.

There followed a round of further statements from various member states. Although the tone varied from strong enthusiasm for the new agreement to a degree of carping about particular aspects (e.g., human rights provisions) that individual member states found problematic, none of the latter comments were presented formally as reservations to the document. By the end of this further round, the consensus among UN member states in favor of the text had been amply demonstrated.

In personal remarks to conclude the session, Ambassador Donoghue expressed warm thanks in a number of directions: to his fellow co-facilitator, Ambassador Kamau; to the individual members of the small but highly effective Irish and Kenyan teams (the listing of each member drew loud and sustained applause); to Amina Mohammed and her team; to the UN secretariat (DESA); and to the several hundred delegates and MGoS representatives who had been part of this process from the outset. It was particularly gratifying, he commented, to see the active engagement of MGoS right to the very end of these long and arduous negotiations.

Dedicating the successful outcome to the memory of his friend, the PR of Djibouti who had died recently, Ambassador Kamau expressed his thanks to Ambassador Donoghue and others and made some stirring final comments that highlighted the enormity of what had just been achieved.

Knowing that many delegates had had nothing to eat that day (but perhaps conscious also that a celebratory glass of champagne might not have suited all tastes in this universal body), Amina Mohammed had thoughtfully arranged for supplies of cookies to be made available to participants. These were extremely welcome and provided a basis for – at least initial – celebration of one of the UN's most significant achievements in recent years.

The enthusiastic acclaim for the new agreement – for what would henceforth be known as the '2030 Agenda' – continued over the days and weeks following Sunday 2 August. One of the more remarkable aspects, and which attracted much comment, was that the negotiations were brought to a successful conclusion only a day and a half over schedule – and a good six weeks ahead of the summit (25 September) toward which they were directed. This was in itself something almost unheard of in UN negotiating history. Senior UN figures who had arranged their schedules on the assumption of a protracted impasse during August expressed pleasant surprise in private at this unexpected turn of events. Although the CoF had signalled that they had flight reservations made for Monday 3 August (which was indeed the case), this was generally not taken seriously, being viewed as a further ploy on the CoFs' part to keep the pressure on for agreement by, or as close as possible to, 31 July.

The likely explanation for the unexpectedly early conclusion to the negotiations was that a combination of factors was at play. Many groups felt that their key concerns, while not addressed perfectly in the text, had nevertheless been treated broadly to their satisfaction (bearing in mind also that this would ultimately have to be a consensus text). They knew also that there was an irresistible political momentum worldwide in favor of the conclusion of a post-2015 development agenda. A summit had been set for 25 September for this purpose. And, while there might have been some short-term tactical gain in resisting agreement on one or other aspect until closer to 25 September, there was realistically very little prospect that such moves would have been successful. In addition, those perceived to be endangering the summit in this way would have paid a heavy political price. Last but not least, the arduous negotiation process over the preceding weeks, and in particular over the last thirty-six hours, had probably induced a degree of fatigue. Delegates may have concluded that a good overall balance had been achieved which could not be improved on significantly and that the process could now be put honorably to bed.

For the full text of "Transforming our world: the 2030 Agenda for Sustainable Development" see the Annex.

FIGURE 3.4 Left to right: Co-facilitators Ambassador David Donoghue (Ireland) and Ambassador Macharia Kamau (Kenya) applauding the adoption of the post-2015 development agenda

Photo by IISD/ENB (www.iisd.ca/post2015/in7–8/images/2aug/Cofacilitators2.jpg)

The Third International Conference on Financing for Development

In parallel to the negotiations that led to the 2030 Agenda, separate intergovernmental negotiations took place at the UN, which prepared an outcome document for the Third International Conference for Development. This conference would take place in Addis Ababa in July 2015.

The Third International Conference on Financing for Development was also a daughter of Rio 1992. As mentioned in Chapter 1, the cost of delivering Agenda 21 had been estimated at US$625 billion a year with a transfer of US$125 billion from developed to developing countries. In 1992 ODA was roughly half what was needed and at the five-year review (1997) of Rio, ODA had actually decreased. One of the outcomes from Rio+5 was a General Assembly discussion on financing, which ultimately became the Monterrey Financing for Development Conference (2002). This conference was timed to take place before the World Summit on Sustainable Development in 2002, and the Secretary General (Nitin Desai) was the same for both conferences. Governments envisaged the Monterrey Conference as helping to fund the implementation of WSSD as well as the MDGs. Monterrey, which for the first time ever brought finance ministers into the development debate at the UN, focused on:

1 Mobilizing domestic financial resources for development.
2 Mobilizing international resources for development: foreign direct investment and other private flows.
3 International trade as an engine for development.
4 Increasing international financial and technical cooperation for development.
5 External debt.
6 Addressing systemic issues: enhancing the coherence and consistency of the international monetary, financial and trading systems in support of development.

As WSSD occurred under the long shadow of 9/11, these agendas began to drift apart, with the second Financing for Development Conference taking place in Doha in March 2008 as the financial crisis started to play out. Doha focused on:

1 Reaffirming the goals and commitments of the Monterrey Consensus.
2 Mobilizing domestic financial resources for development.
3 Mobilizing international resources for development: foreign direct investment and other private flows.
4 International trade as an engine for development.
5 Increasing international financial and technical cooperation for development.
6 External debt.
7 Addressing systemic issues: enhancing the coherence and consistency of the international monetary, financial and trading systems in support of development.
8 Other new challenges and emerging issues.
9 Staying engaged.

Rio+20 did not have the time to address how sustainable development should be financed and so established the Intergovernmental Committee of Experts on Sustainable Development Finance (ICESDF) which is dealt with in Chapter 2. Perhaps it was unrealistic to expect miracles from the ICESDF to change development finance in one year. But it would have perhaps achieved more if it had been open to stakeholders and had a better balance with the experts coming from both sustainable development and traditional development perspectives and without some regions rotating their experts. There were also major differences in the fact that the OWG process was looking at individual sectors and hoping that an FfD process would be developed separately and would help to identify funding for those sectors and their interlinkages.

In October 2014 the PGA appointed the Ambassadors of Norway and Guyana, Geir Pedersen and George Talbot, as co-facilitators for the financing for development process. Initially they were charged with preparing the modalities for these negotiations; in due course leading negotiations for an outcome document for the Addis Ababa conference was entrusted to them.

27–29 January: financing for development meeting

BOX 3.1 WORKSHOP ON GLOBAL FINANCIAL REFORM: HOW MIGHT THE 2015 INTERNATIONAL CONFERENCE ON FINANCING FOR DEVELOPMENT STRENGTHEN REFORM MOMENTUM?

On 20 October 2014, Brot für die Welt and the Financing for Development Office of the UNDESA organized a workshop for member states on 'Global Financial Reform: How might the 2015 International Conference on Financing for Development strengthen reform momentum?'. In the report of the event it said that the:

> linkages between financial systems in emerging and mature markets, which are greater than before the crisis, which implies greater contagion effects should there be disruptions in either group of countries. These linkages have been primarily intensified via capital market credit intermediation, be it bonds or other forms of financing, especially those involving "shadow banking" activities. In 2014, portfolio managers in the West held 4 trillion dollars in assets from Emerging Markets, making up 12 percent of their portfolio, making asset managers in developed countries a main potential conduit for financial instability.
>
> *(Thiemann, 2014)*

The workshop reflected that there was little confidence in the finance sector and in the regulations put in place. Underlining that it was still true that 'banks were too big to fail.' As U.S. Senator Brown of Ohio said:

> The assets of the six largest banks in the United States today total 63 percent of GDP . . . . We've got to deal with risk to be sure, but we've got to deal with the size of these banks, because if one of these banks is in serious trouble, it will have such a ripple effect on the whole economy.
>
> *(Brown, 2010)*

The workshop discussed the need for more regulation and suggested the integration of the 'Ruggie Principles on Business and Human Rights'.[1,2] Another suggestion was that there is a need for a better forum to discuss and bring political guidance, bringing in more voices than the regulators.

From the early stages of the post-2015 development process, it was very clear that the fates of both negotiation tracks – those preparing the outcome for the New York summit in September 2015 and those preparing the outcome for the Addis Ababa conference in July 2015 – were intertwined. For example, the inclusion in the OWG outcome of a significant number of MOI targets as well as Goal 17 was a clear signal that the "how" of achieving the new SDGs would have to be built into the new agenda. The FfD outcome, furthermore, would also have to be coherent with the post-2015 agenda.

Consideration was given early on to holding the Addis Ababa conference after the SDGs summit; it could address the commitments made in New York. This would have mirrored the dynamic between the Monterrey conference and the Millennium Development Goals. It was felt, however, that the confluence of landmark meetings in 2015 could build momentum across the financing, sustainable development and climate change agendas. An ambitious and far-ranging agreement in Addis Ababa could be the first step in a positive chain of breakthroughs running from Addis Ababa to New York to Paris in the space of six months. Ultimately, however, it was decided to hold the Addis Ababa conference just before the post-2015 discussions were due to conclude. This ratcheted up the pressure on the FfD negotiations significantly; a poor outcome, or conceivably no outcome at all, would have perhaps fatally undermined the prospects for agreeing to a transformative 2030 Agenda.

In terms of interaction with the post-2015 negotiations, the phrase "two sides of the same coin" was often used to describe the intertwined dynamic, with perhaps differing perspectives as to which process was heads and which was tails. The four Ambassadors worked closely together throughout the period from October 2014 to July 2015, holding a number of meetings to reflect on interlinkages and how the parallel negotiation tracks would affect each other. As time passed, and responding to many calls from the floor to ensure coherence, the two tracks sat in joint sessions in two instances in April and May 2015. These sessions proved key in unblocking a number of important issues. The April meeting brought clarity to the membership regarding the relationship between the two tracks, and the May discussions saw significant progress on the issue of creating a TFM. This latter point had been kept live and given prominence in both processes, but through the joint session approach it proved possible, working with a small number of key delegations, to address an appropriate way forward. The mechanism was then ultimately established through the Addis Ababa outcome but launched through the 2030 Agenda. Both outcomes also mirrored identical language with regard to the TFM to ensure that there would be no contradictions in the two agreements on this issue.

A notable dimension of the relationship between the two negotiation tracks was the support role played by the UN Secretariat. UNDESA consists of a number of branches, three of which were of particular relevance to the negotiations which took place over the course of 2014 and 2015. These were the branches handling sustainable development, financing for development, and support for ECOSOC. The latter was of particular importance in terms of the UN system and follow-up and review architecture, given the prominent role of the HLPF and UN functional Commission.

A challenge faced by the FfD process was the need to balance specifics with constructive ambiguity. The negotiations on a post-2015 development agenda had the advantage of starting from a strongly aspirational base. Financing for development, on the other hand, does not lend itself to such an approach; discussions inevitably got bogged down in detail around issues such as domestic, international and private resource mobilization, debt forgiveness, multilateral tax policy and the international monetary and financial system.

With this often highly technical subject matter, there were strong and early calls by many member states for line-by-line negotiations. This proved a very difficult dynamic. Following on from a number of informal sessions held in late 2014, the co-facilitators circulated in advance of the first drafting session in January 2015 an elements paper that set out seven "building blocks", namely domestic public finance; domestic and international private finance; international public finance; trade; technology, innovation and capacity building; sovereign debt; and systemic issues. The elements paper highlighted major challenges under each of these headings and included a separate section on monitoring, data and follow-up.

Recognizing that the private sector would play a significant role in funding implementation of the SDGs, UNCTAD with Aviva Investors,[3,4] organized during the first half of 2015, and in the context of the FfD negotiations, a series of briefings for the regional groupings. These focused on the role capital markets might play to support the SDGs. The workshops enabled member states to ask people from the finance sector questions that were specific to their own regions. Applying the conventional definition to capital markets, Aviva pointed out that "capital markets that finance development that meets the needs of the present without compromising the ability of future generations to meet their own needs" (AVIVA, 2014). It also observed that a primary failure of capital markets in relation to sustainable development is that of the misallocation of capital.

The structuring of the first preparatory session in January 2015 was around the elements paper that had been prepared by the co-facilitators. This had the following traditional development sections:

- Domestic Public Finance.
- Domestic and International Private Finance.
- International Public Finance.
- Trade and Technology, Innovation and Capacity Building.
- Sovereign Debt and Systemic Issues.
- Building Synergies with the Post-2015 Development Agenda and Other Issues.
- Monitoring, Data and Follow-Up.

The session had a sharp focus on the links between the post-2015 process and the FfD process and what steps should be taken to build synergies and avoid duplication. Some countries and stakeholders had called for the FfD process to address in much more depth the MoI envisaged for the SDGs. Others wanted to keep FfD entirely separate.

It was clear that FfD would be addressing a number of issues in detail which would not require such close attention in the post-2015 process. FfD would be looking at trade, intellectual property rights (IPRs) and illicit financial flows, and although this was not initially clear, it would become the home for commitments on the Technology Facilitation Mechanism (TFM). The TFM was also a child of Rio+20 and had been put in the FfD process, some people thought, to ensure at least one good outcome. It was unclear how climate finance would be handled within the FfD process given the upcoming Paris UNFCCC.

On the issue of monitoring and follow-up of financing for development, there was a debate about whether a separate mechanism would be needed and whether additional institutions aside from the HLPF would be a required. Given the very substantial agenda represented by the SDGs, the HLPF might not have the resources needed for this task. Whereas the organ of the UN that the HLPF had replaced (the UN Commission on Sustainable Development) had had a total of twenty days available to it each year, the HLPF would only have eight days a year.

13–17 April: financing for development meeting

In March 2015, the co-facilitators circulated a "zero draft" of the Addis Ababa outcome document. This looked to build on the discussions in the previous sessions and other inputs such as the UN Secretary General's synthesis report, the report of the OWG and the report of the Intergovernmental Committee of Experts on Sustainable Development Finance (ICESDF).

The April session opened with the co-facilitators introducing the zero draft of the FfD. This was structured in seven chapters:

- Domestic public resources.
- Domestic and international private business and finance.
- International public finance.
- International trade as an engine for development.
- Debt and debt sustainability.
- Addressing systemic issues.
- Science, technology, innovation (STI) and capacity building.

One of the early differences that emerged was the issue of defining a "global partnership for development". In the MDGs, this had clearly been government-to-government partnerships. What FfD started to discuss was changing this to 'shared responsibility'; the responsibility would be 'by all for all'. Developed countries argued that middle-income countries should take more responsibility in the international development sphere. G77 objected to the idea of moving away from the concept of CBDR. There was much discussion about the concept of "leaving no one behind" and what this would mean for the FfD process. The other conceptual challenge with which the FfD process had not previously dealt was the relationship between poverty eradication and sustainable development.

Another major concern that emerged was whether current institutions were adequate to address new challenges relating to FfD. Developing countries championed the idea of upgrading the UN International Committee on Tax Matters and argued for a new global online platform for infrastructure development.

15–22 June: financing for development meeting

Following three weeks of additional FfD informal discussions, the negotiations resumed for a final round before Addis Ababa. The co-facilitators prepared what they called "bridging paragraphs", which attempted to accommodate differing positions. Work was conducted in smaller informal formats to facilitate frank discussion of key disagreements. During this final eight-day round, two further versions of the draft outcome document were produced.

Key divergences that were a problem at the beginning of the FfD process dogged these negotiations to the end. How much of the agenda should focus on the MOI of the post-2015 development agenda and how much should focus on the traditional Monterrey and Doha agenda? Was ODA now going to be used for sustainable development? Was the private sector now going to play a much more significant role in the implementation of these agendas? What would be the follow-up mechanisms for this process and the MOIs in the post-2015 development agenda? Much was left unresolved and would go to Addis Ababa that way.

13–16 July: financing for development conference, Addis Ababa

With the conference looming (July 13–16) and progress in the formal New York sessions stalling, discussions moved largely to smaller group and bilateral discussions. The co-facilitators presented on 7 July their final effort to secure agreement in advance of Addis Ababa. Although intensive discussions took place on this draft, it ultimately proved impossible to bridge the remaining gaps, and the decision was reluctantly made to take an open text to Addis Ababa for further negotiation. Issues that remained difficult for many in the 7 July draft included the follow-up and review mechanism for tracking implementation of the FfD outcomes, the upgrading of the UN Tax Committee, how to address the issue of CBDR and describing the relationship between the MoI of the post-2015 development agenda and FfD.

There were hopes that with high-level representatives arriving in Addis Ababa, some fresh scope for compromise might emerge in the Ethiopian capital. The Ethiopian Government had its own interest in delivering an agreement and preventing the possible collapse of a conference in which they had invested so much. Its influence within the African group was an important asset.

The outcome from the Addis Ababa conference was to be called the Addis Ababa Action Agenda (AAAA). The conference attracted over 11,000 people, including eighteen heads of state and government as well as many ministers.

The upgrading of the UN Tax Committee quickly became the touchstone issue in the corridors. The G77 wanted to make this committee more intergovernmental in nature. With a large number of NGOs present in Addis Ababa, there was significant media and political pressure on WEOG delegations to show movement. WEOG countries, for their part, felt that the 7 July draft represented the best, or even only, hope for consensus and feared that reopening a key element such as the Tax Committee issue could result in the entire process unraveling.

With pressure building and the conference due to conclude on 16 July, those calling for the New York draft to be largely the basis for the agreed outcome eventually won out.

The final outcome document was agreed on the night of 15 July and subsequently adopted by the conference on 16 July. While not meeting G77 expectations, the Addis Ababa Action Agenda at least kept the Tax Committee issue open for further discussion and elaboration. It also allowed for a review of multilateral development finance, which could assess the functioning of multilateral development banks. In terms of international public resource mobilization, the outcome document did not go further than restating existing ODA commitments.

On the issue of a separate mechanism for reviewing the implementation of FfD commitments, the Addis Ababa Action Agenda reflected the intertwined nature of the two processes, set out for the middle ground by establishing the Financing for Development Forum under ECOSOC that is mandated to review both the FfD and the MoI and global partnership targets of the post-2015 development agenda, and which will report to the HLPF. The discrete but interlinked nature of the forum mirrored the approach taken in the post-2015 agenda, which acknowledged the independence of the FfD process, but also its key contribution to the new agenda.

The Addis Ababa conference will probably be looked at as a turning point for ODA. There was an acceptance by governments, in some cases reluctantly (and with many stakeholders also strongly opposed), of an increased role for the private sector in development finance. This represented a significant shift from ODA being solely understood as a transfer of resources between governments (sometimes through multilateral organizations) to a definition that is more expansive.

The Sustainable Development Solutions Network (SDSN) had estimated that it would cost $US2 to 3 trillion a year to implement the SDGs. Some considered that the Addis Ababa conference had missed an opportunity to suggest in a coherent way how that would happen.

The AAAA also contained many progressive elements that supported and complemented the SDGs. It called for a new social compact to ensure the provision of essential services in the areas of health, education, energy, and water and sanitation. The AAAA also sought to put in place the means to achieve universal secondary education by scaling up international investments. The outcome established also a global infrastructure forum to facilitate synergies in infrastructure development. Also of key importance was the centrality of gender equality and of the empowerment of women and girls. Both Monterrey and Doha had not delivered in terms of applying a gender dimension to financing. In contrast, the Addis Ababa outcome was strong in mainstreaming this perspective throughout, with a focus on equal economic rights for women.

Finally, the establishment of a Technology Facilitation Mechanism, advocated strongly in both the FfD and IGN processes, was an important achievement.

In his press conference at the end of the conference, UN Secretary General Ban Ki-moon said that "the Addis Ababa Action Agenda is a major step forward in building a world of prosperity and dignity for all" (Ki-moon, 2015).

Some important announcements concerning new funding or partnerships were made at the Addis Ababa conference. These included:

- The Bill & Melinda Gates Foundation and the governments of Canada, Japan and the United States announced new financing commitments totaling US$214 million.
- The UN, World Bank and partners launched a global financing facility to reduce maternal health and child mortality. US$12 billion have already been aligned to country-led five-year investment plans for women's, children's and adolescents' health in the Democratic Republic of the Congo, Ethiopia, Kenya and Tanzania in domestic and international, private and public funding.
- The multilateral development banks and the International Monetary Fund committed to extend more than $US400 billion in financing over the next three years.
- The Organization for Economic Co-operation and Development (OECD) and UNDP announced the worldwide launch of the Tax Inspectors Without Borders program, designed to support developing countries to build tax audit capacity.

- The European Investment Bank and the Food and Agricultural Organization signed a five-year agreement to foster investment operations in the field of agriculture, private sector development and value chains to eradicate hunger and ensure food security.
- The G7 also announced an increase of up to US$400 million in the number of people with access to climate insurance.
- UN Women and Member States launched the Addis Ababa Action Plan on Transformative Financing for Gender Equality and Women's Empowerment. The plan aims to outline financing priorities to translate the pledges in the Addis Ababa Action Agenda into actions for meeting new and existing commitments to gender equality and women's empowerment to in the new sustainable development agenda (UN, 2015d).

United Nations Sustainable Development Summit and the Pope's address

On 25–27 September 2015, the United Nations convened the Sustainable Development Summit. The three-day event was an unprecedented gathering with 150 heads of state endorsing the 2030 Agenda for Sustainable Development. The summit was the first step to transforming the new vision into concerted action. The new principles of "leaving no one behind and reaching those that are the farthest away" echoed through the General Assembly hall. All the 193 countries speaking highlighted a deep sense of ownership in this new plan.

Preceding the adoption of the 2030 Agenda, Pope Francis addressed a full General Assembly. This was the fifth time a pope visited the UN in its history. Pope Francis has become a prominent leader in political affairs – from his quiet mediation between Cuba and United States to his published encyclical on climate change – his voice is respected no matter the creed. It was therefore very symbolic that Pope Francis made his address before the adoption of the 2030 Agenda.

At the General Assembly, Pope Francis made a call to end the cycle of exclusion, "The poor are discarded from society, they are forced to live off waste and they have become part of the culture of waste" (UN, 2015e). "The adoption of the 2030 Agenda is "an important sign of hope to the world" (UN, 2015e). Pope Francis conveyed that the best and simplest way to measure progress in the 2030 Agenda is by providing immediate access to all to basic services, such as housing, decent work for all, potable water, nutritious food and freedom of religion (UN, 2015e). Moreover, Pope Francis warned that the international community must avoid the temptation of only working in the world of theory and of ideals, such as drafting long declarations that may have a "soothing effect on the conscience" without any real transformation on the ground (UN, 2015e).

The youngest Nobel laureate, Malala Yousafzai, was also present during the momentous adoption of the 2030 Agenda. She asked of world leaders that all children should have the right to safe, free and quality primary and secondary education.

On the sidelines of the summit, there were multiple events taking place simultaneously. Among them, the heads of state of Sweden, Brazil, Colombia, Liberia,

TABLE 3.1 Summary of incremental SDG investment needs in low- and lower-middle-income countries (average for 2015–2030 in US$2013 billion)

Investment area	"Development" investment needs	Incremental climate mitigation and adaptation investment needs	Total investment needs	Private, commercial financing (%)	Private, commercial financing	Public financing
Health	68–87	1–1.4	69–89	0%	0	69–89
Education	194	0	194	0%	0	194
Social protection	?	?	?	?	?	?
Agriculture and food security	[125]	[22]	[148]	[51%]	[75]	[73]
Access to modern energy	257–278	51–55	308–333	[55–59%]	169–196	137–138
Access to electricity and clean cooking fuels	54–71	10–14	64–85	[40–50%]	26–42	38–42
Power infrastructure	[203–207]	[41]	[244–248]	[59–62%]	[144–154]	[94–100]
Access to water and sanitation	29	13–16	43–46	[5–26%]	2–12	34–40
Basic water supply and adequate sanitation	28	6	34	[0–20%]	0–7	27–34
Water and sanitation infrastructure	[1]	[8–11]	[9–12]	[24–44%]	[2–5]	[7]
Telecommunications Infrastructure	[361]	[72]	[434]	[52–68%]	[225–295]	[139–208]
Transport infrastructure	[189]	[0]	[189]	[54–84%]	[102–159]	[30–87]
Ecosystems, incl. biodiversity	[21–28]	?	[21–28]	[15%]	[3–4]	[18–24]
Data for the SDGs	0.4	0	0.4	[0%]	0	0.4
Emergency response and humanitarian work*	8–23	?	[8–23]	[0%]	[0]	[8–23]
All SDG investment areas**	1253–1316	160–167	1413–1483	[41–50%]	577–741	743–836

Source: Guido Schmidt–Traub calculations and sources identified in the paper

* Emergency response and humanitarian work will be entirely funded by concessional public international financing and cannot be disaggregated by income group.

** This total excludes several SDG investment needs identified in this paper, including social protection and incremental investment needs for climate change mitigation and adaptation for ecosystems. Total does not equal sum of LICs and LMICs because cost of emergency response and humanitarian work is allocated to total only (Shmidt–Traub, 2015).

Tanzania, Germany, Tunisia, Timor-Leste and South Africa launched a High-Level Group to spur implementation of the 2030 Agenda (Sweden, 2015).

Outside the UN walls, the 2015 global citizen festival attracted 60,000 young people, who came to celebrate the adoption of the global goals. One of the mottos was "we are not a generation of bystanders" (Global Citizen, 2015). In order to gain access to this event, participants had to volunteer or prove that they were doing something to change the world. The list of celebrities supporting the festival and performing or speaking was extensive: Radiohead, Beyoncé and Coldplay as well as Leonardo DiCaprio and Michelle Obama. This festival exponentially increased awareness of the SDGs in the public domain and it galvanized early engagement for their implementation. Anyone visiting New York that week, whether it was for the UNGA event or just a tourist passing by, learned of the global goals by the buzz generated by this global event.

This three-day summit was also part of a larger celebration: the UN was turning seventy. In 1956, former Secretary-General Dag Hammarskjold predicted:

> I have no doubt that in 40 years from now we shall be engaged in the same pursuit. How could we expect otherwise? World organization is still a new adventure in human history.
>
> *(Dag Hammarskjold, 1956)*

It has been over forty years, and the UN is still a new experiment evolving through the challenges that it has had to tackle. The 2030 Agenda provides a new platform for the UN – it is a roadmap that, if genuinely implemented, can address the most pressing twenty-first-century challenges.

Indicators: the Statistical Commission 2015

On 25 and 26 February 2015, prior to the UN Statistical Commission, an expert group meeting on the proposed indicator framework for the post-2015 development agenda reached a consensus on the following main points:

- It is necessary to define an architecture for an integrated monitoring framework that would include global indicators and different levels of regional, national and thematic monitoring.
- The global-level monitoring framework should be limited to a small number of indicators.
- Such indicators should be selected on the basis of an agreed-upon set of criteria.
- The initial proposal for indicators to be put forth by the Statistical Commission is expected to be further refined and reviewed by the Commission at its forty-seventh session, to take place in 2016.
- A mechanism such as an Interagency and Expert Group on Sustainable Development Goal (SDG) Indicators (IAEG-SDGs) should be established.

- It is necessary to ensure national ownership of indicators (including of the estimation process).
- It is necessary to ensure disaggregation of indicators and to include a human rights dimension to the indicator framework (following the "no one left behind" principle).
- It is necessary to further strengthen national statistical capacity, including by mobilizing the necessary resources.
- It is important to draw from existing integrated statistical frameworks.
- It is important to build on the Millennium Development Goals' experience and lessons.

It was made plain by member states that any indicators proposed would not redefine any of the targets and that, ultimately, the suggestions by the IAEG-SDGs would still have to be agreed to by member states. Dr. Lisa Grace S. Bersales (Philippines) and Fabiola Riccardini (Italy) were selected by member states to chair the IAEG-SDGs.

In addition to the IAEG the Statistical Commission established two other bodies:

1 High Level Group on Partnership, Coordination and Capacity-Building for post-2015 monitoring. This would have fifteen to twenty representatives from national statistical offices. It would have the following roles:
   - Provide strategic leadership for the SDG implementation process as it concerns statistical monitoring and reporting.
   - Promote national ownership of the post-2015 monitoring system and foster capacity building, partnership and coordination for post-2015 monitoring, including to ensure consistency between national and global monitoring and reporting.
   - Address the need of funding statistical capacity building, including by developing proposals and advocating for resource mobilization and their management and monitoring, and identifying ways to leverage the resources and creativity of the private sector.
   - Advise on how the opportunities of the data revolution can be harnessed to support the SDG implementation process, taking into account the levels of development of the countries.
   - Review and make recommendations, as appropriate, and in cooperation with the IAEG-SDGs, on the issue of common (cross-country) data infrastructures to exploit the possibilities of new technologies.
   - Reach out and promote dialogue and partnerships between the statistical community and other stakeholders working on the implementation and monitoring of globally agreed sustainable development goals and targets (UN Statistical Commission, 2015).
2 A World Forum on Sustainable Development Data. This would bring together the whole data ecosystem to share ideas and experiences for data improvements, innovation, advocacy and technology transfer. The first forum would be in 2016 and should take place every two years.

The Statistical Commission processes the next steps

Now that heads of state have adopted the SDGs, one of the significant issues that needed to be finally addressed was the issue of what indicators there should be for the targets. After the establishment of the IAEG-SDGs by the Statistical Commission in March 2015, an open and transparent process to look for the relevant indicators for the targets was set out. It had three meetings in June 2015, October 2015 and March 2016. The meetings were open to input from member states, UN agencies and relevant stakeholders working on indicators. The co-chairs and the Statistical Division reached out to bring the best ideas forward wherever they might come from. There are targets in the SDGs in which global indicators have never been developed at the international level (i.e., total violent deaths, number of child soldiers). These global indicators represent an important opportunity to measure progress in a comprehensive manner.

The March 2016 Statistical Commission meeting agreed on a set of 226 indicators grouped into three tiers:

Tier I: Indicator conceptually clear, established methodology and standards available and data regularly produced by countries (ninety-eight indicators).

Tier II: Indicator conceptually clear, established methodology and standards available but data are not regularly produced by countries (fifty indicators).

Tier III: Indicator for which there are no established methodology and standards or methodology/standards are being developed/tested (seventy-eight indicators).

The political oversight of this process has been one of the main differences compared to the development of the MDG indicators. The advantage of this is that it will ensure ownership of the eventual indicators by everyone.

Notes

1 Beyond 2015 is a global civil society campaign, pushing for a strong and legitimate successor framework to the Millennium Development Goals.

2 The Ruggie Principles are named after the UN special representative on business and human rights, John Ruggie. The UN Guiding Principles on Business and Human Rights were endorsed by the UN Human Rights Council in June 2011. In the same resolution, the UN Human Rights Council established the UN Working Group on business and human rights. More information is available online at: http://business-humanrights.org/en/un-guiding-principles/text-of-the-un-guiding-principles.

3 Aviva Investors is a global asset management business dedicated to delivering investment outcomes that are central to the well-being and success of customers. They are wholly owned by Aviva plc, the UK's leading insurer, with strong businesses in selected markets in Europe, Asia and Canada.

4 The Committee of Experts on International Cooperation in Tax Matters as a subsidiary body of the Economic and Social Council is responsible for keeping under review and updating, as necessary, the United Nations Model Double Taxation Convention between Developed and Developing Countries and the Manual for the Negotiation of Bilateral Tax Treaties between Developed and Developing Countries. It also provides a framework for

dialogue with a view to enhancing and promoting international tax cooperation among national tax authorities and assessing how new and emerging issues could affect this cooperation. The committee is also responsible for making recommendations on capacity building and the provision of technical assistance to developing countries and countries with economies in transition. In all its activities, the committee gives special attention to developing countries and countries with economies in transition. Information is available online at: www.un.org/esa/ffd/ffd-follow-up/tax-committee.html.

References

AVIVA (2014) A roadmap for sustainable capital markets: How can the UN sustainable development goals harness the global capital markets? Available online at: www.aviva.com/media/upload/Aviva-Roadmap-to-Sustainable-Capital-Markets-updated.pdf

Brown, S. (2010) In an interview on "This Week" reported in POLITIFACT. Available online at: www.politifact.com/truth-o-meter/statements/2010/apr/27/sherrod-brown/six-largest-banks-getting-bigger-brown-said/

Global Citizen Festival (2015) Available online at: www.globalcitizen.org/en/festival/2015/

Hammarskjold, D. (1956) UN Secretary General, UN, New York. Available online at: https://archives.un.org/content/un-secretary-general-dag-hammarskj%C3%B6ld.

Ki-moon, B. (2015) In Addis Ababa conference opens path for robust implementation of new sustainable development agenda. UN Press Release. Available online at: www.un.org/esa/ffd/ffd3/press-release/addis-ababa-conference-opens-path-for-robust-implementation-of-new-sustainable-development-agenda.html

Shmidt-Traub, G. (2015) *Investment Needs to Achieve the Sustainable Development Goals Understanding the Billions and Trillions*, SDSN, New York. Available online at: http://unsdsn.org/wp-content/uploads/2015/09/151112-SDG-Financing-Needs.pdf

Sweden (2015) Press statement. Available online at: www.government.se/press-releases/2015/09/swedish-government-initiates-high-level-group-in-un/

Thiemann, M. (2014) Global financial reform: How might the 2015 International conference on financing for development strengthen reform momentum? Brot fur die Welt. Available online at: http://info.brot-fuer-die-welt.de/sites/default/files/blog-downloads/report_on_global_financial_reform_bfdw_thiemann.pdf

United Nations (2013) *Outcome Document of the Special Event to Follow Up Efforts Made towards Achieving the Millennium Development Goals*, UN, New York. Available online at: www.un.org/en/ga/search/view_doc.asp?symbol=A/RES/68/6

United Nations (2014a) *Report of the Open Working Group on Sustainable Development Goals Established Pursuant to General Assembly Resolution 66/288*, UN, New York. Available online at: www.un.org/en/ga/search/view_doc.asp?symbol=A/RES/68/309

United Nations (2014b) *Report of the Open Working Group on Sustainable Development Goals Established Pursuant to General Assembly Resolution 66/288*, UN, New York. Available online at: www.un.org/en/ga/search/view_doc.asp?symbol=A/RES/68/309

United Nations (2015a) Countries reach historic agreement to generate financing for new sustainable development agenda. UN, Addis Ababa. Available online at: www.un.org/sustainabledevelopment/blog/2015/07/countries-adopt-addis-ababa-action-agenda/

United Nations (2015b) *Elements Paper for Declaration Discussion*, UN, New York. Available online at: https://sustainabledevelopment.un.org/content/documents/5977Intergovernmental%20Negotiations%20Post-2015%20Dev.Agenda%20-%206%20February%202015.pdf

United Nations (2015c) *Food for thought Paper on a Possible Technology Facilitation Mechanism*, UN, New York. Available online at: https://sustainabledevelopment.un.org/content/documents/7167TFM%20Food%20for%20Thought%20Paper.pdf

United Nations (2015d) Highlights from the conference. Available online at: www.un.org/esa/ffd/ffd3/special/highlights-from-the-conference.html

United Nations (2015e) Pope Francis address in the General Assembly. Available online at: http://webtv.un.org/search/address-by-his-holiness-pope-francis-general-assembly-3rd-plenary-meeting-70th-session/4509290546001?term=pope%20francis

UNCTAD/AVIVA (2014) Capital markets and their role in sustainable development finance and the sustainable development goal: Briefing note for regional member state meetings on capital markets. Available online at: www.linkedin.com/pulse/20140908151955–8380295-capital-markets-and-their-role-in-sustainable-development-finance-and-the-sustainable-development-goals

United Nations (2015f) *The World Is Watching and Expectations Are High'*, *Secretary-General Says at Intergovernmental Negotiations on Post-2015 Development Agenda*, UN, New York. Available online at: www.un.org/press/en/2015/sgsm16471.doc.htm

United Nations Archives and Records (1956) Available online at: https://archives.un.org/content/un-secretary-general-dag-hammarskjöld

United Nations President of the General Assembly (2015) *Statement by the President at the Stocktaking Session of Intergovernmental Negotiations on the Post-2015 Development Agenda*, UN, New York. Available online at: www.un.org/pga/190115_statement-stocktaking-session-post-2015/

United Nations Statistical Commission (2015) Terms of reference for the High-level Group for partnership, coordination and capacity-building for post-2015 monitoring. Available online at: http://unstats.un.org/files/HLG%20-%20Terms%20of%20Reference%20(April%202015).pdf

4

A TRANSFORMATIONAL AGENDA

Outcomes from 2015 and what they mean

Introduction

The key to delivering the Sustainable Development Goals in a truly transformational way is how seriously governments, intergovernmental bodies and stakeholders take their role, singularly or in partnership, in their implementation. This section will look at what the outcomes have been and suggest what the next stages could look like for their implementation at the global, regional, national and subnational level. It will also look at what roles different stakeholders, including industry, can play. The SDGs have been framed as a "we the people" document, rather than taking only a state-centric approach. Its achievement will lie in their ability to inspire people around the world.

A journey finished, another one started: a retrospective look at what has been achieved

The agreement reached on the 2030 Agenda for Sustainable Development sets the world on a new course for the next fifteen years and beyond. Breathtaking in its scope and ambition, it amounts to a blueprint for the development of humanity and the planet in the twenty-first century. Never before has a single global agreement connected so clearly and compellingly the major challenges faced by the world today: eradicating poverty, protecting our planet from environmental degradation, creating conditions for balanced and sustainable economic growth. Never before has a set of goals and targets been drawn up for the world which recognizes the indivisibility of these and other challenges and the need to tackle them holistically. Never before has the entire world – all 193 member states of the UN – negotiated and committed itself to a single, universal plan of action of this kind.

The 2030 Agenda is a unique document: unique in its scale, unique in the way in which it was negotiated and unique in its universal applicability. It will, we hope, have a transformative impact on the lives of billions of human beings, in this and future generations. It has been hailed as one of the finest achievements of the United Nations in many years. It is the culmination of a supreme effort by the member states of the UN to agree collectively on the way forward. In a process spanning several years, negotiators used the tools of quiet and patient multilateral diplomacy to construct the new agenda. They benefited richly from a deep engagement throughout this period, on all issues relating to the new agenda, with civil society, the private sector and other vital partners: the Major Groups and Other Stakeholders. Their work was also underpinned by the broadest public consultation process ever undertaken in support of a UN negotiation. The result is a 2030 Agenda for Sustainable Development, adopted by consensus and without reservation, which enjoys unprecedented support and commitment across the world.

With the adoption of this agenda by heads of state and government at the UN on 25 September 2015, one part of the journey has been completed. But another is only just beginning. The new goals and targets came into effect on 1 January 2016. We have all set out now on the "road to 2030". As the agenda makes clear, this is a journey that will involve governments, parliaments, civil society, academia, the research community, the private sector and many other stakeholders. It will also involve countless ordinary people around the world who will make their own contributions to the achievement of the new goals and targets. It is an agenda "by, for and with the people".

There is no time to lose. Fifteen years is a relatively short time for implementation of so vast a set of commitments. But, learning from the experience of the Millennium Development Goals (where insufficient attention was paid to the arrangements for monitoring of implementation and to financing), we are better placed now to move swiftly and effectively into the implementation phase. We must ensure that after the momentous agreements reached last year in New York, Addis Ababa and Paris, there is no loss of momentum as we face up to the huge challenges of implementation and reviews of progress. For the 2030 Agenda, this is Year 1 of implementation; governments and all other stakeholders must waste no time in demonstrating that they have taken the new goals and targets to heart and are translating them into comprehensive national action plans. This will require in many cases the creation of new institutional arrangements to ensure that governments understand and respect the cross-cutting nature of the agenda. Traditional compartmentalized approaches, or "silo" thinking, will no longer be effective; 'whole-of-government' approaches will be needed to do justice to the new agenda and to ensure that it is fully realized.

A number of factors will make the task easier. The agenda contains a set of goals and targets that are specific, action oriented and measurable. A set of global indicators has been prepared that will guide member states as they develop their own indicators to assist in monitoring performance and reviewing implementation. While the bulk of the implementation effort will fall on member states at the national level, a set of follow-up and review arrangements has been included in the agenda to assist member states by promoting exchanges of best practices and mutual learning at the regional and global levels. Specific arrangements have also been made to ensure that commitments made in relation to MoI and Goal 17, and also in the FfD process, are tracked and supported.

The importance of adequate disaggregated data being available to member states to help them measure progress under the individual headings of the agenda cannot be overestimated. This will be a key requirement for effective implementation of the agenda. Many member states with underdeveloped data collection capacity will need significant support in this respect – and will need this at a very early stage.

A key role has been entrusted at the global level to the High-Level Political Forum, meeting under the auspices of ECOSOC every year and under the authority of the General Assembly once every four years. This body will have a central oversight responsibility in relation to implementation of the agenda. While the detail of how it will operate remains to be settled, it is clear that the HLPF will be of pivotal importance in terms of ensuring a comprehensive overview of how the seventeen goals and 169 targets are being implemented and of supporting member states in their implementation efforts. The HLPF's 2016 meeting will consider how to "ensure that we leave nobody behind". This overriding objective for the agenda, which gives it much of its moral impact and resonance, needs to be operationalized; the 2016 meeting will be an important opportunity to explore how member states can in practice ensure that the needs of all vulnerable minorities are addressed. The HLPF was an occasion for member states to signal clearly their commitments to the agenda, with some describing their own initial responses to it with a view to encouraging similar action from others. Strong signals about the integrated and indivisible nature of the new goals and targets may also be expected.

In preparation for the first meeting of the Finance for Development Forum in April 2016 the UN Interagency Task Force on Financing for Development prepared a report, 'Monitoring commitments and actions'. In the report they brought together the outputs from FfD and the SDGs to show where they supported each other. Table 4.1 shows this very well.

TABLE 4.1 Mapping of select Addis Ababa commitments and actions in support of the SDGs

	Domestic public resources	Domestic and international private business and finance	International development cooperation	International trade as an engine for development	Debt and debt sustainability	Addressing systemic issues	Science, technology, innovation and capacity building
Goal 1: End poverty in all its forms everywhere	Social compact (12) progressive tax systems (22)	Financial inclusion (39), remittance (40)	ODA focus on those with greatest needs (52), south–south cooperation and poverty eradication (57)	Trade as engine for poverty eradication, to promote productive employment (79)	Consideration of debt relief for countries experiencing shocks (102)	Coordination to reduce spillovers from financial crisis (105)	Addressing digital (114), research and development vaccines and medicines (121)
Goal 2: End hunger, achieve food security and improve nutrition and promote sustainable agriculture	Increasing public investment in research, infrastructure, pro-poor initiatives (13)	Responsible investments in agriculture (13), support to agricultural banks (39), FDI in agriculture (48)	Coordination of international efforts to support smallholders, women farmers (13)	Correction and prevention of trade restrictions, distortions in world agricultural markets (83)	Borrowing as an important tool for financing SDGs (93)	Measures to ensure proper functioning of food commodity markets (108)	Capacity development for agriculture productivity (115), cooperation for agricultural research (123)
Goal 3: Ensure healthy lives and promote well-being for all at all ages	Investments in public services, including health (12), price and tax measures on tobacco (32)	Foster a dynamic and well-functioning business sector, while protecting health standards (37)	International support to social compact (12), health emergencies (68), strengthening health systems (77)	TRIPS Agreement not to prevent members from taking measures to protect public health (86)	Debt-to-health swaps (102)		Support research and development of vaccines and medicines (121)

(Continued)

TABLE 4.1 (Continued)

	Domestic public resources	Domestic and international private business and finance	International development cooperation	International trade as an engine for development	Debt and debt sustainability	Addressing systemic issues	Science, technology, innovation and capacity building
Goal 4: Ensure Inclusive and equitable quality education and promote life-long learning opportunities for all	Investments in public services, including education (12)		Scaled up international cooperation to allow all children to complete education (78)		Borrowing as an important tool for financing SDGs (93)	Recognition of education of migrants (111)	Scaled up investment in STEM education, enhanced technical, vocational, tertiary education (119)
Goal 5: Achieve gender equality and empower all women and girls	Enforcement of non-discriminatory laws (21), gender responsive budgeting (30)	Removing barriers for women's participation in economy (41), equal rights for women to economic resources (41)	Reporting allocations for gender equality (53), development bank safeguards on gender equality (75)	Address specific challenges of women in trade (90)		Gender-based selection of heads of financial institutions (106), ending human trafficking of women (112)	Promote access to technology for women (114), equal access to STEM education for women and girls (119)
Goal 6: Ensure availability and sustainable management of water and sanitation for all	Investments in public services, including water and sanitation (12), strengthen capacities of municipalities (34)		International support to social compact (12)		Management of contingent liabilities for infrastructure investment (48)		Capacity building for water and sanitation (115)
Goal 7: Ensure access to affordable, reliable, sustainable and modern energy for all	Investments in public services, including energy (12), development bank investment in energy infrastructure (33)	Promoting private investment in clean energy technology, increasing share of renewable technology (49)	International support to social compact (12), MDB financing for infrastructure (75)		Management of contingent liabilities for infrastructure investment (48)	Promote investment in clean energy technologies (49)	Promote investment in clean energy technologies (49)

Goal 8: Promote sustained, inclusive and sustainable economic growth, full and productive employment and decent work for all	Include full and productive employment and decent work for all in national development strategies (18)	Private business as a driver of economic growth and job creation (35)	Lending by MDBs (70)	Trade as an engine for growth (79), regional integration to promote growth (87)	Durable solutions to debt problems to promote growth (99)	Reducing spillover effects of financial crises (104), enhancing global financial and macro stability (105)	Development and diffusion of innovations (114), dissemination of technologies to SMEs (116)
Goal 9: Build resilient infrastructure, promote inclusive and sustainable industrialization and foster innovation	National development bank lending for infrastructure, industrialization (33), support cities in infrastructure (34)	Overcoming impediments to private investments in infrastructure (47), FDI for structural transformation (45)	Blended finance for infrastructure (54), MDB financing (75)	Integration of SMEs in global value chains (87)	Management of contingent liabilities for infrastructure investment (48)		Dissemination of technologies for industrial diversification (116)
Goal 10: Reduce inequality within and among countries	Add social compact (12)	Full and equal access to financial services (39), incentivize FDI to LDCs (45)	Focus of concessional resources on those with greatest needs (52)	Special and differential treatment of developing countries in WTO (84)	Workouts from sovereign debt crises (98)	Voice and participation of developing countries in international economic decision making (106)	Development, dissemination and diffusion and transfer of environmentally sound technologies to developing countries (120)

(Continued)

TABLE 4.1 (Continued)

	Domestic public resources	Domestic and international private business and finance	International development cooperation	International trade as an engine for development	Debt and debt sustainability	Addressing systemic issues	Science, technology, innovation and capacity building
Goal 11: Make cities and human settlements inclusive, safe, resilient and sustainable	Strengthen capacities of municipalities and other local authorities, municipal bond markets (34)	Incentivize private sector to adopt sustainable practices, foster long-term quality investment (36)	Strengthen capacity of local actors to manage and finance disaster risk reduction (62)		Establish or strengthen municipal bond markets (34)		
Goal 12: Ensure sustainable consumption and production patterns	Corporate transparency, accountability in extractive industries (32), rationalize inefficient fossil-fuel subsidies (31)	Businesses to shift to more sustainable consumption and production patterns (35), FDI to promote sustainable patterns of production, consumption (45)	Social and environmental safeguards systems by development banks (75)	Combat poaching, trafficking of protected species, trafficking in hazardous waste (92)		Take account of environmental challenges in enhancing policy coherence (103)	Strengthen scientific, technological and innovative capacity for sustainable patterns of consumption and production (120)
Goal 13: Take urgent action to combat climate change and its impacts	Rationalize inefficient fossil fuel subsidies (31), cities implementing mitigation and adaptation policies (34)	Businesses take account of environmental and social impacts (37)	Meeting climate finance commitments (60), consider climate, disaster resilience in development financing (62)			Take account of climate change in enhancing policy coherence (103)	Capacity building for climate services (115), transfer of environmentally sound technologies (120)
Goal 14: Conserve and sustainably use the oceans, seas and marine resources for sustainable development	Coherent policy, financing, trade and technology frameworks to protect, manage and restore marine ecosystems (17)	Voluntary Guidelines on Responsible Governance of Tenure of Land, Fisheries, Forests (13)	Commit to protecting, and restoring, the health, productivity and resilience of oceans and marine ecosystems (64)	Strengthen disciplines on subsidies in the fisheries sector (83)		Provide access for small-scale artisanal fishers to marine resources and markets (108)	Capacity building for fisheries (115), increase scientific knowledge, research, transfer marine technology (121)

Goal 15: Protect, restore and promote sustainable use of terrestrial ecosystems, sustainably manage forests, combat desertification, and halt and reverse land degradation and halt biodiversity loss	Coherent policy frameworks to protect, manage and restore terrestrial ecosystems (17)	Sustainable corporate practices, integrating environmental, social and governance factors into company reporting (37)	Mobilization of financial resources to conserve and sustainably use biodiversity and ecosystems (63)	Combat poaching and trafficking of protected species, trafficking in hazardous waste, and trafficking in minerals (92)	Debt-to-nature swaps (102)	Strengthen coherence, consistency of multilateral financial, investment . . . environment institutions (113)	Development, dissemination and diffusion and transfer of environmentally sound technologies (120)
Goal 16: Promote peaceful and inclusive societies for sustainable development, provide access to justice for all and build effective, accountable and inclusive institutions at all levels	Strengthen domestic enabling environments, rule of law, combatting corruption (20), supreme audit institutions (30)	Build transparent, predictable investment climates (36)	Coherence of developmental and humanitarian finance (66), financing for peace building and development in the post–conflict context (67)	Commitment to strengthening multilateral trade system (80)		Voice and participation of developing countries in international economic decision making (106)	Capacity building for public finance and administration (115)

Source: 'Monitoring commitments and actions' (UN, 2016)

Climate change and the 2030 agenda: competing or complementary agendas?

The Climate Change Conference in Paris ended in a genuine standing ovation lasting a couple of minutes. Teary-eyed delegates and even ministers stood from their seats in awe that the Paris Agreement had been adopted despite insurmountable odds. Just a week before its adoption, the text looked like it needed another year's worth of work. At the final plenary meeting, world leaders described it as a "major landmark that will provide security and stability" (UN, 2015a).

The implications of this new treaty are far-reaching: once it enters into force, all countries will be bound to take ambitious action at their national level, from the smallest island to the biggest emitter. Contrary to the previous multilateral agreement on climate change, the Kyoto Protocol, the challenge to decarbonize the world economy is a shared responsibility by all countries. Part of the Paris Agreement is the Nationally Determined Contributions (NDCs) – these are national pledges that each country has committed to implement. These national plans will be reviewed every five years, and with each new cycle they will have to become more ambitious.

Several scientists argue that global emissions have reached a point of no return and that it is not possible to stay below the 1.5 C threshold (Sachs, 2016). The year in which the Paris Agreement was adopted was paradoxically the hottest year in recorded history (NOAA, 2016). The only way to stay the course is if energy systems around transform; they need a "radical overhaul" (Sachs, 2016). The use of renewable sources of energy should become the norm instead of the exception.

Contrary to the SDGs, which expire in 2030, the commitments made under the Paris Agreement go beyond 2050. In Paris, leaders agreed to reach "carbon neutrality" by the second half of this century and to hold global average temperature "well below 2C" (UN, 2015b). Countries are starting to work on decarbonization strategies; these plans are paving the way for the transformation of the energy matrix.

Additionally, the way food is produced is at the core of the needed transformation. The Intergovernmental Panel on Climate Change (IPCC) highlighted that industrial revolution is among the top sources of greenhouse gas emissions (Leiva-Roesch & Puri, 2015). With a growing population estimated to reach 10 billion by the end of this century, there will be a need to produce more food, but it will need to happen in a very different way:

> Worldwide, agriculture is pushing into forests, grasslands, wetlands causing extensive global deforestation and soil destruction and degradation. Among the main drivers of this deforestation are the expansion of industrial plantations for the production of commodities such as soy, sugarcane, oil palm and maize.
>
> *(Gopalan, 2016)*

Fortunately the world is aligning to meet these challenges. The Paris Agreement was adopted just a few weeks after the 2030 Agenda for Sustainable Development. There are a number of goals and targets in the SDGs that, if implemented in unison with the Paris Agreement, can have a positive and exponential ripple effect – for example, Goal 2: "End hunger, achieve food security and improved nutrition and promote sustainable agriculture"; Goal 7: "Ensure access to affordable, reliable, sustainable and modern energy for all"; and Goal 12: "Ensure sustainable consumption and production patterns" (UN, 2015d). The question is whether countries are planning to jointly implement the SDGs and the NDCs. If these agendas are implemented in isolation, they risk undermining each other, or worse, they can be at the expense of each other (Phathanothai, 2016). What can be done under the flag of development and poverty eradication can substantially undermine mitigation efforts and vice versa. Moreover, climate change can easily undo gains made to eradicate poverty.

Both agendas were negotiated in parallel, with very little overlap:

> Delivering on both the SDGs and climate objectives will require a new mindset of partnership between two professional and policy communities that to date have been operating largely separately, within distinct bureaucracies and institutions.
>
> *(Phathanothai, 2016)*

It will undoubtedly take more effort to plan and implement joint strategies, but their results will have greater impact. The implementation of both the 2030 Agenda and the Paris Agreement need to spur new policies that are a "win-win" between sustainability and growth.

The integrated and universal characters of the SDGs and of the Paris Agreement make them compatible partners. Both of these agreements are based on a firm commitment to achieve sustainable development and poverty eradication. Both are new "political manifestos" that are galvanizing concerted action at the multilateral, regional, national and local levels.

On 22 April 2016, without breaking the unprecedented momentum achieved in Paris, 175 Parties to the United Nations Framework Convention on Climate Change (UNFCCC) signed the Paris Agreement. Fifteen parties ratified it. The world's largest emitters, the United States and China, were among the signatories (together they represent approximately 38 percent of greenhouse gas emissions). This multilateral treaty broke the record of member states signing on the first available day (Associated Press, 2016). The Paris Agreement will enter into force when it is ratified by fifty-five countries, representing at least 55 percent of global emissions. After the success of the 22 April event, the Paris Agreement will hopefully enter into force earlier than anticipated.

At the signing ceremony, Secretary-General Ban Ki-moon said,

> The window for keeping global temperature rise well-below 2°C, let alone 1.5°C, is rapidly closing. The era of consumption without consequences is over. We must intensify efforts to decarbonize our economies and we must support developing countries in making this transition. The poor and most vulnerable must not suffer further from a problem they did not create.
>
> *(Ki-moon, 2016)*

Is the UN fit to implement the 2030 Agenda?

As the UN celebrated its seventieth anniversary, the majority of member states recognized the need for its reform. The 2030 Agenda clearly states that all the goals and targets are indivisible and should be implemented in an integrated manner. This new policy framework runs contrary to the modus operandi of the organization, which has been working in silos and in sectors.

The current UN system, including its intergovernmental bodies, does not promote integration and does not focus enough on implementation. Moreover, the way funding flows are distributed also encourages more fragmentation. Fortunately, there is renewed momentum to evaluate the UN machinery. A number of ongoing initiatives are looking at how to align the UN to the new priorities set out in the 2030 Agenda. The ECOSOC dialogues on the long-term positioning of the UN system, the Quadrennial Comprehensive Policy Review (QCPR) are only a few examples. Within the UN, the Chief Executives Board (CEB), which is the highest-level coordination body at the UN, is also evaluating how to implement this new vision.

Beyond the UN's structural reform, throughout the 2030 Agenda negotiations, delegations kept repeating that there was a need to change the mind-set. Changing the culture and working methods at the UN might be one of the most difficult but most important tasks ahead. Currently, the General Assembly, the Security Council and the Economic and Social Council work in isolation from each other. Although each charter body has its own mandate, the founding fathers could have never anticipated that there would be such little overlap and communication between them. With sustained leadership by member states and a new Secretary-General, the UN can go through the needed metamorphosis in order to support the implementation of this transformative vision.

Implementation at the national level

If the SDGs are going to be implemented, what happens at the national level will be critical. There are number of ways that this implementation can be accelerated. The best place to start is to learn from what has worked in the past and build on those lessons, both positive and negative.

National Councils for Sustainable Development

Agenda 21 (1992) required governments to produce national strategies on sustainable development as a mechanism for implementing the agreement. To help them do this, over 100 countries established National Councils for Sustainable Development (NCSD) by 2002. The form of the NCSD differed from country to country, but many were multistakeholder platforms which governments would chair or co-chair. They were established by governments in different ways:

- Presidential decree: Argentina and Vietnam.
- Ministerial decree: Niger and Barbados.
- Council of State decision: Finland.

- National law: Mexico and Philippines.
- Letter from the environment minister: Norway.
- Cabinet resolution: Ukraine and Grenada.

After agreeing upon the SDGs, each country would have to develop their National Sustainable Development Goals Strategy (NSDGS). There are considerable lessons to be drawn from the approach taken after the 1992 conference, one being establishing, strengthening or reinvigorating an NCSD to play a role in the development of the NSDGS. This would strengthen national stakeholder engagement as well as implementation.

A lesson from the implementation of the 1992 outcomes is that the NCSD is likely to be more successful if the secretariat is placed within the prime minister or president's office. This will guarantee line ministries' involvement at the highest level.

A NSDGS could become a consolidated and streamlined framework. This could enable coordination among the different national strategies linked to global sustainable development obligations (e.g., biodiversity, climate, Paris Agreements, etc.). This could include a strategy for awareness raising, indicator measurement, data collection, approach to multistakeholder partnerships and implementation. The OECD did a review of sustainable development strategies in 2001 and outlined what made them successful:

- Country ownership and participation, leadership and initiative in developing their strategies.
- Broad consultation, including particularly with the poor and with civil society, to open up debate on new ideas and information, exposing issues to be addressed and building consensus and political support on action.
- Ensuring sustained beneficial impacts on disadvantaged and marginalized groups and on future generations.
- Building on existing strategies and processes, rather than adding additional ones, to enable convergence and coherence.
- A solid analytical basis, taking account also of relevant regional issues, including a comprehensive review of the present situation and forecasts of trends and risks.
- Integration of economic, social and environmental objectives through mutually supportive policies and practices and the management of tradeoffs.
- Realistic targets with clear budgetary priorities (OECD, 2001).

Stakeholder Forum for a Sustainable Future, which acts as the secretariat for the Global Coalition of NCSD, produced a review of the functions that an NCSD can play and suggested the following:

- Strategy creation and advice.
- Policy and implementation.
- Monitoring and scrutiny.
- Stakeholder engagement and capacity building.
- International outreach (Stakeholder Forum, 2015).

In the past, the link between NCSD and local and subnational implementation has been weak – this needs to be looked at.

Adopting multistakeholder processes does not mean that everything will become easy. Engaging stakeholders enables a way for more voices to be heard and for more individuals and organizations to be motivated. Former Minister of Water of South Africa Kadar Asmal put it well:

> A parting warning: [conducting a multi-stakeholder process] is never a neat, organized, tidy concerto. More often, the process becomes a messy, loosely-knit, exasperating, sprawling cacophony. Like pluralist democracy, it is the absolute worst form of consensus building, except for all the others.
>
> *(Asmal, 2000)*

The role of parliaments

Agenda 2030 is one of the first UN documents to recognize the role that national parliaments can play in holding the executive accountable to commitments it has made.

> 79. We also encourage Member States to conduct regular and inclusive reviews of progress at the national and subnational levels which are country-led and country-driven. Such reviews should draw on contributions from indigenous peoples, civil society, the private sector and other stakeholders, in line with national circumstances, policies and priorities. National parliaments as well as other institutions can also support these processes.
>
> *(United Nations, 2015c)*

The experience of previous sustainable development agreements is that the SDGs cannot be implemented without strong political will. The SDGs have a fifteen-year horizon, and in this time, governments may change a number of times. As always, NGOs and other stakeholders will continue to remind governments of the obligations they have made. A robust oversight by parliamentary committees would ensure a higher degree of implementation and ownership by all political parties.

One of the key challenges that implementation will face is returning to a sector approach. The SDGs have been unique in their development by recognizing the interlinkages between the goals, targets and indicators. Parliamentary committees also operate along sector or ministry lines, and so, in addition to different parliamentary committees taking oversight of different goals and targets, there will need to be a committee to facilitate the interlinkages and coordination between the sectors. Some might call this the "SDG committee" but once established, it could play an even broader role in national policy development and oversight. This oversight:

> . . . should include a participatory process allowing for hearings with civil society, the private sector and other groups, direct interaction with all

government departments, as well as the authority to demand reports or convene expert witnesses. It may also need authority to block draft legislation until further review.

(Motter, 2015)

As mentioned earlier, where National Councils of Sustainable Development exist, they should play a role in being an independent review of, or producer of, the national reports to the UN High-Level Political Forum. These reports should also be reviewed by parliaments and, where relevant, the parliamentary committees should monitor the follow-up actions to the reports.

> A similar process is being utilized, with assistance from the Inter-Parliamentary Union (IPU), in the reporting exercise of the CEDAW, as well as that of the Universal Periodic Review. While this practice has yet to mature, it has a great potential to effectively support the implementation of the SDGs in each country.
>
> *(Motter, 2015)*

An annual debate on the SDGs and targets in parliaments would enable stakeholders to mobilize media interest in the implementation of the SDGs, highlighting both successes and remaining challenges.

The ability for parliaments to play this oversight role will vary between countries, and there is clearly a need to build capacity within a number of parliaments. This should be undertaken in partnership with the Inter-Parliamentary Union.

Local and subnational levels

One of the well-recognized successes of the 92 Earth Summit was the engagement with local authorities. Chapter 28 of Agenda 21 identified a key responsibility that local authorities should undertake:

> By 1996, every local authority should have consulted with its citizens, and developed "a local Agenda 21" for the community.
>
> *(UN, 1992)*

By 2002, over 6,000 local Agenda 21s had undertaken that responsibility and created local dialogues on local sustainability issues. At WSSD in 2002, the Network for Regional Government for Sustainable Development (NRG4SD) was launched to take a similar role for subnational governments.

> We believe that the implementation of sustainable development needs a strategic framework for all governments. We believe that this applies strongly in our regional spheres. Regional governments need sustainable development strategies as central frameworks for linking all their other strategies,

ensuring that each is sustainable and that they are mutually supportive of each other.

(NRG4SD, 2002)

The development of NSDGS should link subnational and local SDG strategies together. Each of these levels of government has a role in embedding SDGs in their work, their committee structures and most importantly in developing their own sustainable development councils and strategies. Local and subnational implementation will require the active involvement of all stakeholders.

The role of partnerships

Shortly after the heads of state left New York in September 2015, member states started their work on the UN resolution 'Towards Global Partnerships'. They defined these partnerships as:

voluntary and collaborative relationships between various parties, both public and non-public, in which all participants agree to work together to achieve a common purpose or undertake a specific task and, as mutually agreed, to share risks and responsibilities, resources and benefits.

(UN, 2015e)

Some of the delivery of targets of the SDGs can be undertaken by multistakeholder partnerships (MSPs). In 2002 WSSD recognized that involving stakeholders in the implementation of the global agreements increased the likelihood of their implementation. At WSSD the outcomes were seen as two different types:

Type 1 were policy agreements and commitments.
Type 2 were commitments and action-oriented multistakeholder platforms focused on deliverables and that would contribute in translating political commitments into action.

A set of principles was developed at the last preparatory meeting for WSSD in June 2002, which was known as the Bali Guidelines on Partnerships. They covered:

- Objective of partnerships.
- Voluntary in nature/respect for fundamental principles and values.
- Link with globally agreed outcomes.
- Integrated approach to sustainable development.
- Transparency and accountability.
- Tangible results.
- Funding agreements.
- New/value-added partnerships.
- Local involvement and international impact.

(UN, 2002)

These were then developed further at the Commission on Sustainable Development in 2003, which decided on the criteria and guidelines for partnerships as follows:

- Voluntary initiatives undertaken by governments and relevant stakeholders.
- Contribute to the implementation Agenda 21, JPoI.
- Not intended to substitute commitments made by governments.
- Bear in mind the economic, social and environmental dimensions.
- Predictable and sustained resources for their implementation should include the mobilization of new resources and, where relevant, should result in the transfer of technology to, and capacity building in, developing countries.
- Designed and implemented in a transparent and accountable manner.
- Should be consistent with national laws and national strategies.
- Providing information and reporting by partnerships registered with the CSD.

(UN, 2003)

The 2030 Agenda partnerships should learn from the lessons of the WSSD partnerships. For example, one of the challenges identified was an inability to delist partnerships that were not achieving their aims. This time around there is a stronger commitment for robust partnerships to be applied through a SMART criterion (commitments = specific, measureable, achievable, resource based, with timelines).

At present, there are a series of so-called 'partnerships' reflected on the UN website that would benefit from a clearer delineation. First, it's clear that private–public partnerships should not be on the website, as they represent a financial and legal relationship between a form of government and usually a company to deliver services. Second, voluntary initiatives by a particular stakeholder are also not partnerships. Voluntary initiatives, in particular, were made around the follow-up to the Rio+20 conference and should be separated out.

What should be left are three types of partnerships:

1 UN-organized partnerships.
2 UN-facilitated or supported partnerships.
3 Partnerships that have no involvement by the UN.

There should be mandatory reporting of UN-led MSPs to the relevant UN body and probably for UN-facilitated or supported partnerships. Type 3 partnerships where the UN is not involved should publicly report self-assessment requirements on at least a biennial basis. The need for a coherent and strengthened due-diligence process needs to be established.

Perhaps even some independent auditing of partnerships could be envisioned, for example, by creating a partnership standard – possibly through the International Standards Organization (ISO) or an equivalent body. This might enable some form of quality standard or rating for partnerships to indicate if they are delivering against their objectives. This kind of transparency would be very useful.

A UN task team made up of the relevant UN agencies, funds and programs could support an annual or biannual meeting of the individual SDGs and the partnerships working on their particular targets.

This 'meta-partnership' approach of those interested in contributing to deliver on the targets for a particular SDG and report could be done at the relevant sector meeting for each goal where there is one, such as WHO for health. Each of these could be supported by the different UN task teams, therefore enhancing the coordination and impact of partnerships. It would ensure the initial review was undertaken by parts of the UN with relevance to those partnerships and build a strong knowledge management of the successes and challenges faced by those partnerships.

In general, all those MSPs that are not publicly reporting their progress could be delisted or flagged and then delisted. If there is a rating system, then it could be that their rating is lowered.

Adequate and additional funding would need to be made available for the UN agencies, funds and programs assigned to be part of the different UN task teams and for the meta-partnership hubs and their meetings. At the UN, the ECOSOC Partnership Forum would play a critical role:

> The ECOSOC Partnership Forum could discuss lessons learned and evaluate the effectiveness of established guidelines and policy frameworks. A report on the results could inform the HLPF.
>
> *(Beisheim & Nils, 2016)*

An effective way to look at partnerships in the UN can be seen in Figure 4.1.

If partnerships are to play this critical role, then the approach should be one of building on learning lessons and scaling up successes.

The private sector

> Now a new generation of policy innovation is aiming to ensure that the financial system serves the needs of inclusive, environmentally-sustainable, economic development. These innovations in financial and monetary policies and regulations, along with wider market standards are creating a critical nexus between the rules that govern the financial system and sustainable development.
>
> *(UNEP, 2015)*

To deliver the AAAA, SDGs and the Paris Climate Agreement, it has been recognized that the private sector will have to play a much more significant role.

The UN started an effective engagement with the private sector in 2000. The UN Global Compact was launched as a voluntary initiative based on CEO commitments to implement universal sustainability principles and to take steps to support UN objectives. In 2016, its membership includes over 8,000 companies and 4,000 nonbusiness participants.

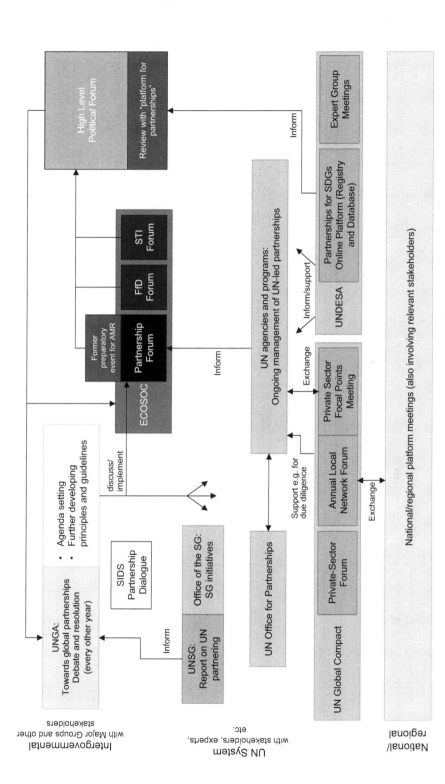

FIGURE 4.1 Multistakeholder partnerships for implementing the 2030 Agenda: improving accountability and transparency (Beisheim & Nils, 2016)

To join the Global Compact, companies have to show they are delivering on the ten principles. The UN Global Compact's Ten Principles are derived from the Universal Declaration of Human Rights, the International Labour Organization's Declaration on Fundamental Principles and Rights at Work, the Rio Declaration on Environment and Development and the United Nations Convention Against Corruption. The principles are discussed in the following sections.

Human rights

- Principle 1: Businesses should support and respect the protection of internationally proclaimed human rights.
- Principle 2: make sure that they are not complicit in human rights abuses.

Labour

- Principle 3: Businesses should uphold the freedom of association and the effective recognition of the right to collective bargaining.
- Principle 4: the elimination of all forms of forced and compulsory labor.
- Principle 5: the effective abolition of child labor.
- Principle 6: the elimination of discrimination in respect of employment and occupation.

Environment

- Principle 7: Businesses should support a precautionary approach to environmental challenges.
- Principle 8: undertake initiatives to promote greater environmental responsibility.
- Principle 9: encourage the development and diffusion of environmentally friendly technologies.

Anticorruption

- Principle 10: Businesses should work against corruption in all its forms, including extortion and bribery.

Back in 2000, the UN General Assembly agreed to the Guidelines on Cooperation between the UN and the Business Community in order to enhance their cooperation. These have subsequently been strengthened in 2009 and in 2015.

The purpose of these guidelines was to provide a framework to facilitate the formulation and implementation of partnerships between the United Nations and the business sector, while safeguarding the integrity, impartiality and independence of the United Nations and preventing and mitigating potential risks of adverse impacts on people and the environment.

The guidelines only apply to the UN and its separately administrated organs, funds and programs. They were intended to serve as a common framework for the whole UN, but it is up to those UN Agencies (e.g., World Health Organization [WHO], UNESCO, FAO) that have their own governing bodies to decide if they take them up. Governments and stakeholders should ensure that they are taken up.

The comprehensive agenda agreed upon in 2015 recognized that to enable the finance needed to deliver it, there needs to be access to the global capital market. If this was done, then there needs to be some form of corporate accountability. One suggestion that has been tabled at Rio+20 and at the FfD process is that of reporting by companies listed on the stock exchanges on their environment, social and governance (ESG).

The share of investment subject to environmental social and governance reporting considerations remains small relative to global capital markets. It is at present only 7 per-cent, or US$611 trillion of investments in a global capital market of US$12,143 trillion in 2010. It is clear that there are trillions in the capital market that could be focused on helping us to move quicker to living on the planet in a more sustainable way.

The work of UNEP in its Inquiry into the Design of a Sustainable Financial System (2015) has pointed the way to mobilizing the capital required and suggested the reforms needed which are in line with what was listed earlier.

Over the last four years, member states have moved closer to agreeing on a set of regulatory instruments such as the requirement that companies listed on stock exchanges should publish their ESG report or explain why not. Building on the excellent work of the Sustainable Stock Exchanges (SSE) and other stakeholders from the investors and civil society community, there is support for stock exchanges that go down this path. A full list of UN Policies on Corporate Reporting and Sus-tainable Private Finance can be found in the Annex.

This still remains unfinished business from 2015, and member states and stake-holders are looking at avenues to address this with the finance sector.

References

Asmal, K. (2000) First World Chaos, Third World Calm: A Multi-Stakeholder Process to Part the Waters in the Debate Over Dams. *Le Monde*, November 15.

Associated Press (2016) 175 nations sign historic Paris climate deal on earth day. Available online at: www.usatoday.com/story/news/world/2016/04/22/paris-climate-agreement-signing-united-nations-new-york/83381218/

Beisheim, M. and Nils, S. (2016) Multi-stakeholder partnerships for implementing the 2030 agenda: Improving accountability and transparency. Independent analytical paper for the 2016 ECOSOC partnership forum, New York, UN. Available online at: www.un.org/ecosoc/sites/www.un.org.ecosoc/files/files/en/2016doc/partnership-forum-beisheim-simon.pdf

Gopalan, Radha (2016) The winter of our disconnect and the neglect of soil. Available online at: http://thewire.in/2016/01/13/the-winter-of-our-disconnect-and-the-neglect-of-soil-19179/

Ki-moon, B. (2016) *Declaring Era of Consumption without Consequences Over, Secretary-General Commends Paris Climate Agreement Signatories for Making Historic Pledge to Protect Planet*, UN, New York. Available online at: www.un.org/press/en/2016/sgsm17695.doc.htm

Leiva Roesch, Jimena and Puri, Hardeep (2015) Leaps of Faith. *Horizons Winter Journal*, Available online at: www.cirsd.org/publications/magazines_article_view_short/english/129

Motter, A. (2015) *Parliaments Role in Monitoring Implementation of the SDGs in Governance for Sustainable Development*, edited by Luna, S., Lim, H., Rebedea, O., Banisar, D., Dodds, F. and McKew, Q., Apex, New World Frontiers. Available online at: http://friendsofgovernance. org/index.php/books/

Network for Regional Government for Sustainable Development (2002) *Gauteng Declaration*, Network for Regional Government for Sustainable Development, Brussels.

NOAA (2016) Global summary information. Available online at: www.ncdc.noaa.gov/sotc/ summary-info/global/201601

OECD (2001) *The DAC guidelines: Strategies for sustainable development*, OECD, Paris. Available online at: www.oecd.org/dac/environment-development/2669958.pdf

Phathanothai, Leo-Horn (2016) Bridging development goals. Available online at: www. sustainablegoals.org.uk/wp-content/uploads/2016/03/080–084-HORN-PHAT_ Partners-in-action_2016.pdf

Sachs, J. (2016) Implementing the Paris Climate Agreement, *Horizons Winter Journal*, Available online at: www.cirsd.org/publications/magazines_article_view_short/english/128

Stakeholder Forum (2015) *National Councils for Sustainable Development: Lessons from the Past and Present in Governance for Sustainable Development*, edited by Luna, S., Lim, H., Rebedea, O., Banisar, D., Dodds, F. and McKew, Q., Apex, New World Frontiers. Available online at: http://friendsofgovernance.org/index.php/books/

UNEP (2015) *The Financial System We Need: Aligning the Financial System with Sustainable Development*, UNEP, Geneva. Available online at: http://web.unep.org/inquiry#sthash. vehflT3z.dpuf

United Nations (1992) *Agenda 21 Chapter 28*, UN, New York. Available online at: www. un-documents.net/a21–28.htm

United Nations (2002) Bali guidelines on partnerships. Available online at: https:// sustainabledevelopment.un.org/content/dsd/dsd_aofw_par/par_mand_baliguidprin. shtml

United Nations (2003) Commission on sustainable development decision on criteria and guidelines for partnerships. Available online at: https://sustainabledevelopment.un.org/ content/dsd/dsd_aofw_par/par_critguid.shtml

United Nations (2015a) Adoption of the Paris agreement, EU statement. Available online at: http://unfccc6.meta-fusion.com/cop21/events/2015–12–12–17–26-conference-of- the-parties-cop-11th-meeting

United Nations (2015b) Paris agreement. Available online at: https://unfccc.int/resource/ docs/2015/cop21/eng/l09r01.pdf

United Nations (2015c) *Transforming Our World: The 2013 Agenda for Sustainable Development*, UN, New York. Available online at: https://sustainabledevelopment.un.org/post2015/ transformingourworld

United Nations (2015d) Transforming our world: 2030 agenda for sustainable development. Available online at: https://sustainabledevelopment.un.org/post2015/transformingourworld

United Nations (2015e) General assembly resolution towards global partnerships. Available online at: www.unglobalcompact.org/docs/news_events/9.6/GA_TowardsGlobal Partnerships_2015.pdf

United Nations (2016) Monitoring commitments and actions appendix C mapping of select Addis commitments ad actions in support of the SDGs. Available online at: www.un.org/ esa/ffd/wp-content/uploads/2016/03/Report_IATF-2016-full.pdf

5

UNDERSTANDING THE FUTURE

From 2015 to 2030, the challenges ahead

Introduction

Over the next fifteen years the Sustainable Development Goals (SDGs) will be implemented in a more and more insecure world. This chapter suggests what the emerging issues that will have an impact on the SDGs might be. It will look at these challenges and how this "transformational agenda" could be adjusted so that it might address these challenges while still securing the goals and targets agreed to in 2015.

Global migration, forced displacement: a new phenomenon

> We will endeavour to reach the furthest behind first.
>
> *(2030 Agenda)*

In the fall of 2015, the international community celebrated the adoption of the 2030 Agenda and the Paris Agreement. Among the many new elements that the agenda presented was the positive contribution made by migrants in many societies. The needs of refugees, internally displaced persons (IDPs) and migrants were also noted at various points. A clear place was given to these groups within the new Sustainable Development Agenda.

In stark contrast, the humanitarian system was sounding alarm bells at the same time the number of forced displaced persons had hit a record high. The only other time in recent history with a similar exodus was after World War II. Former Secretary-General Kofi Annan remarked that current crises "have renewed attention on one of mankind's oldest activities: migration" (Annan, 2015).

According to UN agencies, there are approximately 65 million forcibly displaced persons (UNHCR, UNRWA, 2015a). Humanitarian agencies are running at maximum capacity to cope with multiple crises erupting in Africa, the Middle

East, Southeast Asia and Central America. Although the countries of origin are the epicenters of the unfolding tragedy, the impacts are rippling throughout the world.

Antonio Guterres, who served as head of UNHCR until recently, commented that the humanitarian system is "financially broke" and is no longer capable of proving basic services (Guterres, 2015). He argued that the UN's 'siloed' approach, which separates humanitarian action from development, is no longer suitable for a crisis of this magnitude. Moreover, crises are lasting longer, and the average time a refugee or IDP spends in a 'provisional' camp is seventeen years.

The consequences of this global crisis are still unfolding. These massive movements are shaping a new world in which walls are being erected. This 'closed-door' approach and the toxic narrative against migrants and refugees in many countries run contrary to the spirit of the 2030 Agenda. Although the most highlighted cause of desperate migration is flagrant human rights violations and armed conflict, the underlying causes are often more complex. In the Sahel and Syria, prolonged droughts caused hunger and unrest before internal conflicts erupted (Friedman, 2016).

Currently the UN has no coherent strategy to deal with what could be the most tragic humanitarian crisis in the twenty-first century. U2 singer Bono has proposed a Marshall Plan for refugees (Bono, 2016). The UN is the right place to craft such a global strategy. On 19 September this year, the UN convened a high-level meeting to address large movements of refugees and migrants. Early in 2016 the PGA appointed the Ambassadors of Ireland and Jordan, Ambassador David Donoghue and Dina Kawar, as co-facilitators for this meeting, initially to lead negotiations with member states on its modalities and thereafter to lead the negotiations to produce an outcome document for the meeting. These negotiations concluded successfully in August 2016. The meeting of Heads of State and Government on 19 September was the first high-level UN meeting to address comprehensively the challenges posed by large movements of refugees and migrants. Building on a report produced by the Secretary General in May and on the outcomes of several recent conferences, it delivered strong political messages and a wide range of detailed policy commitments aimed at ensuring a more humane, dignified and compassionate regime for refugees and migrants.

Nexus: climate, water, energy, food

Agenda 21, which had been agreed to in 1992, was expected to be the sustainable development blueprint into the first decade of the twenty-first century. However, over the following twenty years, there was very little implementation of that agenda and a lack of decisive action on climate change. As a consequence, policy makers were faced with multiple challenges, and by 2010, the flaws to a sectoral approach to policy making and implementation became clearer. The 1990s and 2000s may be looked back on as the lost decades for sustainable development.

The financial crisis exposed the link between energy and food, because when energy prices went up, so did food prices. Due to the rising oil prices (October 2006 US$60 a barrel, October 2007 US$90 a barrel and by July 2008 it was at US$145 a barrel), prices for food were increasing. By December 2007 the UN (FAO) was projecting a 49 percent increase in African cereal prices through July

2008. At the UN on 16 October 2008, at the height of the crisis, former President Clinton made the following comment on the global food crisis:

> "[W]e all blew it, including me", by treating food crops "like color TVs" instead of as a vital commodity for the world's poor . . . Clinton criticized decades of policymaking by the World Bank, the International Monetary Fund and others, encouraged by the U.S., that pressured Africans in particular into dropping government subsidies for fertilizer, improved seed and other farm inputs as a requirement to get aid. Africa's food self-sufficiency declined and food imports rose. Now skyrocketing prices in the international grain trade – on average more than doubling between 2006 and early 2008 – have pushed many in poor countries deeper into poverty.
>
> *(Clinton, 2008)*

The Intergovernmental Panel on Climate Change's (IPCC) 5th Assessment (2008) raised the issue that water availability would be affected by climate change. It stated that "hundreds of millions of people will be exposed to increased water stress" (IPCC, 2008).

The Water and Climate Coalition, coordinated by Stakeholder Forum for a Sustainable Future (SFSF) and the Stockholm International Water Institute (SIWI), worked for three years (2009–11) at the UNFCCC meetings to persuade government negotiators that they should address water urgently in both their mitigation and adaptation policies. By the 2010 meeting in Cancun, the UNFCCC took up the agenda and incorporated it into their instructions for national climate plans.

At the same time, the German Government took the bold step of trying to address not just two interlinkages between two sectors, but rather three: water, food and energy. In November 2011, it held the Bonn 2011 Nexus Conference. In preparation, the Stockholm Environment Institute (SEI) prepared the background paper 'Understanding the Nexus', which outlined four key reasons for why a nexus approach is needed:

- Urbanization: Now at 50 percent of the global population, it is expected to rise to 70 percent by 2050. Urban areas account for around 75 percent of all greenhouse gas emissions and will face ever-increasing demand for water and food.
- Globalization: The integration of markets has enabled increased international trade and foreign direct investments in sectors such as food and water. Although positive to mitigate local scarcities, trade has also put pressure on land, water and livelihoods in some developing countries due to higher demand from more affluent consumers in other regions. Additionally, emissions go higher as energy demand for transport intensifies.
- Population: Population growth is expected to add another billion people by 2030 with all the additional pressures that will bring on resource use.

- Climate change: Driven by energy use and changes in land use, climate measures need to take into account the impact of increasing production and supply of food and water (e.g., methane release, fertilizer use, water- and energy-intensive technologies) and, on the other hand, the impact of climate measures on water and food (e.g., biofuels demand on water and land).

The SEI paper and the conference acknowledged that there is no place in an interlinked world for isolated solutions aimed at just one sector. This was very similar to the approach being taken elsewhere by the governments of Colombia, Guatemala, Peru and the UAE.

A sector approach can often have fatal consequences in other sectors. If the world is going to reduce hunger and eradicate poverty, then achieving security for water, energy and food for people is critical. This challenge is becoming even more urgent with the impacts of climate change and the fact that water will be the medium by which we will address much of this nexus. If things continue this way:

- Agriculture will have to produce 70 percent more food by 2050.
- Primary energy needs will increase by 50 percent by 2035.
- Demand for water will exceed global availability by 40 percent in 2030.

(SEI, 2011)

During the negotiations for the SDGs, there was strong input from stakeholders and governments that a more interlinked approach between goals and targets would be critical to a transformational agenda. In early 2014, the second Nexus Conference was held in Chapel Hill, North Carolina. In its declaration, which was submitted to member states and the UN Secretary General, it said:

> An integrative approach is a valuable strategic tool for operationalizing the goals and targets of the Sustainable Development Goals and the post-2015 development agenda. Constructing integrated goals and targets presents challenges but also clear opportunities for policy makers.
>
> *(Water Institute, 2014)*

The SDGs were able to catch some of the interlinkages between the sectors in their targets, but not all of them.

The final selection of indicators for the SDG targets will be able to address this more, and so will the follow-up. In particular, it will be important that the national implementation embraces this 'interlinked' approach.

Trade-offs

As the move to implement the SDGs starts in 2016, it is clear that the nexus approach will need to be integrated into planning at all levels: regional, national, subnational and local.

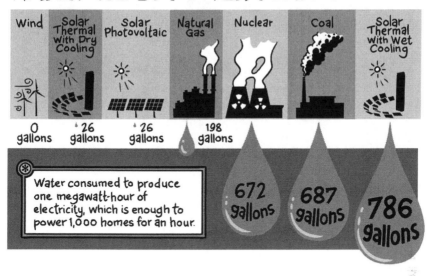

WATER USE BY POWER PLANTS*

FIGURE 5.1   Water use by power plants

Source: National Renewable Energy Laboratory; illustration by Andy Warner

One of the consequences of moving from fossil fuels to renewable energy (RE) is that RE uses much less water (except biofuels). The rapidly reducing costs of RE has made them comparable with fossil fuel costs. If fossil fuel costs increase again, the argument for renewables will be very difficult to counter.

Agriculture consumes around 70 percent of the water used in the world and therefore offers the greatest opportunity to reduce water use. This can be achieved particularly in water-stressed areas by growing crops that use less water, as well as utilizing irrigation with precision. It was estimated in 2013 that half of all food is wasted worldwide (British Institute of Mechanical Engineers, 2013). A move to reduce food waste could also have positive impacts on the amount of food and water needed, and some countries are already starting to move that way. In France, starting 1 January 2016, for example, all supermarkets will be:

> banned from throwing away or destroying unsold food and must instead donate it to charities or for animal feed, under a law set to crack down on food waste.
>
> *(Chrisafis, 2015)*

This approach may soon be taken by other European countries.

At the national level, governments will need to play an enabling role in ensuring they give the right financial incentives for an integrated approach, as the 2014 Global Sustainable Development Report concluded:

Innovative Climate, Land, Energy and Water (CLEW) nexus solutions are "cheaper" in terms of mitigation costs, but may mean shifts of investments across sectors. There are typically both "winners" and "losers" from integrated solutions, potentially leading to political economy issues. Since components of CLEW nexus solutions depend on what happens in other parts of the system, investors may face additional uncertainty and risks, which might make nexus solutions less attractive to them. Benefits of integrated approaches differ greatly between and within countries and thus good financing strategies have to be tailored to country situations. CLEW nexus projects are expected to face important challenges in tapping into financial resources provided by local and international financing institutions and funds due to the existing fragmentation by narrowly defined sectors and activities.

(UN, 2014)

Urban impacts

In 2013, Barnhart, a West Texas town, ran out of water while another twenty-nine towns in Texas risked the same fate due to fracking. This highlighted the link between water and energy very dramatically.

A recent study, 'Operationalizing the Urban Nexus: Towards resource-efficient and integrated cities and metropolitan regions', by Jeb Brugmann and Katherine Brekke for Deutsche Gesellschaft für Internationale Zusammenarbeit (GIZ) and International Council for Local Environmental Initiatives (ICLEI) looked at the critical role that subnational and local policy making will play. They concluded that the success factors based on case studies for addressing the Urban Nexus were:

Identify 'hotspots'. When identifying priorities for Urban NEXUS projects, consider the areas, or 'hotspots', where this approach would have the most multiplier or ripple effects to maximize the reach and benefit of the initiative.

Bring all stakeholders around the same table by creating 'Urban NEXUS Task Forces'. Urban NEXUS Task Forces created to oversee Urban NEXUS projects at the urban and regional level serve the purpose of linking relevant departments and levels of government together with other key stakeholders (experts, civil society, private business, NGOs and multilateral organizations). Urban NEXUS Task Forces are a simple way to kick off, strengthen and sustain cross-departmental collaboration, offering stakeholders a taste of 'breaking the silos'. Eventually, the goal is to institutionalize such multistakeholder collaboration.

Encourage governmental authorities and stakeholders at all levels to be part of Urban NEXUS solutions, which should reconnect scales and optimize complex cross-boundary resource flows (e.g., river basin management).

Promote supportive framework conditions for Urban NEXUS solutions at all levels. Urban NEXUS projects, regardless of their size and scope, are embedded in regulatory and administrative frameworks. For example, national 'silos' in regulation, public procurement, budgeting and accounting processes, etc., can hinder innovative integrated approaches and cross-departmental cooperation at the local level. Supportive national and decentralized frameworks regarding legislative mandates, financial support and incentives are therefore crucial for the scaling up of successful local and regional Urban NEXUS initiatives.

(Brugmann & Brekke, 2016)

Addressing the Nexus by working out the best trade-offs will be vital at the local and subnational level, and this will be best achieved through the proactive engagement of local and subnational government and relevant stakeholders. Underpinning this is the use of water and the need to reduce it wherever possible.

As oil was in the 20th century – the key resource, a focus of tension, even conflict – so water will be of the 21st, as states, countries, and industries compete over the ever-more-precious resource.

(Brookes, 2011)

From exclusion to inclusion: a new policy response to peace and security challenges

The 2030 Agenda and the Paris Agreement were born in troubled times. As leaders celebrated the culmination of the 2015 agreements, the international community was also grappling with a new wave of security and humanitarian challenges. Terrorist attacks struck Paris just two weeks before the Climate Change Conference (COP 21). Undeterred by these attacks, citizens from around the world pressed on, as global leaders met in Paris and adopted a new and universal agreement. The attacks in Paris brought to light a new reality in which peace and sustainable development can no longer be treated in isolation.

The state as the principal actor of implementing the Paris Agreement and the SDGs is under multiple pressures. Armed nonstate actors are often filling up a vacuum in ungoverned territories and are challenging state authority. The Islamic State (IS), Boko Haram and al-Qaida affiliations have caused "wars, state collapse and geopolitical upheaval in the Middle East, gained new footholds in Africa and pose new threats elsewhere" (International Crisis Group, 2016). These groups are testing the core values for which the UN stands. Can the 2030 Agenda, with its embedded principle of inclusion across all the goals, be part of the solution to these growing crises?

The instability provoked by these groups is spreading beyond borders. Violent extremists have recruited over 30,000 foreign terrorist fighters from over 100 member states to travel to Syria, Libya, Yemen and Afghanistan (UN, 2015). Most of these recruits are young people, many of whom are educated and are between 18 and 29 years old (Williams, 2016). What is driving youth to join armed nonstate actors is a deep sense of alienation from the current governance establishment. Although the response to these growing crises has been militarized, an ideology can only be countered with new and powerful ideas, as well as with concrete responses that address the dignity deficits felt by the young.

The UN and its member states are moving toward a new policy framework that calls for inclusion and for wider participation in peace building and state building. As an example of this shift, Security Council Resolution 2250 (2015) urges member states to elevate the voices of youth in decision making at all levels. This is the first resolution on youth adopted by the Security Council. In parallel, SDG target 16.7 calls on states to "ensure an inclusive, participatory and representative decision-making at all levels" (UN, 2015a).

To transform these new policies into action, a new kind of governance is needed. Efforts such as the Open Governance Partnership, a coalition of sixty-nine countries, have committed to making their government more open, accountable and responsive to citizens.

> If the goals and targets of the SDGs are understood solely as the concern of governments, multilateral agencies, and experts, the cynical spirit of the times will be reinforced. But if governance can be transformed and leadership nurtured then at all levels of society, there is reason to believe that the SDGs can become authentic goals for popular movements, local communities and all manner of networks.
>
> *(Mahmoud et al., 2014)*

Health

We live in an increasingly interdependent world, and the health challenges that will bring will also increase. By 2030 an additional 1 billion people will be on the planet and over 1.5 billion of those will be over 60 years old. The SDGs are an attempt to help deliver healthy lives and health security for all people.

Present challenges over increased obesity and diabetes, cancer, tobacco and alcohol, as well as malaria, HIV/AIDS, tuberculosis, hepatitis, Ebola and other communicable diseases will be added to by new challenges.

One of the emerging ones recognized in the Transforming Our World is:

> 26 . . . including by addressing growing anti-microbial resistance and the problem of unattended diseases affecting developing countries.
>
> *(UN, 2015f)*

Antimicrobial resistance is growing according to a number of reports published in 2014 and 2015. It means that people and animals are becoming resistant to antibacterial drugs. Antimicrobial resistance is a broader term then antibiotic as it includes parasites and viruses.

In May 2016 Jim O'Neill was appointed by the United Kingdom to chair a review on antimicrobial resistance (AR). In one of his scenarios he suggested that there could be up to 300 million premature deaths due to AR. Some of the best approaches to addressing this includes preventative messages. This is an example of a different nexus around health: water and sanitation, employment, as unemployment is associated with doubling the risk of illness and 60 percent less likelihood of recovery from disease (WHO, 2012).

The Sustainable Development Goals call for an interlinkage approach, and so do the health challenges of the next fifteen years. This should be supported by multistakeholder partnerships such as Gavi the Vaccine Alliance, Global Alliance for Improved Nutrition (GAIN) and the Global Fund to Fight AIDS, Tuberculosis and Malaria. Only by working at the local, national and international levels together will the resources and capacity be created to address these new challenges.

Disruptive industries

There have always been disruptive industries throughout history: the car replaced the horse-drawn carriage, Wikipedia replaced traditional encyclopedias, the computer replaced the typewriter, digital music replaced CDs, Amazon is replacing book shops, etc.

The general view of economists is that as new technologies are introduced, some industries are being destroyed. But at the same time, those new industries will create new jobs to fill the ones lost. It is no longer true that enough jobs will be filled to take the place of those being lost because technological advances are happening on too many fronts at the same time. This is increasingly becoming no longer true. However, many countries struggle with high rates of youth unemployment. In the United States, for example, youth unemployment is running at 10.30 percent in 2016, over twice the quoted national unemployment rate of 4.9 percent. In Europe it is even starker, with rates of 48 percent in Greece, 46 percent in Spain, 37 percent in Italy, 25 percent in France and in the European region as a whole the average youth unemployment is 22 percent (Statista, 2015).

> The world is facing a worsening youth employment crisis: young people are three times more likely to be unemployed than adults and almost 73 million youth worldwide are looking for work. The ILO has warned of a "scarred" generation of young workers facing a dangerous mix of high unemployment, increased inactivity and precarious work in developed countries, as well as persistently high working poverty in the developing world.
>
> *(ILO, 2015)*

The Canadian government's foresight organization, 'Policy Horizons Canada', has brought out two very important reports: Metascan 2: Building Resilience in the Transition to a Digital Economy and a Networked Society and Metascan 3: Emerging Technologies. In the Metascan 3 report it identified the most disruptive technologies for the next fifteen years:

- Emerging biotechnologies: Synthetic biology, bioinformatics, tissue engineering.
- Emerging nanotechnologies: Nanomaterials, nanodevices and nanosensors, nanotechnology for energy.

- Emerging neuroscience technologies: Neurostimulation, brain–computer interface.
- Emerging digital technologies: Artificial intelligence, robotics.

(Policy Horizon Canada, 2014)

Most of these are not in the general public discourse, yet every government and policy maker should be looking at them and their impacts. Thomas Frey, editor of *The Futurist* magazine, has tried to quantify the potential job losses; his estimate is that "over 2 billion jobs will disappear by 2030" (Frey, 2012).

He goes on to identify where there will be job losses and what kinds of new jobs will be created (see Table 5.1).

TABLE 5.1 Jobs going away and new jobs created

Industry	Jobs going away	New jobs created
Power	• Power generation plants will begin to close down. • Coal plants will begin to close down. • Many railroad and transportation workers will no longer be needed. • Even wind farms, natural gas, and bio-fuel generators will begin to close down. • Ethanol plants will be phased out or repurposed. • Utility company engineers will be gone. • Line repairmen will be gone.	• Manufacturing power generation units the size of air conditioning units will go into full production. • Installation crews will begin to work around the clock. • The entire national grid will need to be taken down (a twenty-year project). Much of it will be recycled, and the recycling process alone will employ many thousands of people. • Micro-grid operations will open in every community, requiring a new breed of engineers, managers and regulators.
Automobile transportation	• Taxi and limo drivers will be gone. • Bus drivers will be gone. • Truck drivers will be gone. • Gas stations, parking lots, traffic cops and traffic courts will be gone. • Fewer doctors and nurses will be needed to treat injuries. • Pizza (and other food) delivery drivers will be gone. • Mail delivery drivers will be gone. • FedEx and UPS delivery jobs will be gone. • As people shift from owning their own vehicles to a transportation-on-demand system, the total number of vehicles manufactured will also begin to decline.	• Delivery dispatchers. • Traffic monitoring systems, although automated, will require a management team. • Automated traffic designers, architects and engineers. • Driverless "ride experience" people. • Driverless operating system engineers. • Emergency crews for when things go wrong.

Education	• Teachers. • Trainers. • Professors.	• Coaches. • Course designers. • Learning camps.
3D printers	• If we can print our own clothes and they fit perfectly, clothing manufacturers and clothing retailers will quickly go away. • Similarly, if we can print our own shoes, shoe manufacturers and shoe retailers will cease to be relevant. • If we can print construction material, the lumber, rock, drywall, shingle, concrete, and various other construction industries will go away.	• 3D printer design, engineering and manufacturing. • 3D printer repairmen will be in big demand. • Product designers, stylists and engineers for 3D printers. • 3D printer "ink" sellers.
Bots	• Fishing bots will replace fishermen. • Mining bots will replace miners. • Ag bots will replace farmers. • Inspection bots will replace human inspectors. • Warrior drones will replace soldiers. • Robots can pick up building material coming out of the 3D printer and begin building a house with it.	• Robot designers, engineers, repairmen. • Robot dispatchers. • Robot therapists. • Robot trainers. • Robot fashion designers.

Synthetic biology (SB)

What is possibly the least known and potentially most disruptive of the emerging technologies is developing new biological systems, including new foods. It uses:

> genetically engineered organisms to manufacture a growing range of materials such as bio plastics, biofuels, bio rubber, bio steel, spider silk and industrial chemicals. Industries that may be disrupted include pulp and paper, building materials, chemical manufacturing, pharmaceuticals, agriculture and fossil fuel extraction.
>
> *(Policy Horizon Canada, 2014)*

Policy challenges: This would include regulating the creation of genetically modified foods (GMOs). At present, this is covered under the Convention on Biological Diversity (CBD). The convention requires contracting parties:

> 8(g) . . . to regulate, manage or control the risks associated with the use and release of living modified organisms resulting from biotechnology which are

likely to have adverse environmental impacts that could affect the conservation and sustainable use of biological diversity . . . .

(CBD, 1992)

The CBD has been ratified by all UN member states except the United States.

In 2000 the Cartagena Protocol on Biosafety of the CBD went much further. The protocol protects biological diversity from the potential risks posed by safe transfer, handling and use of living modified organisms (LMOs) resulting from modern biotechnology. The protocol is applicable to all LMOs with the exception of pharmaceuticals for humans; these are addressed by other international agreements.

The other major policy challenge will be the continued move to the automation of farms into smart farms. In an article on technology news and trends Taylor Dobbs argues:

With automated farming, workers and traditional family farmers will be quickly and easily excessed. The race will be on to completely subsume small farms into giant corporate farms that exercise monopoly control over food production, and advanced technology will drive the whole process. Those who have the technology will thrive; those who don't will wither away.

(Dobbs, 2015)

Large farms are now using drones to collect aerial analysis of a farm and feed it into big data databases to be able to address what in the past had been seen as intuitive. This is coupled with using robotics to do manual work. The results, as in many of the examples, will be a reduction of labor as the farms become more automatized. On the positive side, it also enables savings in water and fertilizer use.

Bioinformations

The Metascan 3 report suggests that 'do it yourself' surveillance and weapons systems will become common – the example used is the Switchblade drone, which is lethal at short distances and fits into a small backpack. These are going to cause huge problems for the police and military. With open-source material and personal information on all of us accessible on the Web, the issue of privacy will need redefining. The report says:

Smart devices will routinely know a person's movement, and location to within 10 cms, which will make it possible to infer a person's activity, behavior, interactions and relationships.

(Policy Horizon Canada, 2014)

Policy challenges: How to prepare and legislate nationally and globally for the spread of cheap but lethal do-it-yourself weapons. As this book is being written, Connecticut has become another regional government to consider banning drones that are armed with guns and even flamethrowers. They follow similar bans in Nevada (2015), North Carolina (2014) and Oregon (2013).

Privacy is also coming under increased stress with the collection of so-called big data by companies, governments and stakeholders. Much of this is happening without a real debate within the general public. At times it is as if people are prepared to give away information about themselves without considering the implications, provided they can get access to something on the Web. Big data will also have impacts on patents and copyrights, which may become irrelevant, as it will be difficult to know if a submitted patent is unique. A major challenge ahead for governments will be what regulation and safeguards can be put in place to balance privacy with the need for big data.

3D printing

3D printing will have a huge impact on employment in the manufacturing industry where it will reduce the need for transportation from overseas and it will move away from assembly line workers to robots. In the area of health, 3D printing will also enable some amazing advancements with the printing of veins, hearts and other organs. In the aerospace industry the development will include creating parts that are at present made up of many components being produced in one item.

Basic 3D printers are already moving to the high street and retailing for under US$500. In 2014 a Chinese company, WinSun, printed and built ten basic houses in one day with a cement-based mixture containing construction waste and glass fiber. The houses still need plumbing, electrical wiring and insulation added after construction, but the printing of the house cost only US$5,000 (Scott, 2014).

Policy challenges: The impact of 3D printing could be huge as the printers become more and more refined. Consumer goods and clothes that have traditionally been produced in developing countries could in the next ten years be on any desktop in any home.

There will be issues around intellectual property (IP), which will be difficult to control. All children in the future will need to be taught programming as they are taught English and mathematics today to ensure they have skills for jobs. These skills will give them a chance to be designers taking basic products and adding some code to produce more unique items.

In 2012, the US company Defense Distributed announced that they were working on a plastic gun that could be downloaded by anybody. In 2013 a Texas company, Solid Concepts, printed a 3D version of an M1911 gun. Foreseeing this in 1988 the US Congress had passed the Undetectable Firearms Act, which makes it illegal for the manufacture of firearms that a metal detector cannot detect. In 2013 there was an unsuccessful attempt to toughen the law. The US Department of Homeland Security and the Joint Regional Intelligence Center released a memo stating:

> Significant advances in three-dimensional (3D) printing capabilities, availability of free digital 3D printer files for firearms components, and difficulty

> regulating file sharing may present public safety risks from unqualified gun seekers who obtain or manufacture 3D printed guns," and that "proposed legislation to ban 3D printing of weapons may deter, but cannot completely prevent their production. Even if the practice is prohibited by new legislation, online distribution of these digital files will be as difficult to control as any other illegally traded music, movie or software files.
>
> *(Kleinman, 2013)*

There are issues around IP but also around quality, standard setting and safety. One of the vital questions will be: What will be the rules that govern what you can or cannot print?

Artificial intelligence

An example is found within the transportation industries with the development of the Google/Uber driverless car. This will have an effect on taxi drivers, lorry drivers and bus drivers first, but then personal cars where perhaps in the future people move away from owning cars to just telephoning for one when you need it. A Columbia University study has suggested that only 9,000 driverless Ubers could replace all taxis in New York and that the average waiting time would be only thirty-six seconds (Burns et al., 2013).

It has been estimated that the impact of the driverless vehicles in the United States alone could see up to 10 million job losses in vehicle drivers, production, dealers and maintenance (Kanter, 2015).

Uber's CEO Travis Kalanick's said, "Getting Google's cars to a 90 percent solution is going to happen soon". But he predicted Google wouldn't get to a "99.99 percent success level" for another fifteen or twenty years (Kalanick, 2015). Others put that timeline closer to ten to fifteen years.

Another example is 'Sophie'. There are two laboratories working on producing humanlike robots. These are Hanson Robotics and Hiroshi Ishiguro. Sophie was created by Dr. David Hanson and his team. The design is based on his wife and Audrey Hepburn (Taylor, 2016).

In an interview with CNBC's Harriet Taylor, Dr. Hanson said:

> Our goal is that she will be as conscious, creative and capable as any human. We are designing these robots to serve in health care, therapy, education and customer service applications. The artificial intelligence will evolve to the point where they will truly be our friends. Not in ways that dehumanize us, but in ways the re-humanize us, that decrease the trend of the distance between people and instead connect us with people as well as with robots. That can really help to prevent some of the disconnect and possible dangers of developing super intelligent or human-level machines that don't care.
>
> *(Hanson, 2016)*

Policy challenges: How will infrastructure need to change to accommodate driverless vehicles?

Implications of new technology

What we might be seeing is a perfect storm as many new industries come to the forefront at the same time. Several of these new technologies will be environmentally friendly (though not all) but they will affect employment, social cohesion and stability in all countries.

The future for many will be a move to temporary jobs and portfolio jobs, where someone will have a number of jobs and for a shorter time. There will be many more freelance jobs. One of the biggest websites out there, and growing, is Freelance.com – in 2015, there were nearly 16 million people registered.

A shrinking tax base with fewer jobs is a recipe for instability and increased inequality. Governments need to prepare people for the changes coming and the skill base and mind-set to be able to change jobs regularly. Some people are even suggesting that the state should provide a minimum living wage for people and that jobs post-2030 may be shared among people. There are huge challenges ahead, so what could the intergovernmental process do to help address these challenges?

Policy recommendation: The UN Secretary General with the UN General Assembly set up a Commission into New Technologies and their Impacts on Social Cohesion and Employment. This should not be a short-time Commission but one that is built on the approach taken by the United Nations Commission on Environment and Development, otherwise known as the Brundtland Commission. This should be a three-year Commission with open hearings, and its members should include some of the people engaged in the emerging and disruptive technologies.

The relevant UN agencies and programs should work together, looking at the impacts on specific sectors and reporting through the Technology Facilitation Mechanism.

The Global Sustainable Development Report should have a section dealing with emerging technologies and their impact on the SDGs. The HLPF should ensure that this impact is reviewed annually and could look at the areas where there may need to be new international regulation.

Afterword: 2030 Agenda adoption poem

I can now see
With brilliant clarity
A vision of the World,
Not as it is or was,
But as it should be.
One free of sin and injustice,
Full of peace and fairness;
Where all are given ample chance
To make the planet
Even better and healthier
For the generations to come.
Unveiled by disappearing smog,
We shall call this place paradise,
Colored by the bluest of blues,
And the greenest of greens.
Talk will be solely of abundance,
And the only food and knowledge
That shall be sought
Will be for that of thought;
Thirst shall only be
For matters concerning the heart.
Every person will have a home
Which they will proudly call their own,
Be they in the grandest cities
Or smallest of villages.
Every child and adult
Shall have a hand to hold
Through all their pursuits.
No more he or she,
Them or me,
But only we.

By Ryan Lee Hom, Advisor and negotiator for the 2030 Agenda,
Permanent Mission of Papua New Guinea to the United Nations, 2 August 2015

References

Annan, K. (2015) Migration realism, project syndicate. Available online at: www.project-syndicate.org/commentary/human-migration-reality-by-kofi-a-annan-2015–06?barrier=true

Bono (2016) Time to Think Bigger about the Refugee Crisis, *New York Times*, Available online at: www.nytimes.com/2016/04/12/opinion/bono-time-to-think-bigger-about-the-refugee-crisis.html?_r=0

British Institute of Mechanical Engineers (2013) Food Waste: Half of All Food Ends Up Thrown Away, *Huffington Post*, January 10, 2013.

Brookes, J. (2011) Why water is the new oil, rolling stone. Available online at: www.rollingstone.com/politics/news/why-water-is-the-new-oil-20110707

Brugmann, J. and Brekke, K. (2016) *Operationalizing the Urban Nexus in the Water, Food, Energy and Climate Nexus: Challenges and an Agenda for Action*, edited by Dodds, F. and Bartram, J., Routledge, Oxford.

Burns, D. L., Jordan, C. W. and Scarborough, A. B. (2013) *Transforming Personal Mobility*, The Earth Institute Colombia University, New York. Available online at: http://sustainablemobility.ei.columbia.edu/files/2012/12/Transforming-Personal-Mobility-Jan-27-20132.pdf

Chrisafis, A. (2015) *France to Force Big Supermarkets to Give Unsold Food to Charities*, Guardian, London. Available online at: www.theguardian.com/world/2015/may/22/france-to-force-big-supermarkets-to-give-away-unsold-food-to-charity

Clinton, B. (2008) Speech at the UN on the 16 October 2008 reported by Hanley, C., J. (October 23, 2008). "We blew it on global food, says Bill Clinton". The San Francisco Chronicle. Associated Press.

Convention on Biological Diversity (1992) Article 8g. Available online at: www.cbd.int/convention/articles/default.shtml?a=cbd-08

Dobbs, T. (2015) The future of food: Completely automated farms run by robots, technology news and trends. Available online at: www.technocracy.news/index.php/2015/12/29/the-future-of-food-completely-automated-farms-run-by-robots/

Frey, T. (2012) 2 billion jobs to disappear by 2030. Available online at: www.wfs.org/content/2-billion-jobs-disappear-2030

Friedman, Thomas L. (2016) Out of Africa, *New York Times*, Available online at: http://mobile.nytimes.com/2016/04/13/opinion/out-of-africa.html?smid=tw-tomfriedman&smtyp=cur&_r=1&referer

Guterres, A. (2015) Humanitarian response system is "broke". Available online at: www.ipinst.org/2015/11/leadership-and-global-partnerships-in-the-face-of-todays-refugee-crisis#2

Hanson, D. (2016) In article by Harriet Taylor, could you fall in love with this robot, CNBC March 16, 2016. Available online at: www.cnbc.com/2016/03/16/could-you-fall-in-love-with-this-robot.html

ILO (2015) Youth employment. Available online at: www.ilo.org/global/topics/youth-employment/lang—en/index.htm

International Crisis Group Special Report (2016) Exploiting disorder: al-Qaida and the Islamic State. Available online at: www.crisisgroup.org/en/regions/global/exploiting-disorder-al-qaeda-and-the-islamic-state.aspx

IPCC (2008) Synthesis report, Geneva, IPCC, p. 10. Available online at: www.ipcc.ch/pdf/assessment-report/ar4/syr/ar4_syr_spm.pdf

Kalanick, T. (2015) In Google vs. Uber and the race to self-driving taxis by Hawkins, A. The Verge. Available online at: www.theverge.com/2015/12/16/10309960/google-vs-uber-competition-self-driving-cars

Kanter, Z. (2015) *How Uber's Autonomous Cars Will Destroy 10 Million Jobs and Reshape the Economy by 2025*, CBS, San Francisco. Available online at: http://sanfrancisco.cbslocal.com/2015/01/27/how-ubers-autonomous-cars-will-destroy-10-million-jobs-and-reshape-the-economy-by-2025-lyft-google-zack-kanter/

Kleinman, A. (2013) Homeland security is worried limiting 3D-printing guns 'may be impossible': Report. Available online at: www.huffingtonpost.com/news/Homeland%20Security

Leiva Roesch, Jimena, Puri, Hardeep, Leaps of Faith, *Horizons Winter Journal*, Available online at: www.cirsd.org/publications/magazines_article_view_short/english/129

Mahmoud, Y., Nation, S., and Leiva-Roesch, R. J. (2014) Building a sustainable future requires leadership from state to citizen. Available online at: https://theglobalobservatory.org/2014/09/sustainable-future-leadership-state-citizen/

Policy Horizon Canada (2014) MetaScan 3: Emerging technologies, Ottawa Government of Canada. Available online at: www.horizons.gc.ca/eng/content/metascan-3-emerging-technologies-0

Scott, R. (2014) A Giant 3D Printer Builds Ten Houses in One Day, *Huffington Post*, Available online at: www.huffingtonpost.com/2014/09/08/3d-printed-houses_n_5773408.html

Statista (2015) The statistics portal: Youth employment as of December 2015. Available online at: www.statista.com/statistics/266228/youth-unemployment-rate-in-eu-countries/

Stockholm Environment Institute (2011) Understanding the Nexus, Stockholm, SEI. Available online at: www.sei-international.org/publications?pid=1977

Taylor, H. (2016) Could you fall in love with this robot, CNBC March 16, 2016. Available online at: www.cnbc.com/2016/03/16/could-you-fall-in-love-with-this-robot.html

United Nations (2014) *Chapter 6: Special Theme: The Climate-Land-Energy-Water—Development Nexus in the Global Sustainable Development Report 2014*, UN, New York. Available online at: https://sustainabledevelopment.un.org/globalsdreport/2014

United Nations (2015a) Adoption of the Paris agreement, EU statement. Available online at: http://unfccc6.meta-fusion.com/cop21/events/2015-12-12-17-26-conference-of-the-parties-cop-11th-meeting

UNRWA (2015a) The 65 million figure is the sum of UNHCR's people of concern, UNWRA's statistics and the Internal Displacement Monitoring Centre of Global Figures. See UNHCR mid-year trends 2015. Available online at: www.unhcr.org/56701b969.html

Water Institute (2014) Building integrated approaches into the sustainable development goals: A declaration from the Nexus 2014: Water, food, climate and energy conference, Chapel Hill, Water Institute. Available online at: http://nexusconference.web.unc.edu/files/2014/08/nexus-declaration.pdf

Williams, M. (2016) Long considered a threat, can youth take the lead in peacebuilding? Available online at: https://theglobalobservatory.org/2016/01/youth-countering-violent-extremism-resolution-2250/

World Health Organization (2012) *Facing Challenges for Global Health*, WHO, Geneva. Available online at: www.who.int/whr/2003/chapter1/en/

ANNEX – TRANSFORMING OUR WORLD

The 2030 Agenda for Sustainable Development

Preamble

This Agenda is a plan of action for people, planet and prosperity. It also seeks to strengthen universal peace in larger freedom. We recognise that eradicating poverty in all its forms and dimensions, including extreme poverty, is the greatest global challenge and an indispensable requirement for sustainable development. All countries and all stakeholders, acting in collaborative partnership, will implement this plan. We are resolved to free the human race from the tyranny of poverty and want and to heal and secure our planet. We are determined to take the bold and transformative steps which are urgently needed to shift the world onto a sustainable and resilient path. As we embark on this collective journey, we pledge that no one will be left behind. The 17 Sustainable Development Goals and 169 targets which we are announcing today demonstrate the scale and ambition of this new universal Agenda. They seek to build on the Millennium Development Goals and complete what these did not achieve. They seek to realize the human rights of all and to achieve gender equality and the empowerment of all women and girls. They are integrated and indivisible and balance the three dimensions of sustainable development: the economic, social and environmental.

The Goals and targets will stimulate action over the next fifteen years in areas of critical importance for humanity and the planet:

People

We are determined to end poverty and hunger, in all their forms and dimensions, and to ensure that all human beings can fulfil their potential in dignity and equality and in a healthy environment.

Planet

We are determined to protect the planet from degradation, including through sustainable consumption and production, sustainably managing its natural resources and taking urgent action on climate change, so that it can support the needs of the present and future generations.

Prosperity

We are determined to ensure that all human beings can enjoy prosperous and fulfilling lives and that economic, social and technological progress occurs in harmony with nature.

Peace

We are determined to foster peaceful, just and inclusive societies which are free from fear and violence. There can be no sustainable development without peace and no peace without sustainable development.

Partnership

We are determined to mobilize the means required to implement this Agenda through a revitalised Global Partnership for Sustainable Development, based on a spirit of strengthened global solidarity, focused in particular on the needs of the poorest and most vulnerable and with the participation of all countries, all stakeholders and all people.

The interlinkages and integrated nature of the Sustainable Development Goals are of crucial importance in ensuring that the purpose of the new Agenda is realised. If we realize our ambitions across the full extent of the Agenda, the lives of all will be profoundly improved and our world will be transformed for the better.

Declaration

Introduction

1 We, the Heads of State and Government and High Representatives, meeting at the United Nations Headquarters in New York from 25–27 September 2015 as the Organization celebrates its seventieth anniversary, have decided today on new global Sustainable Development Goals.

2 On behalf of the peoples we serve, we have adopted a historic decision on a comprehensive, far-reaching and people-centred set of universal and transformative Goals and targets. We commit ourselves to working tirelessly for the full implementation of this Agenda by 2030. We recognize that eradicating poverty in all its forms and dimensions, including extreme poverty, is the greatest global

challenge and an indispensable requirement for sustainable development. We are committed to achieving sustainable development in its three dimensions – economic, social and environmental – in a balanced and integrated manner. We will also build upon the achievements of the Millennium Development Goals and seek to address their unfinished business.

3 We resolve, between now and 2030, to end poverty and hunger everywhere; to combat inequalities within and among countries; to build peaceful, just and inclusive societies; to protect human rights and promote gender equality and the empowerment of women and girls; and to ensure the lasting protection of the planet and its natural resources. We resolve also to create conditions for sustainable, inclusive and sustained economic growth, shared prosperity and decent work for all, taking into account different levels of national development and capacities.

4 As we embark on this great collective journey, we pledge that no one will be left behind. Recognizing that the dignity of the human person is fundamental, we wish to see the Goals and targets met for all nations and peoples and for all segments of society. And we will endeavour to reach the furthest behind first.

5 This is an Agenda of unprecedented scope and significance. It is accepted by all countries and is applicable to all, taking into account different national realities, capacities and levels of development and respecting national policies and priorities. These are universal goals and targets which involve the entire world, developed and developing countries alike. They are integrated and indivisible and balance the three dimensions of sustainable development.

6 The Goals and targets are the result of over two years of intensive public consultation and engagement with civil society and other stakeholders around the world, which paid particular attention to the voices of the poorest and most vulnerable. This consultation included valuable work done by the General Assembly Open Working Group on Sustainable Development Goals and by the United Nations, whose Secretary-General provided a synthesis report in December 2014.

Our vision

7 In these Goals and targets, we are setting out a supremely ambitious and transformational vision. We envisage a world free of poverty, hunger, disease and want, where all life can thrive. We envisage a world free of fear and violence. A world with universal literacy. A world with equitable and universal access to quality education at all levels, to health care and social protection, where physical, mental and social well-being are assured. A world where we reaffirm our commitments regarding the human right to safe drinking water and sanitation and where there is improved hygiene; and where food is sufficient, safe, affordable and nutritious. A world where human habitats are safe, resilient and sustainable and where there is universal access to affordable, reliable and sustainable energy.

8 We envisage a world of universal respect for human rights and human dignity, the rule of law, justice, equality and non-discrimination; of respect for race, ethnicity and cultural diversity; and of equal opportunity permitting the full realization of human potential and contributing to shared prosperity. A world which invests in its children and in which every child grows up free from violence and exploitation. A world in which every woman and girl enjoys full gender equality and all legal, social and economic barriers to their empowerment have been removed. A just, equitable, tolerant, open and socially inclusive world in which the needs of the most vulnerable are met.

9 We envisage a world in which every country enjoys sustained, inclusive and sustainable economic growth and decent work for all. A world in which consumption and production patterns and use of all natural resources – from air to land, from rivers, lakes and aquifers to oceans and seas – are sustainable. One in which democracy, good governance and the rule of law as well as an enabling environment at national and international levels, are essential for sustainable development, including sustained and inclusive economic growth, social development, environmental protection and the eradication of poverty and hunger. One in which development and the application of technology are climate-sensitive, respect biodiversity and are resilient. One in which humanity lives in harmony with nature and in which wildlife and other living species are protected.

Our shared principles and commitments

10 The new Agenda is guided by the purposes and principles of the Charter of the United Nations, including full respect for international law. It is grounded in the Universal Declaration of Human Rights, international human rights treaties, the Millennium Declaration and the 2005 World Summit Outcome Document. It is informed by other instruments such as the Declaration on the Right to Development.

11 We reaffirm the outcomes of all major UN conferences and summits which have laid a solid foundation for sustainable development and have helped to shape the new Agenda. These include the Rio Declaration on Environment and Development; the World Summit on Sustainable Development; the World Summit for Social Development; the Programme of Action of the International Conference on Population and Development, the Beijing Platform for Action; and the United Nations Conference on Sustainable Development ("Rio+ 20"). We also reaffirm the follow-up to these conferences, including the outcomes of the Fourth United Nations Conference on the Least Developed Countries, the Third International Conference on Small Island Developing States; the Second United Nations Conference on Landlocked Developing Countries; and the Third UN World Conference on Disaster Risk Reduction.

12 We reaffirm all the principles of the Rio Declaration on Environment and Development, including, inter alia, the principle of common but differentiated responsibilities, as set out in principle 7 thereof.

13 The challenges and commitments contained in these major conferences and summits are interrelated and call for integrated solutions. To address them effectively, a new approach is needed. Sustainable development recognizes that eradicating poverty in all its forms and dimensions, combatting inequality within and among countries, preserving the planet, creating sustained, inclusive and sustainable economic growth and fostering social inclusion are linked to each other and are interdependent.

Our world today

14 We are meeting at a time of immense challenges to sustainable development. Billions of our citizens continue to live in poverty and are denied a life of dignity. There are rising inequalities within and among countries. There are enormous disparities of opportunity, wealth and power. Gender inequality remains a key challenge. Unemployment, particularly youth unemployment, is a major concern. Global health threats, more frequent and intense natural disasters, spiralling conflict, violent extremism, terrorism and related humanitarian crises and forced displacement of people threaten to reverse much of the development progress made in recent decades. Natural resource depletion and adverse impacts of environmental degradation, including desertification, drought, land degradation, freshwater scarcity and loss of biodiversity, add to and exacerbate the list of challenges which humanity faces. Climate change is one of the greatest challenges of our time and its adverse impacts undermine the ability of all countries to achieve sustainable development. Increases in global temperature, sea level rise, ocean acidification and other climate change impacts are seriously affecting coastal areas and low-lying coastal countries, including many Least Developed Countries and Small Island Developing States. The survival of many societies, and of the biological support systems of the planet, is at risk.

15 It is also, however, a time of immense opportunity. Significant progress has been made in meeting many development challenges. Within the past generation, hundreds of millions of people have emerged from extreme poverty. Access to education has greatly increased for both boys and girls. The spread of information and communications technology and global interconnectedness has great potential to accelerate human progress, to bridge the digital divide and to develop knowledge societies, as does scientific and technological innovation across areas as diverse as medicine and energy.

16 Almost fifteen years ago, the Millennium Development Goals were agreed. These provided an important framework for development and significant progress has been made in a number of areas. But the progress has been uneven, particularly in Africa, Least Developed Countries, landlocked developing countries, and small island developing States, and some of the MDGs remain off-track, in particular those related to maternal, newborn and child health and to reproductive health. We recommit ourselves to the full realization of all the MDGs, including the off-track MDGs, in particular by providing focused

and scaled-up assistance to Least Developed Countries and other countries in special situations, in line with relevant support programmes. The new Agenda builds on the Millennium Development Goals and seeks to complete what these did not achieve, particularly in reaching the most vulnerable.

17 In its scope, however, the framework we are announcing today goes far beyond the MDGs. Alongside continuing development priorities such as poverty eradication, health, education and food security and nutrition, it sets out a wide range of economic, social and environmental objectives. It also promises more peaceful and inclusive societies. It also, crucially, defines means of implementation. Reflecting the integrated approach that we have decided on, there are deep interconnections and many cross-cutting elements across the new Goals and targets.

The new agenda

18 We are announcing today 17 Sustainable Development Goals with 169 associated targets which are integrated and indivisible. Never before have world leaders pledged common action and endeavour across such a broad and universal policy agenda. We are setting out together on the path towards sustainable development, devoting ourselves collectively to the pursuit of global development and of "win-win" cooperation which can bring huge gains to all countries and all parts of the world. We reaffirm that every State has, and shall freely exercise, full permanent sovereignty over all its wealth, natural resources and economic activity. We will implement the Agenda for the full benefit of all, for today's generation and for future generations. In doing so, we reaffirm our commitment to international law and emphasize that the Agenda is to be implemented in a manner that is consistent with the rights and obligations of states under international law.

19 We reaffirm the importance of the Universal Declaration of Human Rights, as well as other international instruments relating to human rights and international law. We emphasize the responsibilities of all States, in conformity with the Charter of the United Nations, to respect, protect and promote human rights and fundamental freedoms for all, without distinction of any kind as to race, colour, sex, language, religion, political or other opinion, national or social origin, property, birth, disability or other status.

20 Realizing gender equality and the empowerment of women and girls will make a crucial contribution to progress across all the Goals and targets. The achievement of full human potential and of sustainable development is not possible if one half of humanity continues to be denied its full human rights and opportunities. Women and girls must enjoy equal access to quality education, economic resources and political participation as well as equal opportunities with men and boys for employment, leadership and decision-making at all levels. We will work for a significant increase in investments to close the gender gap and strengthen support for institutions in relation to gender equality and the

empowerment of women at the global, regional and national levels. All forms of discrimination and violence against women and girls will be eliminated, including through the engagement of men and boys. The systematic mainstreaming of a gender perspective in the implementation of the Agenda is crucial.

21 The new Goals and targets will come into effect on 1 January 2016 and will guide the decisions we take over the next fifteen years. All of us will work to implement the Agenda within our own countries and at the regional and global levels, taking into account different national realities, capacities and levels of development and respecting national policies and priorities We will respect national policy space for sustained, inclusive and sustainable economic growth, in particular for developing states, while remaining consistent with relevant international rules and commitments. We acknowledge also the importance of the regional and sub-regional dimensions, regional economic integration and interconnectivity in sustainable development. Regional and sub-regional frameworks can facilitate the effective translation of sustainable development policies into concrete action at national level.

22 Each country faces specific challenges in its pursuit of sustainable development. The most vulnerable countries and, in particular, African countries, Least Developed Countries, landlocked developing countries and small island developing states deserve special attention, as do countries in situations of conflict and post-conflict countries. There are also serious challenges within many middle-income countries.

23 People who are vulnerable must be empowered. Those whose needs are reflected in the Agenda include all children, youth, persons with disabilities (of whom more than 80% live in poverty), people living with HIV/AIDS, older persons, indigenous peoples, refugees and internally displaced persons and migrants. We resolve to take further effective measures and actions, in conformity with international law, to remove obstacles and constraints, strengthen support and meet the special needs of people living in areas affected by complex humanitarian emergencies and in areas affected by terrorism.

24 We are committed to ending poverty in all its forms and dimensions, including by eradicating extreme poverty by 2030. All people must enjoy a basic standard of living, including through social protection systems. We are also determined to end hunger and to achieve food security as a matter of priority and to end all forms of malnutrition. In this regard, we reaffirm the important role and inclusive nature of the Committee on World Food Security and welcome the Rome Declaration on Nutrition and Framework for Action. We will devote resources to developing rural areas and sustainable agriculture and fisheries, supporting smallholder farmers, especially women farmers, herders and fishers in developing countries, particularly Least Developed Countries.

25 We commit to providing inclusive and equitable quality education at all levels – early childhood, primary, secondary, tertiary, technical and vocational training. All people, irrespective of sex, age, race, ethnicity, and persons with disabilities, migrants, indigenous peoples, children and youth, especially those in vulnerable

situations, should have access to life-long learning opportunities that help them acquire the knowledge and skills needed to exploit opportunities and to participate fully in society. We will strive to provide children and youth with a nurturing environment for the full realization of their rights and capabilities, helping our countries to reap the demographic dividend including through safe schools and cohesive communities and families.

26 To promote physical and mental health and well-being, and to extend life expectancy for all, we must achieve universal health coverage and access to quality health care. No one must be left behind. We commit to accelerating the progress made to date in reducing newborn, child and maternal mortality by ending all such preventable deaths before 2030. We are committed to ensuring universal access to sexual and reproductive health-care services, including for family planning, information and education. We will equally accelerate the pace of progress made in fighting malaria, HIV/AIDS, tuberculosis, hepatitis, Ebola and other communicable diseases and epidemics, including by addressing growing anti-microbial resistance and the problem of unattended diseases affecting developing countries. We are committed to the prevention and treatment of non-communicable diseases, including behavioural, developmental and neurological disorders, which constitute a major challenge for sustainable development.

27 We will seek to build strong economic foundations for all our countries. Sustained, inclusive and sustainable economic growth is essential for prosperity. This will only be possible if wealth is shared and income inequality is addressed. We will work to build dynamic, sustainable, innovative and people-centred economies, promoting youth employment and women's economic empowerment, in particular, and decent work for all. We will eradicate forced labour and human trafficking and end child labour in all its forms. All countries stand to benefit from having a healthy and well-educated workforce with the knowledge and skills needed for productive and fulfilling work and full participation in society. We will strengthen the productive capacities of least-developed countries in all sectors, including through structural transformation. We will adopt policies which increase productive capacities, productivity and productive employment; financial inclusion; sustainable agriculture, pastoralist and fisheries development; sustainable industrial development; universal access to affordable, reliable, sustainable and modern energy services; sustainable transport systems; and quality and resilient infrastructure.

28 We commit to making fundamental changes in the way that our societies produce and consume goods and services. Governments, international organizations, the business sector and other non-state actors and individuals must contribute to changing unsustainable consumption and production patterns, including through the mobilization, from all sources, of financial and technical assistance to strengthen developing countries' scientific, technological and innovative capacities to move towards more sustainable patterns of consumption and production. We encourage the implementation of the 10-Year Framework of Programmes on Sustainable Consumption and Production. All countries

take action, with developed countries taking the lead, taking into account the development and capabilities of developing countries.

29 We recognize the positive contribution of migrants for inclusive growth and sustainable development. We also recognize that international migration is a multi-dimensional reality of major relevance for the development of countries of origin, transit and destination, which requires coherent and comprehensive responses. We will cooperate internationally to ensure safe, orderly and regular migration involving full respect for human rights and the humane treatment of migrants regardless of migration status, of refugees and of displaced persons. Such cooperation should also strengthen the resilience of communities hosting refugees, particularly in developing countries. We underline the right of migrants to return to their country of citizenship, and recall that States must ensure that their returning nationals are duly received.

30 States are strongly urged to refrain from promulgating and applying any unilateral economic, financial or trade measures not in accordance with international law and the Charter of the United Nations that impede the full achievement of economic and social development, particularly in developing countries.

31 We acknowledge that the UNFCCC is the primary international, intergovernmental forum for negotiating the global response to climate change. We are determined to address decisively the threat posed by climate change and environmental degradation. The global nature of climate change calls for the widest possible international cooperation aimed at accelerating the reduction of global greenhouse gas emissions and addressing adaptation to the adverse impacts of climate change. We note with grave concern the significant gap between the aggregate effect of Parties' mitigation pledges in terms of global annual emissions of greenhouse gases by 2020 and aggregate emission pathways consistent with having a likely chance of holding the increase in global average temperature below 2 °C or 1.5 °C above pre-industrial levels.

32 Looking ahead to the COP 21 conference in Paris in December, we underscore the commitment of all States to work for an ambitious and universal climate agreement. We reaffirm that the protocol, another legal instrument or agreed outcome with legal force under the Convention applicable to all Parties shall address in a balanced manner, inter alia, mitigation, adaptation, finance, technology development and transfer, and capacity-building, and transparency of action and support.

33 We recognise that social and economic development depends on the sustainable management of our planet's natural resources. We are therefore determined to conserve and sustainably use oceans and seas, freshwater resources, as well as forests, mountains and drylands and to protect biodiversity, ecosystems and wildlife. We are also determined to promote sustainable tourism, tackle water scarcity and water pollution, to strengthen cooperation on desertification, dust storms, land degradation and drought and to promote resilience and disaster risk reduction. In this regard, we look forward to COP13 of the Convention on Biological Diversity to be held in Mexico in 2016.

34 We recognize that sustainable urban development and management are crucial to the quality of life of our people. We will work with local authorities and communities to renew and plan our cities and human settlements so as to foster community cohesion and personal security and to stimulate innovation and employment. We will reduce the negative impacts of urban activities and of chemicals which are hazardous for human health and the environment, including through the environmentally sound management and safe use of chemicals, the reduction and recycling of waste and more efficient use of water and energy. And we will work to minimize the impact of cities on the global climate system. We will also take account of population trends and projections in our national, rural and urban development strategies and policies. We look forward to the upcoming United Nations Conference on Housing and Sustainable Urban Development in Quito, Ecuador.

35 Sustainable development cannot be realized without peace and security; and peace and security will be at risk without sustainable development. The new Agenda recognizes the need to build peaceful, just and inclusive societies that provide equal access to justice and that are based on respect for human rights (including the right to development), on effective rule of law and good governance at all levels and on transparent, effective and accountable institutions. Factors which give rise to violence, insecurity and injustice, such as inequality, corruption, poor governance and illicit financial and arms flows, are addressed in the Agenda. We must redouble our efforts to resolve or prevent conflict and to support post-conflict countries, including through ensuring that women have a role in peace-building and state-building. We call for further effective measures and actions to be taken, in conformity with international law, to remove the obstacles to the full realization of the right of self-determination of peoples living under colonial and foreign occupation, which continue to adversely affect their economic and social development as well as their environment.

36 We pledge to foster inter-cultural understanding, tolerance, mutual respect and an ethic of global citizenship and shared responsibility. We acknowledge the natural and cultural diversity of the world and recognize that all cultures and civilizations can contribute to, and are crucial enablers of, sustainable development.

37 Sport is also an important enabler of sustainable development. We recognize the growing contribution of sport to the realization of development and peace in its promotion of tolerance and respect and the contributions it makes to the empowerment of women and of young people, individuals and communities as well as to health, education and social inclusion objectives.

38 We reaffirm, in accordance with the Charter of the United Nations, the need to respect the territorial integrity and political independence of States.

Means of implementation

39 The scale and ambition of the new Agenda requires a revitalized Global Partnership to ensure its implementation. We fully commit to this. This Partnership will work in a spirit of global solidarity, in particular solidarity with the poorest

and with people in vulnerable situations. It will facilitate an intensive global engagement in support of implementation of all the Goals and targets, bringing together Governments, the private sector, civil society, the United Nations system and other actors and mobilizing all available resources.

40 The means of implementation targets under Goal 17 and under each SDG are key to realising our Agenda and are of equal importance with the other Goals and targets. The Agenda, including the SDGs, can be met within the framework of a revitalized global partnership for sustainable development, supported by the concrete policies and actions as outlined in the outcome document of the Third International Conference on Financing for Development, held in Addis Ababa from 13–16 July 2015. We welcome the endorsement by the General Assembly of the Addis Ababa Action Agenda, which is an integral part of the 2030 Agenda for Sustainable Development. We recognize that the full implementation of the Addis Ababa Action Agenda is critical for the realization of the Sustainable Development Goals and targets.

41 We recognize that each country has primary responsibility for its own economic and social development. The new Agenda deals with the means required for implementation of the Goals and targets. We recognize that these will include the mobilization of financial resources as well as capacity-building and the transfer of environmentally sound technologies to developing countries on favourable terms, including on concessional and preferential terms, as mutually agreed. Public finance, both domestic and international, will play a vital role in providing essential services and public goods and in catalyzing other sources of finance. We acknowledge the role of the diverse private sector, ranging from micro-enterprises to cooperatives to multinationals, and that of civil society organizations and philanthropic organizations in the implementation of the new Agenda.

42 We support the implementation of relevant strategies and programmes of action, including the Istanbul Declaration and Programme of Action, the SIDS Accelerated Modalities of Action (SAMOA) Pathway, the Vienna Programme of Action for Landlocked Developing Countries for the Decade 2014–2024, and reaffirm the importance of supporting the African Union's Agenda 2063 and the programme of the New Partnership for Africa's Development (NEPAD), all of which are integral to the new Agenda. We recognize the major challenge to the achievement of durable peace and sustainable development in countries in conflict and post-conflict situations.

43 We emphasize that international public finance plays an important role in complementing the efforts of countries to mobilize public resources domestically, especially in the poorest and most vulnerable countries with limited domestic resources. An important use of international public finance, including ODA, is to catalyse additional resource mobilization from other sources, public and private. ODA providers reaffirm their respective commitments, including the commitment by many developed countries to achieve the target of 0.7% of ODA/GNI to developing countries and 0.15% to 0.2% of ODA/GNI to Least Developed Countries.

44 We acknowledge the importance for international financial institutions to support, in line with their mandates, the policy space of each country, in particular developing countries. We recommit to broadening and strengthening the voice and participation of developing countries – including African countries, Least Developed Countries, land-locked developing countries, small-island developing States and middle-income countries – in international economic decision-making, norm-setting and global economic governance.

45 We acknowledge also the essential role of national parliaments through their enactment of legislation and adoption of budgets and their role in ensuring accountability for the effective implementation of our commitments. Governments and public institutions will also work closely on implementation with regional and local authorities, sub-regional institutions, international institutions, academia, philanthropic organisations, volunteer groups and others.

46 We underline the important role and comparative advantage of an adequately resourced, relevant, coherent, efficient and effective UN system in supporting the achievement of the SDGs and sustainable development. While stressing the importance of strengthened national ownership and leadership at country level, we express our support for the ongoing ECOSOC Dialogue on the longer-term positioning of the United Nations development system in the context of this Agenda.

Follow-up and review

47 Our Governments have the primary responsibility for follow-up and review, at the national, regional and global levels, in relation to the progress made in implementing the Goals and targets over the coming fifteen years. To support accountability to our citizens, we will provide for systematic follow-up and review at the various levels, as set out in this Agenda and the Addis Ababa Action Agenda. The High Level Political Forum under the auspices of the General Assembly and the Economic and Social Council will have the central role in overseeing follow-up and review at the global level.

48 Indicators are being developed to assist this work. Quality, accessible, timely and reliable disaggregated data will be needed to help with the measurement of progress and to ensure that no one is left behind. Such data is key to decision-making. Data and information from existing reporting mechanisms should be used where possible. We agree to intensify our efforts to strengthen statistical capacities in developing countries, particularly African countries, Least Developed Countries, landlocked Developing Countries, Small Island Developing States and Middle-Income countries. We are committed to developing broader measures of progress to complement gross domestic product (GDP).

A call for action to change our world

49 Seventy years ago, an earlier generation of world leaders came together to create the United Nations. From the ashes of war and division they fashioned this

Organization and the values of peace, dialogue and international cooperation which underpin it. The supreme embodiment of those values is the Charter of the United Nations.

50   Today we are also taking a decision of great historic significance. We resolve to build a better future for all people, including the millions who have been denied the chance to lead decent, dignified and rewarding lives and to achieve their full human potential. We can be the first generation to succeed in ending poverty; just as we may be the last to have a chance of saving the planet. The world will be a better place in 2030 if we succeed in our objectives.

51   What we are announcing today – an Agenda for global action for the next fifteen years – is a charter for people and planet in the twenty-first century. Children and young women and men are critical agents of change and will find in the new Goals a platform to channel their infinite capacities for activism into the creation of a better world.

52   "We the Peoples" are the celebrated opening words of the UN Charter. It is "We the Peoples" who are embarking today on the road to 2030. Our journey will involve Governments as well as Parliaments, the UN system and other international institutions, local authorities, indigenous peoples, civil society, business and the private sector, the scientific and academic community – and all people. Millions have already engaged with, and will own, this Agenda. It is an Agenda of the people, by the people, and for the people – and this, we believe, will ensure its success.

53   The future of humanity and of our planet lies in our hands. It lies also in the hands of today's younger generation who will pass the torch to future genera-tions. We have mapped the road to sustainable development; it will be for all of us to ensure that the journey is successful and its gains irreversible.

Sustainable development goals and targets

54   Following an inclusive process of intergovernmental negotiations, and based on the Proposal of the Open Working Group on Sustainable Development Goals, which includes a chapeau contextualising the latter, the following are the Goals and targets which we have agreed.

55   The SDGs and targets are integrated and indivisible, global in nature and univer-sally applicable, taking into account different national realities, capacities and levels of development and respecting national policies and priorities. Targets are defined as aspirational and global, with each government setting its own national targets guided by the global level of ambition but taking into account national circum-stances. Each government will also decide how these aspirational and global targets should be incorporated in national planning processes, policies and strategies. It is important to recognize the link between sustainable development and other relevant ongoing processes in the economic, social and environmental fields.

56   In deciding upon these Goals and targets, we recognise that each country faces specific challenges to achieve sustainable development, and we underscore the

special challenges facing the most vulnerable countries and, in particular, African countries, Least Developed Countries, Landlocked Developing Countries and Small Island Developing States, as well as the specific challenges facing the Middle-Income Countries. Countries in situations of conflict also need special attention.

57 We recognize that baseline data for several of the targets remain unavailable, and we call for increased support for strengthening data collection and capacity building in Member States, to develop national and global baselines where they do not yet exist. We commit to addressing this gap in data collection so as to better inform the measurement of progress, in particular for those targets below which do not have clear numerical targets.

58 We encourage ongoing efforts by states in other fora to address key issues which pose potential challenges to the implementation of our Agenda; and we respect the independent mandates of those processes. We intend that the Agenda and its implementation would support, and be without prejudice to, those other processes and the decisions taken therein.

59 We recognise that there are different approaches, visions, models and tools available to each country, in accordance with its national circumstances and priorities, to achieve sustainable development; and we reaffirm that planet Earth and its ecosystems are our common home and that 'Mother Earth' is a common expression in a number of countries and regions.

Sustainable Development Goals

Goal 1: End poverty in all its forms everywhere.

Goal 2: End hunger, achieve food security and improved nutrition and promote sustainable agriculture.

Goal 3: Ensure healthy lives and promote well-being for all at all ages.

Goal 4: Ensure inclusive and equitable quality education and promote lifelong learning opportunities for all.

Goal 5: Achieve gender equality and empower all women and girls.

Goal 6: Ensure availability and sustainable management of water and sanitation for all.

Goal 7: Ensure access to affordable, reliable, sustainable and modern energy for all.

Goal 8: Promote sustained, inclusive and sustainable economic growth, full and productive employment and decent work for all.

Goal 9: Build resilient infrastructure, promote inclusive and sustainable industrialization and foster innovation.

Goal 10: Reduce inequality within and among countries.

Goal 11: Make cities and human settlements inclusive, safe, resilient and sustainable.

Goal 12: Ensure sustainable consumption and production patterns.

Goal 13: Take urgent action to combat climate change and its impacts*.

Goal 14: Conserve and sustainably use the oceans, seas and marine resources for sustainable development.

Goal 15: Protect, restore and promote sustainable use of terrestrial ecosystems, sustainably manage forests, combat desertification, and halt and reverse land degradation and halt biodiversity loss.

Goal 16: Promote peaceful and inclusive societies for sustainable development, provide access to justice for all and build effective, accountable and inclusive institutions at all levels.

Goal 17: Strengthen the means of implementation and revitalize the global partnership for sustainable development.

Goal 1: End poverty in all its forms everywhere.

1.1 By 2030, eradicate extreme poverty for all people everywhere, currently measured as people living on less than $1.25 a day.

1.2 By 2030, reduce at least by half the proportion of men, women and children of all ages living in poverty in all its dimensions according to national definitions.

1.3 Implement nationally appropriate social protection systems and measures for all, including floors, and by 2030 achieve substantial coverage of the poor and the vulnerable.

1.4 By 2030, ensure that all men and women, in particular the poor and the vulnerable, have equal rights to economic resources, as well as access to basic services, ownership and control over land and other forms of property, inheritance, natural resources, appropriate new technology and financial services, including microfinance.

1.5 By 2030, build the resilience of the poor and those in vulnerable situations and reduce their exposure and vulnerability to climate-related extreme events and other economic, social and environmental shocks and disasters.

    1.a Ensure significant mobilization of resources from a variety of sources, including through enhanced development cooperation, in order to provide adequate and predictable means for developing countries, in particular Least Developed Countries, to implement programmes and policies to end poverty in all its dimensions.

    1.b Create sound policy frameworks at the national, regional and international levels, based on pro-poor and gender-sensitive development strategies, to support accelerated investment in poverty eradication actions.

*Acknowledging that the United Nations Framework Convention on Climate Change is the primary international, intergovernmental forum for negotiating the global response to climate change.

Goal 2: End hunger, achieve food security and improved nutrition and promote sustainable agriculture.

2.1 By 2030, end hunger and ensure access by all people, in particular the poor and people in vulnerable situations, including infants, to safe, nutritious and sufficient food all year round.

2.2 By 2030, end all forms of malnutrition, including achieving, by 2025, the internationally agreed targets on stunting and wasting in children under 5 years of age, and address the nutritional needs of adolescent girls, pregnant and lactating women and older persons.

2.3 By 2030, double the agricultural productivity and incomes of small-scale food producers, in particular women, indigenous peoples, family farmers, pastoralists and fishers, including through secure and equal access to land, other productive resources and inputs, knowledge, financial services, markets and opportunities for value addition and non-farm employment.

2.4 By 2030, ensure sustainable food production systems and implement resilient agricultural practices that increase productivity and production, that help maintain ecosystems, that strengthen capacity for adaptation to climate change, extreme weather, drought, flooding and other disasters and that progressively improve land and soil quality.

2.5 By 2020, maintain the genetic diversity of seeds, cultivated plants and farmed and domesticated animals and their related wild species, including through soundly managed and diversified seed and plant banks at the national, regional and international levels, and promote access to and fair and equitable sharing of benefits arising from the utilization of genetic resources and associated traditional knowledge, as internationally agreed.

2.a Increase investment, including through enhanced international cooperation, in rural infrastructure, agricultural research and extension services, technology development and plant and livestock gene banks in order to enhance agricultural productive capacity in developing countries, in particular Least Developed Countries.

2.b Correct and prevent trade restrictions and distortions in world agricultural markets, including through the parallel elimination of all forms of agricultural export subsidies and all export measures with equivalent effect, in accordance with the mandate of the Doha Development Round.

2.c Adopt measures to ensure the proper functioning of food commodity markets and their derivatives and facilitate timely access to market information, including on food reserves, in order to help limit extreme food price volatility.

Goal 3: Ensure healthy lives and promote well-being for all at all ages.

3.1 By 2030, reduce the global maternal mortality ratio to less than 70 per 100,000 live births.

3.2 By 2030, end preventable deaths of newborns and children under 5 years of age, with all countries aiming to reduce neonatal mortality to at least as low as 12 per 1,000 live births and under-5 mortality to at least as low as 25 per 1,000 live births.

3.3 By 2030, end the epidemics of AIDS, tuberculosis, malaria and neglected tropical diseases and combat hepatitis, water-borne diseases and other communicable diseases.

3.4 By 2030, reduce by one third premature mortality from non-communicable diseases through prevention and treatment and promote mental health and well-being.

3.5 Strengthen the prevention and treatment of substance abuse, including narcotic drug abuse and harmful use of alcohol.

3.6 By 2020, halve the number of global deaths and injuries from road traffic accidents.

3.7 By 2030, ensure universal access to sexual and reproductive health-care services, including for family planning, information and education, and the integration of reproductive health into national strategies and programmes.

3.8 Achieve universal health coverage, including financial risk protection, access to quality essential health-care services and access to safe, effective, quality and affordable essential medicines and vaccines for all.

3.9 By 2030, substantially reduce the number of deaths and illnesses from hazardous chemicals and air, water and soil pollution and contamination.

   3.a Strengthen the implementation of the World Health Organization Framework Convention on Tobacco Control in all countries, as appropriate.

   3.b Support the research and development of vaccines and medicines for the communicable and non-communicable diseases that primarily affect developing countries, provide access to affordable essential medicines and vaccines, in accordance with the Doha Declaration on the TRIPS Agreement and Public Health, which affirms the right of developing countries to use to the full the provisions in the Agreement on Trade-Related Aspects of Intellectual Property Rights regarding flexibilities to protect public health, and, in particular, provide access to medicines for all.

   3.c Substantially increase health financing and the recruitment, development, training and retention of the health workforce in developing countries, especially in Least Developed Countries and Small Island Developing States.

   3.d Strengthen the capacity of all countries, in particular developing countries, for early warning, risk reduction and management of national and global health risks.

Goal 4: Ensure inclusive and equitable quality education and promote lifelong learning opportunities for all.

4.1 By 2030, ensure that all girls and boys complete free, equitable and quality primary and secondary education leading to relevant and effective learning outcomes.

4.2 By 2030, ensure that all girls and boys have access to quality early child-hood development, care and pre-primary education so that they are ready for primary education.

4.3 By 2030, ensure equal access for all women and men to affordable and quality technical, vocational and tertiary education, including university.

4.4 By 2030, substantially increase the number of youth and adults who have relevant skills, including technical and vocational skills, for employment, decent jobs and entrepreneurship.

4.5 By 2030, eliminate gender disparities in education and ensure equal access to all levels of education and vocational training for the vulnerable, including persons with disabilities, indigenous peoples and children in vulnerable situations.

4.6 By 2030, ensure that all youth and a substantial proportion of adults, both men and women, achieve literacy and numeracy.

4.7 By 2030, ensure that all learners acquire the knowledge and skills needed to promote sustainable development, including, among others, through education for sustainable development and sustainable lifestyles, human rights, gender equality, promotion of a culture of peace and non-violence, global citizenship and appreciation of cultural diversity and of culture's contribution to sustainable development.

4.a Build and upgrade education facilities that are child, disability and gender sensitive and provide safe, non-violent, inclusive and effective learning environments for all.

4.b By 2020, substantially expand globally the number of scholarships available to developing countries, in particular Least Developed Countries, Small Island Developing States and African countries, for enrolment in higher education, including vocational training and information and communications technology, technical, engineering and scientific pro-grammes, in developed countries and other developing countries.

4.c By 2030, substantially increase the supply of qualified teachers, including through international cooperation for teacher training in developing countries, especially Least Developed Countries and Small Island Developing States.

Goal 5: Achieve gender equality and empower all women and girls.

5.1 End all forms of discrimination against all women and girls everywhere.

5.2 Eliminate all forms of violence against all women and girls in the public and private spheres, including trafficking and sexual and other types of exploitation.

5.3 Eliminate all harmful practices, such as child, early and forced marriage and female genital mutilation.

5.4 Recognize and value unpaid care and domestic work through the provision of public services, infrastructure and social protection policies and the promotion of shared responsibility within the household and the family as nationally appropriate.

5.5 Ensure women's full and effective participation and equal opportunities for leadership at all levels of decision-making in political, economic and public life.

5.6 Ensure universal access to sexual and reproductive health and reproductive rights as agreed in accordance with the Programme of Action of the International Conference on Population and Development and the Beijing Platform for Action and the outcome documents of their review conferences.

5.a Undertake reforms to give women equal rights to economic resources, as well as access to ownership and control over land and other forms of property, financial services, inheritance and natural resources, in accordance with national laws.

5.b Enhance the use of enabling technology, in particular information and communications technology, to promote the empowerment of women.

5.c Adopt and strengthen sound policies and enforceable legislation for the promotion of gender equality and the empowerment of all women and girls at all levels.

Goal 6: Ensure availability and sustainable management of water and sanitation for all.

6.1 By 2030, achieve universal and equitable access to safe and affordable drinking water for all.

6.2 By 2030, achieve access to adequate and equitable sanitation and hygiene for all and end open defecation, paying special attention to the needs of women and girls and those in vulnerable situations.

6.3 By 2030, improve water quality by reducing pollution, eliminating dumping and minimizing release of hazardous chemicals and materials, halving the proportion of untreated wastewater and substantially increasing recycling and safe reuse globally.

6.4 By 2030, substantially increase water-use efficiency across all sectors and ensure sustainable withdrawals and supply of freshwater to address water scarcity and substantially reduce the number of people suffering from water scarcity.

6.5 By 2030, implement integrated water resources management at all levels, including through transboundary cooperation as appropriate.

6.6 By 2020, protect and restore water-related ecosystems, including mountains, forests, wetlands, rivers, aquifers and lakes.

6.a By 2030, expand international cooperation and capacity-building support to developing countries in water- and sanitation-related activities and programmes, including water harvesting, desalination, water efficiency, wastewater treatment, recycling and reuse technologies.

6.b Support and strengthen the participation of local communities in improving water and sanitation management.

Goal 7: Ensure access to affordable, reliable, sustainable and modern energy for all.

7.1 By 2030, ensure universal access to affordable, reliable and modern energy services.

7.2 By 2030, increase substantially the share of renewable energy in the global energy mix.

7.3 By 2030, double the global rate of improvement in energy efficiency.

    7.a By 2030, enhance international cooperation to facilitate access to clean energy research and technology, including renewable energy, energy efficiency and advanced and cleaner fossil-fuel technology, and promote investment in energy infrastructure and clean energy technology.

    7.b By 2030, expand infrastructure and upgrade technology for supplying modern and sustainable energy services for all in developing countries, in particular Least Developed Countries, Small Island Developing States, and Land-Locked Developing Countries, in accordance with their respective programmes of support.

Goal 8: Promote sustained, inclusive and sustainable economic growth, full and productive employment and decent work for all.

8.1 Sustain per capita economic growth in accordance with national circumstances and, in particular, at least 7 per cent gross domestic product growth per annum in the Least Developed Countries.

8.2 Achieve higher levels of economic productivity through diversification, technological upgrading and innovation, including through a focus on high-value added and labour-intensive sectors.

8.3 Promote development-oriented policies that support productive activities, decent job creation, entrepreneurship, creativity and innovation, and encourage the formalization and growth of micro-, small- and medium-sized enterprises, including through access to financial services.

8.4 Improve progressively, through 2030, global resource efficiency in consumption and production and endeavour to decouple economic growth from environmental degradation, in accordance with the 10-year framework of programmes on sustainable consumption and production, with developed countries taking the lead.

8.5 By 2030, achieve full and productive employment and decent work for all women and men, including for young people and persons with disabilities, and equal pay for work of equal value.

8.6 By 2020, substantially reduce the proportion of youth not in employment, education or training.

8.7 Take immediate and effective measures to eradicate forced labour, end modern slavery and human trafficking and secure the prohibition and elimination of the worst forms of child labour, including recruitment and use of child soldiers, and by 2025 end child labour in all its forms.

8.8 Protect labour rights and promote safe and secure working environments for all workers, including migrant workers, in particular women migrants, and those in precarious employment.

8.9 By 2030, devise and implement policies to promote sustainable tourism that creates jobs and promotes local culture and products.

8.10 Strengthen the capacity of domestic financial institutions to encourage and expand access to banking, insurance and financial services for all.

8.a Increase Aid for Trade support for developing countries, in particular Least Developed Countries, including through the Enhanced Integrated Framework for Trade-Related Technical Assistance to Least Developed Countries.

8.b By 2020, develop and operationalize a global strategy for youth employment and implement the Global Jobs Pact of the International Labour Organization.

Goal 9: Build resilient infrastructure, promote inclusive and sustainable industrialization and foster innovation.

9.1 Develop quality, reliable, sustainable and resilient infrastructure, including regional and transborder infrastructure, to support economic development and human well-being, with a focus on affordable and equitable access for all.

9.2 Promote inclusive and sustainable industrialization and, by 2030, significantly raise industry's share of employment and gross domestic product, in line with national circumstances, and double its share in Least Developed Countries.

9.3 Increase the access of small-scale industrial and other enterprises, in particular in developing countries, to financial services, including affordable credit, and their integration into value chains and markets.

9.4 By 2030, upgrade infrastructure and retrofit industries to make them sustainable, with increased resource-use efficiency and greater adoption of clean and environmentally sound technologies and industrial processes, with all countries taking action in accordance with their respective capabilities.

9.5 Enhance scientific research, upgrade the technological capabilities of industrial sectors in all countries, in particular developing countries, including, by 2030, encouraging innovation and substantially increasing the number of research and development workers per 1 million people and public and private research and development spending.

9.a Facilitate sustainable and resilient infrastructure development in developing countries through enhanced financial, technological and technical support to African countries, Least Developed Countries, Landlocked Developing Countries and Small Island Developing States.

9.b Support domestic technology development, research and innovation in developing countries, including by ensuring a conducive policy environment for, inter alia, industrial diversification and value addition to commodities.

9.c Significantly increase access to information and communications technology and strive to provide universal and affordable access to the Internet in Least Developed Countries by 2020.

Goal 10: Reduce inequality within and among countries.

10.1 By 2030, progressively achieve and sustain income growth of the bottom 40 per cent of the population at a rate higher than the national average.

10.2 By 2030, empower and promote the social, economic and political inclusion of all, irrespective of age, sex, disability, race, ethnicity, origin, religion or economic or other status.

10.3 Ensure equal opportunity and reduce inequalities of outcome, including by eliminating discriminatory laws, policies and practices and promoting appropriate legislation, policies and action in this regard.

10.4 Adopt policies, especially fiscal, wage and social protection policies, and progressively achieve greater equality.

10.5 Improve the regulation and monitoring of global financial markets and institutions and strengthen the implementation of such regulations.

10.6 Ensure enhanced representation and voice for developing countries in decision-making in global international economic and financial institutions in order to deliver more effective, credible, accountable and legitimate institutions.

10.7 Facilitate orderly, safe, regular and responsible migration and mobility of people, including through the implementation of planned and well-managed migration policies.

10.a Implement the principle of special and differential treatment for developing countries, in particular Least Developed Countries, in accordance with World Trade Organization agreements.

10.b Encourage official development assistance and financial flows, including foreign direct investment, to States where the need is greatest, in particular Least Developed Countries, African countries, small island developing States and landlocked developing countries, in accordance with their national plans and programmes.

10.c By 2030, reduce to less than 3 per cent the transaction costs of migrant remittances and eliminate remittance corridors with costs higher than 5 per cent.

Goal 11: Make cities and human settlements inclusive, safe, resilient and sustainable.

11.1 By 2030, ensure access for all to adequate, safe and affordable housing and basic services and upgrade slums.

11.2 By 2030, provide access to safe, affordable, accessible and sustainable transport systems for all, improving road safety, notably by expanding public transport, with special attention to the needs of those in vulnerable situations, women, children, persons with disabilities and older persons.

11.3 By 2030, enhance inclusive and sustainable urbanization and capacity for participatory, integrated and sustainable human settlement planning and management in all countries.

11.4 Strengthen efforts to protect and safeguard the world's cultural and natural heritage.

11.5 By 2030, significantly reduce the number of deaths and the number of people affected and substantially decrease the direct economic losses relative to global gross domestic product caused by disasters, including water-related disasters, with a focus on protecting the poor and people in vulnerable situations.

11.6 By 2030, reduce the adverse per capita environmental impact of cities, including by paying special attention to air quality and municipal and other waste management.

11.7 By 2030, provide universal access to safe, inclusive and accessible, green and public spaces, in particular for women and children, older persons and persons with disabilities.

　11.a Support positive economic, social and environmental links between urban, peri-urban and rural areas by strengthening national and regional development planning.

　11.b By 2020, substantially increase the number of cities and human settlements adopting and implementing integrated policies and plans towards inclusion, resource efficiency, mitigation and adaptation to climate change, resilience to disasters, and develop and implement, in line with the Sendai Framework for Disaster Risk Reduction 2015–2030, holistic disaster risk management at all levels.

　11.c Support Least Developed Countries, including through financial and technical assistance, in building sustainable and resilient buildings utilizing local materials.

Goal 12: Ensure sustainable consumption and production patterns.

12.1 Implement the 10-year framework of programmes on sustainable consumption and production, all countries taking action, with developed countries taking the lead, taking into account the development and capabilities of developing countries.

12.2 By 2030, achieve the sustainable management and efficient use of natural resources.

12.3 By 2030, halve per capita global food waste at the retail and consumer levels and reduce food losses along production and supply chains, including post-harvest losses.

12.4 By 2020, achieve the environmentally sound management of chemicals and all wastes throughout their life cycle, in accordance with agreed international frameworks, and significantly reduce their release to air, water and soil in order to minimize their adverse impacts on human health and the environment.

12.5 By 2030, substantially reduce waste generation through prevention, reduction, recycling and reuse.

12.6 Encourage companies, especially large and transnational companies, to adopt sustainable practices and to integrate sustainability information into their reporting cycle.

12.7 Promote public procurement practices that are sustainable, in accordance with national policies and priorities.

12.8 By 2030, ensure that people everywhere have the relevant information and awareness for sustainable development and lifestyles in harmony with nature.

12.a Support developing countries to strengthen their scientific and technological capacity to move towards more sustainable patterns of consumption and production.

12.b Develop and implement tools to monitor sustainable development impacts for sustainable tourism that creates jobs and promotes local culture and products.

12.c Rationalize inefficient fossil-fuel subsidies that encourage wasteful consumption by removing market distortions, in accordance with national circumstances, including by restructuring taxation and phasing out those harmful subsidies, where they exist, to reflect their environmental impacts, taking fully into account the specific needs and conditions of developing countries and minimizing the possible adverse impacts on their development in a manner that protects the poor and the affected communities.

Goal 13: Take urgent action to combat climate change and its impacts*.

13.1 Strengthen resilience and adaptive capacity to climate-related hazards and natural disasters in all countries.

13.2 Integrate climate change measures into national policies, strategies and planning.

13.3 Improve education, awareness-raising and human and institutional capacity on climate change mitigation, adaptation, impact reduction and early warning.

13.a Implement the commitment undertaken by developed-country parties to the United Nations Framework Convention on Climate Change to a goal of mobilizing jointly $100 billion annually by 2020 from all sources to address the needs of developing countries in the context of meaningful mitigation actions and transparency on implementation and fully operationalize the Green Climate Fund through its capitalization as soon as possible.

13.b Promote mechanisms for raising capacity for effective climate change-related planning and management in Least Developed Countries and Small Island Developing States, including focusing on women, youth and local and marginalized communities.

*Acknowledging that the United Nations Framework Convention on Climate Change is the primary international, intergovernmental forum for negotiating the global response to climate change.

Goal 14: Conserve and sustainably use the oceans, seas and marine resources for sustainable development.

14.1 By 2025, prevent and significantly reduce marine pollution of all kinds, in particular from land-based activities, including marine debris and nutrient pollution.

14.2 By 2020, sustainably manage and protect marine and coastal ecosystems to avoid significant adverse impacts, including by strengthening their resilience, and take action for their restoration in order to achieve healthy and productive oceans.

14.3 Minimize and address the impacts of ocean acidification, including through enhanced scientific cooperation at all levels.

14.4 By 2020, effectively regulate harvesting and end overfishing, illegal, unreported and unregulated fishing and destructive fishing practices and implement science-based management plans, in order to restore fish stocks in the shortest time feasible, at least to levels that can produce maximum sustainable yield as determined by their biological characteristics.

14.5 By 2020, conserve at least 10 per cent of coastal and marine areas, consistent with national and international law and based on the best available scientific information.

14.6 By 2020, prohibit certain forms of fisheries subsidies which contribute to overcapacity and overfishing, eliminate subsidies that contribute to illegal, unreported and unregulated fishing and refrain from introducing new such subsidies, recognizing that appropriate and effective special and differential treatment for developing and Least Developed Countries should be an integral part of the World Trade Organization fisheries subsidies negotiation.

14.7 By 2030, increase the economic benefits to Small Island developing States and Least Developed Countries from the sustainable use of marine resources, including through sustainable management of fisheries, aquaculture and tourism.

14.a Increase scientific knowledge, develop research capacity and transfer marine technology, taking into account the Intergovernmental Oceanographic Commission Criteria and Guidelines on the Transfer of Marine Technology, in order to improve ocean health and to enhance the contribution of marine biodiversity to the development of developing countries, in particular small island developing States and Least Developed Countries.

14.b Provide access for small-scale artisanal fishers to marine resources and markets.

14.c Enhance the conservation and sustainable use of oceans and their resources by implementing international law as reflected in UNCLOS, which provides the legal framework for the conservation and sustainable use of oceans and their resources, as recalled in paragraph 158 of The Future We Want.

Goal 15: Protect, restore and promote sustainable use of terrestrial ecosystems, sustainably manage forests, combat desertification, and halt and reverse land degradation and halt biodiversity loss.

15.1 By 2020, ensure the conservation, restoration and sustainable use of terrestrial and inland freshwater ecosystems and their services, in particular forests, wetlands, mountains and drylands, in line with obligations under international agreements.

15.2 By 2020, promote the implementation of sustainable management of all types of forests, halt deforestation, restore degraded forests and substantially increase afforestation and reforestation globally.

15.3 By 2030, combat desertification, restore degraded land and soil, including land affected by desertification, drought and floods, and strive to achieve a land degradation-neutral world.

15.4 By 2030, ensure the conservation of mountain ecosystems, including their biodiversity, in order to enhance their capacity to provide benefits that are essential for sustainable development.

15.5 Take urgent and significant action to reduce the degradation of natural habitats, halt the loss of biodiversity and, by 2020, protect and prevent the extinction of threatened species.

15.6 Promote fair and equitable sharing of the benefits arising from the utilization of genetic resources and promote appropriate access to such resources, as internationally agreed.

15.7 Take urgent action to end poaching and trafficking of protected species of flora and fauna and address both demand and supply of illegal wildlife products.

15.8 By 2020, introduce measures to prevent the introduction and significantly reduce the impact of invasive alien species on land and water ecosystems and control or eradicate the priority species.

15.9 By 2020, integrate ecosystem and biodiversity values into national and local planning, development processes, poverty reduction strategies and accounts.

15.a Mobilize and significantly increase financial resources from all sources to conserve and sustainably use biodiversity and ecosystems.

15.b Mobilize significant resources from all sources and at all levels to finance sustainable forest management and provide adequate incentives to developing countries to advance such management, including for conservation and reforestation.

15.c Enhance global support for efforts to combat poaching and trafficking of protected species, including by increasing the capacity of local communities to pursue sustainable livelihood opportunities.

Goal 16: Promote peaceful and inclusive societies for sustainable development, provide access to justice for all and build effective, accountable and inclusive institutions at all levels.

16.1 Significantly reduce all forms of violence and related death rates everywhere.

16.2 End abuse, exploitation, trafficking and all forms of violence against and torture of children.

16.3 Promote the rule of law at the national and international levels and ensure equal access to justice for all.

16.4 By 2030, significantly reduce illicit financial and arms flows, strengthen the recovery and return of stolen assets and combat all forms of organized crime.

16.5 Substantially reduce corruption and bribery in all their forms.

16.6 Develop effective, accountable and transparent institutions at all levels.

16.7 Ensure responsive, inclusive, participatory and representative decision-making at all levels.

16.8 Broaden and strengthen the participation of developing countries in the institutions of global governance.

16.9 By 2030, provide legal identity for all, including birth registration.

16.10 Ensure public access to information and protect fundamental freedoms, in accordance with national legislation and international agreements.

16.a Strengthen relevant national institutions, including through international cooperation, for building capacity at all levels, in particular in developing countries, to prevent violence and combat terrorism and crime.

16.b Promote and enforce non-discriminatory laws and policies for sustainable development.

Goal 17: Strengthen the means of implementation and revitalize the global partnership for sustainable development.

Finance

17.1 Strengthen domestic resource mobilization, including through international support to developing countries, to improve domestic capacity for tax and other revenue collection.

17.2 Developed countries to implement fully their official development assistance commitments, including the commitment by many developed countries to achieve the target of 0.7 per cent of ODA/GNI to developing countries and 0.15 to 0.20 per cent of ODA/GNI to Least Developed Countries; ODA providers are encouraged to consider setting a target to provide at least 0.20 per cent of ODA/GNI to Least Developed Countries.

17.3 Mobilize additional financial resources for developing countries from multiple sources.

17.4 Assist developing countries in attaining long-term debt sustainability through coordinated policies aimed at fostering debt financing, debt relief and debt restructuring, as appropriate, and address the external debt of highly indebted poor countries to reduce debt distress.

17.5 Adopt and implement investment promotion regimes for Least Developed Countries.

Technology

17.6 Enhance North-South, South-South and triangular regional and international cooperation on and access to science, technology and innovation and enhance knowledge sharing on mutually agreed terms, including through improved coordination among existing mechanisms, in particular at the United Nations level, and through a global Technology Facilitation Mechanism.

17.7 Promote the development, transfer, dissemination and diffusion of environmentally sound technologies to developing countries on favourable terms, including on concessional and preferential terms, as mutually agreed.

17.8 Fully operationalize the technology bank and science, technology and innovation capacity-building mechanism for Least Developed Countries by 2017 and enhance the use of enabling technology, in particular information and communications technology.

Capacity-building

17.9 Enhance international support for implementing effective and targeted capacity-building in developing countries to support national plans to implement all the sustainable development goals, including through North-South, South-South and triangular cooperation.

Trade

17.10 Promote a universal, rules-based, open, non-discriminatory and equitable multilateral trading system under the World Trade Organization, including through the conclusion of negotiations under its Doha Development Agenda.

17.11 Significantly increase the exports of developing countries, in particular with a view to doubling the Least Developed Countries' share of global exports by 2020.

17.12 Realize timely implementation of duty-free and quota-free market access on a lasting basis for all Least Developed Countries, consistent with World Trade Organization decisions, including by ensuring that preferential rules of origin applicable to imports from Least Developed Countries are transparent and simple, and contribute to facilitating market access.

Systemic issues

Policy and institutional coherence

17.13 Enhance global macroeconomic stability, including through policy coordination and policy coherence.

17.14 Enhance policy coherence for sustainable development.

17.15 Respect each country's policy space and leadership to establish and implement policies for poverty eradication and sustainable development.

Multistakeholder partnerships

17.16 Enhance the global partnership for sustainable development, complemented by multistakeholder partnerships that mobilize and share knowledge, expertise, technology and financial resources, to support the achievement of the sustainable development goals in all countries, in particular developing countries.

17.17 Encourage and promote effective public, public-private and civil society partnerships, building on the experience and resourcing strategies of partnerships.

Data, monitoring and accountability

17.18 By 2020, enhance capacity-building support to developing countries, including for Least Developed Countries and small island developing States, to increase significantly the availability of high-quality, timely and reliable data disaggregated by income, gender, age, race, ethnicity, migratory status, disability, geographic location and other characteristics relevant in national contexts.

17.19 By 2030, build on existing initiatives to develop measurements of progress on sustainable development that complement gross domestic product, and support statistical capacity-building in developing countries.

Means of implementation and the global partnership

60 We reaffirm our strong commitment to the full implementation of this new Agenda. We recognize that we will not be able to achieve our ambitious Goals and targets without a revitalized and enhanced Global Partnership and comparably ambitious means of implementation. The revitalized Global Partnership will facilitate an intensive global engagement in support of implementation of all the goals and targets, bringing together Governments, civil society, the private sector, the United Nations system and other actors and mobilizing all available resources.

61 The Agenda's Goals and targets deal with the means required to realise our collective ambitions. The means of implementation targets under each SDG and Goal 17, which are referred to above, are key to realising our Agenda and are of equal importance with the other Goals and targets. We shall accord them equal priority in our implementation efforts and in the global indicator framework for monitoring our progress.

62 This Agenda, including the SDGs, can be met within the framework of a revitalized global partnership for sustainable development, supported by the concrete policies and actions outlined in the Addis Ababa Action Agenda, which is an integral part of the 2030 Agenda for sustainable development. The Addis Ababa Action Agenda supports, complements and helps contextualize the 2030 Agenda's means of implementation targets. These relate to domestic public resources, domestic and international private business and finance, international development cooperation, international trade as an engine for development, debt and debt sustainability, addressing systemic issues and science, technology, innovation and capacity-building, and data, monitoring and follow-up.

63 Cohesive nationally owned sustainable development strategies, supported by integrated national financing frameworks, will be at the heart of our efforts. We reiterate that each country has primary responsibility for its own economic and social development and that the role of national policies and development strategies cannot be overemphasized. We will respect each country's policy space and leadership to implement policies for poverty eradication and sustainable development, while remaining consistent with relevant international rules and commitments. At the same time, national development efforts need to be supported by an enabling international economic environment, including coherent and mutually supporting world trade, monetary and financial systems, and strengthened and enhanced global economic governance. Processes to develop and facilitate the availability of appropriate knowledge and technologies globally, as well as capacity-building, are also critical. We commit to pursuing policy coherence and an enabling environment for sustainable

development at all levels and by all actors, and to reinvigorating the global partnership for sustainable development.

64 We support the implementation of relevant strategies and programmes of action, including the Istanbul Declaration and Programme of Action, the SIDS Accelerated Modalities of Action (SAMOA) Pathway, the Vienna Programme of Action for Landlocked Developing Countries for the Decade 2014–2024, and reaffirm the importance of supporting the African Union's Agenda 2063 and the programme of the New Partnership for Africa's Development (NEPAD), all of which are integral to the new Agenda. We recognize the major challenge to the achievement of durable peace and sustainable development in countries in conflict and post-conflict situations.

65 We recognize that middle-income countries still face significant challenges to achieve sustainable development. In order to ensure that achievements made to date are sustained, efforts to address ongoing challenges should be strengthened through the exchange of experiences, improved coordination, and better and focused support of the United Nations Development System, the international financial institutions, regional organizations and other stakeholders.

66 We underscore that, for all countries, public policies and the mobilization and effective use of domestic resources, underscored by the principle of national ownership, are central to our common pursuit of sustainable development, including achieving the sustainable development goals. We recognize that domestic resources are first and foremost generated by economic growth, supported by an enabling environment at all levels.

67 Private business activity, investment and innovation are major drivers of productivity, inclusive economic growth and job creation. We acknowledge the diversity of the private sector, ranging from micro-enterprises to cooperatives to multinationals. We call on all businesses to apply their creativity and innovation to solving sustainable development challenges. We will foster a dynamic and well-functioning business sector, while protecting labour rights and environmental and health standards in accordance with relevant international standards and agreements and other on-going initiatives in this regard, such as the Guiding Principles on Business and Human Rights and the labour standards of ILO, the Convention on the Rights of the Child and key multilateral environmental agreements, for parties to those agreements.

68 International trade is an engine for inclusive economic growth and poverty reduction, and contributes to the promotion of sustainable development. We will continue to promote a universal, rules-based, open, transparent, predictable, inclusive, non-discriminatory and equitable multilateral trading system under the World Trade Organization (WTO), as well as meaningful trade liberalization. We call on all WTO members to redouble their efforts to promptly conclude the negotiations on the Doha Development Agenda. We attach great importance to providing trade-related capacity-building for developing countries, including African countries, least-developed countries, landlocked developing countries, small island developing states and middle-income countries,

including for the promotion of regional economic integration and interconnectivity.

69 We recognize the need to assist developing countries in attaining long-term
debt sustainability through coordinated policies aimed at fostering debt financing, debt relief, debt restructuring and sound debt management, as appropriate.
Many countries remain vulnerable to debt crises and some are in the midst of
crises, including a number of Least Developed Countries, Small-Island Developing States and some developed countries. We reiterate that debtors and credi-
tors must work together to prevent and resolve unsustainable debt situations.
Maintaining sustainable debt levels is the responsibility of the borrowing countries; however we acknowledge that lenders also have a responsibility to lend in
a way that does not undermine a country's debt sustainability. We will support
the maintenance of debt sustainability of those countries that have received
debt relief and achieved sustainable debt levels.

70 We hereby launch a Technology Facilitation Mechanism which was established
by the Addis Ababa Action Agenda in order to support the sustainable development goals. The Technology Facilitation Mechanism will be based on a multistakeholder collaboration between Member States, civil society, private sector,
scientific community, United Nations entities and other stakeholders and will
be composed of: a United Nations Interagency Task Team on Science, Technology and Innovation for the SDGs, a collaborative Multistakeholder Forum on
Science, Technology and Innovation for the SDGs and an on-line platform.

- The United Nations Interagency Task Team on Science, Technology and
  Innovation for the SDGs will promote coordination, coherence, and cooperation within the UN System on STI related matters, enhancing synergy
  and efficiency, in particular to enhance capacity-building initiatives. The
  Task Team will draw on existing resources and will work with 10 representatives from the civil society, private sector, the scientific community,
  to prepare the meetings of the Multistakeholder Forum on Science, Technology and Innovation for the SDGs, as well as in the development and
  operationalization of the on-line platform, including preparing proposals
  for the modalities for the Forum and the on-line platform. The 10 representatives will be appointed by the Secretary General, for periods of two
  years. The Task Team will be open to the participation of all UN agencies,
  funds and programmes, and ECOSOC functional commissions and it will
  initially be composed by the entities that currently integrate the informal
  working group on technology facilitation, namely: UN Department of
  Economic and Social Affairs, United Nations Environment Programme,
  UNIDO, United Nations Educational Scientific and Cultural Organization, UNCTAD, International Telecommunication Union, WIPO and the
  World Bank.
- The on-line platform will be used to establish a comprehensive mapping of, and serve as a gateway for, information on existing STI initiatives,
  mechanisms and programmes, within and beyond the UN. The on-line

platform will facilitate access to information, knowledge and experience, as well as best practices and lessons learned, on STI facilitation initiatives and policies. The online platform will also facilitate the dissemination of relevant open access scientific publications generated worldwide. The online platform will be developed on the basis of an independent technical assessment which will take into account best practices and lessons learned from other initiatives, within and beyond the United Nations, in order to ensure that it will complement, facilitate access to and provide adequate information on existing STI platforms, avoiding duplications and enhancing synergies.

- The Multistakeholder Forum on Science Technology and Innovation for the SDGs will be convened once a year, for a period of two days, to discuss STI cooperation around thematic areas for the implementation of the SDGs, congregating all relevant stakeholders to actively contribute in their area of expertise. The Forum will provide a venue for facilitating interaction, matchmaking and the establishment of networks between relevant stakeholders and multistakeholder partnerships in order to identify and examine technology needs and gaps, including on scientific cooperation, innovation and capacity building, and also in order to help facilitate development, transfer and dissemination of relevant technologies for the SDGs. The meetings of the Forum will be convened by the President of the ECOSOC before the meeting of the High Level Political Forum under the auspices of ECOSOC or, alternatively, in conjunction with other fora or conferences, as appropriate, taking into account the theme to be considered and on the basis of a collaboration with the organizers of the other fora or conference. The meetings of the Forum will be co-chaired by two Member States and will result in a summary of discussions elaborated by the two co-chairs, as an input to the meetings of the High Level Political Forum, in the context of the follow-up and review of the implementation of the Post-2015 Development Agenda.
- The meetings of the HLPF will be informed by the summary of the Multistakeholder Forum. The themes for the subsequent Multistakeholder Forum on Science Technology and Innovation for the SDGs will be considered by the High Level Political Forum on sustainable development, taking into account expert inputs from the Task Team.

71 We reiterate that this Agenda and the Sustainable Development Goals and targets, including the means of implementation are universal, indivisible and interlinked.

Follow-up and review

72 We commit to engage in systematic follow-up and review of implementation of this Agenda over the next fifteen years. A robust, voluntary, effective, participatory, transparent and integrated follow-up and review framework will make a

vital contribution to implementation and will help countries to maximize and track progress in implementing this Agenda in order to ensure that no one is left behind.

73 Operating at the national, regional and global levels, it will promote accountability to our citizens, support effective international cooperation in achieving this Agenda and foster exchanges of best practices and mutual learning. It will mobilize support to overcome shared challenges and identify new and emerging issues. As this is a universal Agenda, mutual trust and understanding among all nations will be important.

74 Follow-up and review processes at all levels will be guided by the following principles:

a They will be voluntary and country-led, will take into account different national realities, capacities and levels of development and will respect policy space and priorities. As national ownership is key to achieving sustainable development, the outcome from national level processes will be the foundation for reviews at regional and global levels, given that the global review will be primarily based on national official data sources.

b They will track progress in implementing the universal Goals and targets, including the means of implementation, in all countries in a manner which respects their universal, integrated and interrelated nature and the three dimensions of sustainable development.

c They will maintain a longer-term orientation, identify achievements, challenges, gaps and critical success factors and support countries in making informed policy choices. They will help mobilize the necessary means of implementation and partnerships, support the identification of solutions and best practices and promote coordination and effectiveness of the international development system.

d They will be open, inclusive, participatory and transparent for all people and will support the reporting by all relevant stakeholders.

e They will be people-centred, gender-sensitive, respect human rights and have a particular focus on the poorest, most vulnerable and those furthest behind.

f They will build on existing platforms and processes, where these exist, avoid duplication and respond to national circumstances, capacities, needs and priorities. They will evolve over time, taking into account emerging issues and the development of new methodologies, and will minimize the reporting burden on national administrations.

g They will be rigorous and based on evidence, informed by country-led evaluations and data which is high-quality, accessible, timely, reliable and disaggregated by income, sex, age, race, ethnicity, migration status, disability and geographic location and other characteristics relevant in national contexts.

h They will require enhanced capacity-building support for developing countries, including the strengthening of national data systems and evaluation programs, particularly in African countries, LDCs, SIDS and LLDCs and middle-income countries.

i   They will benefit from the active support of the UN system and other multilateral institutions.

75 The Goals and targets will be followed-up and reviewed using a set of global indicators. These will be complemented by indicators at the regional and national levels which will be developed by member states, in addition to the outcomes of work undertaken for the development of the baselines for those targets where national and global baseline data does not yet exist. The global indicator framework, to be developed by the Inter Agency and Expert Group on SDG Indicators, will be agreed by the UN Statistical Commission by March 2016 and adopted thereafter by the Economic and Social Council and the General Assembly, in line with existing mandates. This framework will be simple yet robust, address all SDGs and targets including for means of implementation, and preserve the political balance, integration and ambition contained therein.

76 We will support developing countries, particularly African countries, LDCs, SIDS and LLDCs, in strengthening the capacity of national statistical offices and data systems to ensure access to high-quality, timely, reliable and disaggregated data. We will promote transparent and accountable scaling-up of appropriate public-private cooperation to exploit the contribution to be made by a wide range of data, including earth observation and geo-spatial information, while ensuring national ownership in supporting and tracking progress.

77 We commit to fully engage in conducting regular and inclusive reviews of progress at sub-national, national, regional and global levels. We will draw as far as possible on the existing network of follow-up and review institutions and mechanisms. National reports will allow assessments of progress and identify challenges at the regional and global level. Along with regional dialogues and global reviews, they will inform recommendations for follow-up at various levels.

National level

78 We encourage all member states to develop as soon as practicable ambitious national responses to the overall implementation of this Agenda. These can support the transition to the SDGs and build on existing planning instruments, such as national development and sustainable development strategies, as appropriate.

79 We also encourage member states to conduct regular and inclusive reviews of progress at the national and sub-national levels which are country-led and country-driven. Such reviews should draw on contributions from indigenous peoples, civil society, the private sector and other stakeholders, in line with national circumstances, policies and priorities. National parliaments as well as other institutions can also support these processes.

Regional level

80 Follow-up and review at the regional and sub-regional levels can, as appropriate, provide useful opportunities for peer learning, including through voluntary reviews, sharing of best practices and discussion on shared targets. We welcome in this respect the cooperation of regional and sub-regional commissions and organizations. Inclusive regional processes will draw on national-level reviews and contribute to follow-up and review at the global level, including at the High Level Political Forum on sustainable development (HLPF).

81 Recognizing the importance of building on existing follow-up and review mechanisms at the regional level and allowing adequate policy space, we encourage all member states to identify the most suitable regional forum in which to engage. UN regional commissions are encouraged to continue supporting member states in this regard.

Global level

82 The HLPF will have a central role in overseeing a network of follow-up and review processes at the global level, working coherently with the General Assembly, ECOSOC and other relevant organs and forums, in accordance with existing mandates. It will facilitate sharing of experiences, including successes, challenges and lessons learned, and provide political leadership, guidance and recommendations for follow-up. It will promote system-wide coherence and coordination of sustainable development policies. It should ensure that the Agenda remains relevant and ambitious and should focus on the assessment of progress, achievements and challenges faced by developed and developing countries as well as new and emerging issues. Effective linkages will be made with the follow-up and review arrangements of all relevant UN Conferences and processes, including on LDCs, SIDS and LLDCs.

83 Follow-up and review at the HLPF will be informed by an annual SDG Progress Report to be prepared by the Secretary General in cooperation with the UN System, based on the global indicator framework and data produced by national statistical systems and information collected at the regional level. The HLPF will also be informed by the Global Sustainable Development Report, which shall strengthen the science-policy interface and could provide a strong evidence-based instrument to support policy-makers in promoting poverty eradication and sustainable development. We invite the President of ECOSOC to conduct a process of consultations on the scope, methodology and frequency of the Report as well as its relation to the SDG Progress Report, the outcome of which should be reflected in the Ministerial Declaration of the HLPF session in 2016.

84 The HLPF, under the auspices of ECOSOC, shall carry out regular reviews, in line with Resolution 67/290. Reviews will be voluntary, while encouraging reporting, and include developed and developing countries as well as relevant

UN entities and other stakeholders, including civil society and the private sector. They shall be state-led, involving ministerial and other relevant high-level participants. They shall provide a platform for partnerships, including through the participation of major groups and other relevant stakeholders.

85 Thematic reviews of progress on the Sustainable Development Goals, including cross-cutting issues, will also take place at the HLPF. These will be supported by reviews by the ECOSOC functional commissions and other inter-governmental bodies and forums which should reflect the integrated nature of the goals as well as the interlinkages between them. They will engage all relevant stakeholders and, where possible, feed into, and be aligned with, the cycle of the HLPF.

86 We welcome, as outlined in the Addis Ababa Action Agenda, the dedicated follow-up and review for the Financing for Development outcomes as well as all the means of implementation of the SDGs which is integrated with the follow-up and review framework of this Agenda. The intergovernmentally agreed conclusions and recommendations of the annual ECOSOC Forum on Financing for Development will be fed into the overall follow-up and review of the implementation of this Agenda in the HLPF.

87 Meeting every four years under the auspices of the General Assembly, the HLPF will provide high-level political guidance on the Agenda and its implementation, identify progress and emerging challenges and mobilize further actions to accelerate implementation. The next HLPF, under the auspices of the General Assembly, will take place in 2019, with the cycle of meetings thus reset, in order to maximize coherence with the Quadrennial Comprehensive Policy Review process.

88 We also stress the importance of system-wide strategic planning, implementation and reporting in order to ensure coherent and integrated support to implementation of the new Agenda by the UN development system. The relevant governing bodies should take action to review such support to implementation and to report on progress and obstacles. We welcome the ongoing ECOSOC Dialogues on the longer term positioning of the UN development system and look forward to taking action on these issues, as appropriate.

89 The HLPF will support participation in follow-up and review processes by the major groups and other relevant stakeholders in line with Resolution 67/290. We call on these actors to report on their contribution to the implementation of the Agenda.

90 We request the Secretary General, in consultation with Member States, to prepare a report, for consideration at the 70th session of the General Assembly in preparation for the 2016 meeting of the HLPF, which outlines critical milestones towards coherent efficient, and inclusive follow-up and review at the global level. This report should include a proposal on the organizational arrangements for state-led reviews at the HLPF under the auspices of ECOSOC, including recommendations on a voluntary common reporting guidelines. It should clarify institutional responsibilities and provide guidance on annual themes, on a sequence of thematic reviews, and on options for periodic reviews for the HLPF.

91 We reaffirm our unwavering commitment to achieving this Agenda and utilizing it to the full to transform our world for the better by 2030.

Reference

United Nations (2015) Transforming our world: The 2030 agenda for sustainable development. Available online at: https://sustainabledevelopment.un.org/post2015/transformingourworld

INDEX

Page numbers in *italics* indicate figures, tables and boxes.